"What if a good urban solution doesn't involve 'fitting into existing conditions' but adding a clear and articulate voice to barely audible communications about ways of living that could be less wasteful, more humane, and just? Read this forward-looking book to discover modern architecture's positive contribution to the city and the cultures it embodies."

David Leatherbarrow, *Emeritus Professor of Architecture, University of Pennsylvania*

"This is a thesis that takes architectural scholarship and criticism to an entirely new level, in part because of the exceptionally sensitive talent and inventive energy of Sverre Fehn, and in part because of Anderson's comparable sensitivity and profound erudition, influenced as it has been by the architectural phenomenologies of Dalibor Vesely and David Leatherbarrow. This is a truly important work."

Kenneth Frampton, *Emeritus Professor of Architecture, Columbia University*

Sverre Fehn and the City

The urban attentions of Pritzker Laureate Sverre Fehn (1924–2009) are extensive, but as yet virtually unexplored. This book examines ten select projects to illuminate Fehn's approach to the city, the embodiment of that thinking in his designs, and the broader lessons those efforts offer for better understanding the relationship between architecture and urban life, with unignorable implications for emergent urban architecture and its address of sociological and ecological crises. Wary of large-scale planning proposals or the erasure of existing urban patterns, Fehn offered an uncommon and profoundly vibrant approach to urbanism at the scale of the single architectural project. His writings, constructed buildings, competition entries, and lectures suggest opportunities for reinvigorating architecture's engagement with the city, and provoke a rethinking of concepts foundational to its theorization. What is the nature of urbanity? What is the relationship of urbanity to the natural world? What is the role of architecture in the provision and sustenance of urban life? While exploring this territory will expand our knowledge of an architect central to key developments of late modernism, the range of the book and the arguments developed therein delineate far broader aims: a fuller understanding of architecture's urban promise.

Stephen M. Anderson is an associate professor in Architecture and Environmental Design in the Tyler School of Art and Architecture, Temple University, Philadelphia, where he teaches architectural theory and graduate design.

Routledge Research in Architecture

The *Routledge Research in Architecture* series provides the reader with the latest scholarship in the field of architecture. The series publishes research from across the globe and covers areas as diverse as architectural history and theory, technology, digital architecture, structures, materials, details, design, monographs of architects, interior design and much more. By making these studies available to the worldwide academic community, the series aims to promote quality architectural research.

Architecture of Threshold Spaces
A Critique of the Ideologies of Hyperconnectivity and Segregation in the Socio-Political Context
Laurence Kimmel

Pyrotechnic Cities
Architecture, Fire-Safety and Standardisation
Liam Ross

Architecture and the Housing Question
Edited by Can Bilsel and Juliana Maxim

Architecture and the Housing Question
Edited by Can Bilsel and Juliana Maxim

Mies at Home
From Am Karlsbad to the Tugendhat House
Xiangnan Xiong

The Philadelphia School and the Future of Architecture
John Lobell

For more information about this series, please visit: https://www.routledge.com/Routledge-Research-in-Architecture/book-series/RRARCH

Sverre Fehn and the City
Rethinking Architecture's Urban Premises

Stephen M. Anderson

LONDON AND NEW YORK

Cover image: Sketch of New York City. Sverre Fehn, 1977. National Museum archives. Archive ID: NMK.2008.0734.141.004.

First published 2023
by Routledge
4 Park Square, Milton Park, Abingdon, Oxon OX14 4RN

and by Routledge
605 Third Avenue, New York, NY 10158

Routledge is an imprint of the Taylor & Francis Group, an informa business

© 2023 Stephen M. Anderson

The right of Stephen M. Anderson to be identified as author of this work has been asserted in accordance with sections 77 and 78 of the Copyright, Designs and Patents Act 1988.

All rights reserved. No part of this book may be reprinted or reproduced or utilised in any form or by any electronic, mechanical, or other means, now known or hereafter invented, including photocopying and recording, or in any information storage or retrieval system, without permission in writing from the publishers.

Trademark notice: Product or corporate names may be trademarks or registered trademarks, and are used only for identification and explanation without intent to infringe.

British Library Cataloguing-in-Publication Data
A catalogue record for this book is available from the British Library

ISBN: 978-1-032-36651-7 (hbk)
ISBN: 978-1-032-38133-6 (pbk)
ISBN: 978-1-003-34364-6 (ebk)

DOI: 10.4324/9781003343646

Typeset in Sabon
by codeMantra

 Printed in the United Kingdom by Henry Ling Limited

Contents

List of figures ix
Acknowledgments xv

1 Fehn in the City: "What Makes This All So Alive" 1

2 Opened Ground 17

3 Sverre Fehn's Ambient Urbanity 61

4 Sverre Fehn, the City, and the Architecture of Participation 95

5 More Oslo 132

Afterword 153
Appendix 1: The Building Will Reflect the Drama of the City 155
Appendix 2: Lecture Transcript 160
Index 175

Figures

1.1 Nasjonalmuseet-Arkitektur, looking west. Photograph by the author — 2
1.2 Glacier Museum, Fjærland, Norway. Photograph by Josh Mings — 2
1.3 Sketch section of street in NYC, by Fehn, from sketchbook, 1977. Compare to Fehn's well-known sketches depicting caves as originary architecture. Fehn's handwriting is difficult to decipher but the top line seems to be, *hva gjør det hele så levende*: "what makes this all so alive." © Sverre Fehn/BONO. Courtesy of National Museum, Architecture Collections — 9
2.1 Vasa Museum, site plan and building section. © Sverre Fehn. Photo: Veiby, Jeanette. Courtesy of National Museum, Architecture Collections — 19
2.2 Vasa Museum, floor plans. North at left. © Sverre Fehn. Photo: Veiby, Jeanette. Courtesy of National Museum, Architecture Collections — 21
2.3 Galärvarvskyrkogården. 100 m east of drydock, view toward Nordic Museum. Cemetery extends to within 5 m of museum. Photograph courtesy of First Morning travel blog, www.firstmorning.se — 22
2.4 Sketch of sailing vessel from aft, by Fehn, from sketchbook, 1993. © Sverre Fehn. Courtesy of National Museum, Architecture Collections — 24
2.5 Hedmark Museum, site plan of peninsula (north at top). © Sverre Fehn. Photo: Ivarsøy, Dag Andre. Courtesy of National Museum, Architecture Collections — 26
2.6 Hedmark Museum, concrete ramp at courtyard. © Ukjent. Courtesy of National Museum, Architecture Collections — 28
2.7 Hedmark Museum, view through aperture at southwest interior, looking north. © Helene Binet — 29
2.8 Hedmark Museum, plan of second level (north at left). Main entry into lobby area on the first level is below large opening shown here in west wall, with access to courtyard directly opposite. Three small rooms referred to in the text

x *Figures*

	as "reliquaries" can be seen here, dotted-in to the south of the entrance. © Sverre Fehn. Photo: Ivarsøy, Dag Andre. Courtesy of National Museum, Architecture Collections	30
2.9	Hedmark Museum, glazing detail at entry. Photo by author	31
2.10	Hedmark Museum, roof support detail, by-passing medieval wall. Photo by author	33
2.11	Hedmark Museum, roof support detail, bearing on medieval rubble wall. Photo by author	33
2.12	Hedmark Museum, view of three "vaults," looking south. Photo by author	34
2.13	Hedmark Museum, view under ramp toward landscape. Photo by author	34
2.14	Hedmark Museum, display of crucifix and sepulcher fragment. Photo by author	37
2.15	Hedmark Museum, construction drawing of display. © Sverre Fehn. Courtesy of National Museum, Architecture Collections	38
2.16	Hedmark Museum, detail of sepulcher fragment. Photo by Geir Ove Andreassen, Anno Domkirkeodden	38
2.17	Hedmark Museum, display of plow. Photo by author	39
2.18	Hedmark Museum, exhibit of glassware. Photo by author	40
2.19	Trondheim Library, plan of second level, showing pedestrian street and connections to adjoining existing buildings. Exterior ruins at sunken court are visible to the left. Interior ruins, to be adapted as children's spaces, are visible in the main reading room at lower right. © Sverre Fehn. Courtesy of National Museum, Architecture Collections	43
2.20	Trondheim Library, detail of building section. Existing town hall at left. © Sverre Fehn. Courtesy of National Museum, Architecture Collections	44
2.21	Trondheim Library, cross-section, looking south. River at far left. © Sverre Fehn. Courtesy of National Museum, Architecture Collections	45
2.22	Trondheim, detail of Cicignon's Baroque plan, after fire of 1681. North at right. Modern library site highlighted by author with dotted oval. Remnant of medieval Krambugata visible as an alley at interior of adjacent blocks to north	46
2.23	Sketch of globe, featuring Villa Rotonda. © Sverre Fehn. Courtesy of National Museum, Architecture Collections	50
2.24	Sketch, Sverre Fehn. Text reads: "That is architecture." The image includes symbols of Fehn's Vasa and Hedmark projects, a pyramid, a jar, with various relationships to a ground plane. © Sverre Fehn. Courtesy of National Museum, Architecture Collections	51

2.25 Sketch, Sverre Fehn. Sketch of Villa Savoye, from under main floor, looking out toward the landscape. © Sverre Fehn. Courtesy of National Museum, Architecture Collections 55
3.1 Foto Huset, interior at night, view toward street, with back of store reflected in storefront. Entrance at right. © Tiegens/DEXTRA Photo. Courtesy of Norsk Teknisk Museum 62
3.2 Foto Huset, detail of staircase, looking up. © Tiegens/DEXTRA Photo. Courtesy of Norsk Teknisk Museum 63
3.3 Foto Huset, view from curb, looking through to back of shop. © Tiegens/DEXTRA Photo. Courtesy of Norsk Teknisk Museum 64
3.4 Foto Huset, main floorplan. © Tiegens/DEXTRA Photo. Courtesy of Norsk Teknisk Museum 65
3.5 Foto Huset, glass display case projecting into sidewalk. © Tiegens/DEXTRA Photo. Courtesy of Norsk Teknisk Museum 65
3.6 Foto Huset, entry and glass display case, looking east. © Tiegens/DEXTRA Photo. Courtesy of Norsk Teknisk Museum 66
3.7 Foto Huset, glass display case, from interior. © Tiegens/DEXTRA Photo. Courtesy of Norsk Teknisk Museum 67
3.8 Villa Norrköping, plan. © Tiegens/DEXTRA Photo. Courtesy of Norsk Teknisk Museum 69
3.9 Villa Norrköping, view from southwest. © Ukjent. Courtesy of Norsk Teknisk Museum 70
3.10 Villa Norrköping, view from street. Front door is visible to right of glazing at center of lower image. Photos from *Bauen + Wohnen* article on the project, 1964 71
3.11 Villa Norrköping, east corner 74
3.12 Villa Norrköping, west corner. © Sverre Fehn. Courtesy of National Museum, Architecture Collections 74
3.13 Villa Norrköping, view from carport through living area to landscape beyond. Note coarseness of brickwork. © Tiegens/DEXTRA Photo. Courtesy of Norsk Teknisk Museum 75
3.14 Villa Norrköping, corner cabinet, one of two panels open, view into kitchen. © Tiegens/DEXTRA Photo. Courtesy of Norsk Teknisk Museum 77
3.15 Villa Norrköping, cross-section and detail at kitchen. Casework at right adjoins dining area. © Tiegens/DEXTRA Photo. Courtesy of Norsk Teknisk Museum 78
3.16 Villa Norrköping, casework at bath, view from hall, outer door closed. © Per Berntsen 79
3.17 Villa Norrköping, casework at bath, view from hall, both doors open. © Tiegens/DEXTRA Photo. Courtesy of Norsk Teknisk Museum 80
3.18 Nordic Pavilion, looking east. © Tiegens/DEXTRA Photo. Courtesy of Norsk Teknisk Museum 81

xii *Figures*

3.19	Nordic Pavilion, interior	83
3.20	Nordic Pavilion, plan, final version, with American and Danish pavilions to west and north, with courtyard penciled in. Primary promenade at right-most edge of drawing. © Sverre Fehn. Courtesy of National Museum, Architecture Collections	84
3.21	Nordic Pavilion, competition drawing, section. © Sverre Fehn. Courtesy of National Museum, Architecture Collections	87
3.22	San Giorgio Maggiore from the Giardini. Sketch, Sverre Fehn, 1993. © Sverre Fehn. Courtesy of National Museum, Architecture Collections	88
3.23	Nordic Pavilion, view from portico of Danish pavilion, looking south. © Ferruzzi, 1962. Courtesy of National Museum, Architecture Collections	89
3.24	Nordic Pavilion, north elevation, American pavilion to the left, Danish pavilion and its portico drawn in cross-section to the right. © Sverre Fehn. Courtesy of National Museum, Architecture Collections	90
3.25	Nordic Pavilion, looking south from garden court, Danish pavilion just out of frame to the right. © Ferruzzi, 1962. Courtesy of National Museum, Architecture Collections	90
3.26	Nordic Pavilion, proposed exhibition configurations. © Tiegens/DEXTRA Photo. Courtesy of Norsk Teknisk Museum	92
4.1	Tullinløkka, looking north, 1906. The square is visible as a grassy square right of the center of image; a diagonal path is barely discernible; university buildings in foreground. A small portion of the street-park axis that defines the heart of the city can be seen at bottom left. Photo by Narve Skarpmoen	96
4.2	Tullinløkka, interior perspective, mixed media. © Sverre Fehn. Courtesy of National Museum, Architecture Collections	98
4.3	Tullinløkka, site plan featuring diagonal pedestrian street and amphitheater. Note over-street walkway at Kristian IV Gate connecting University Hall to proposed museum addition. At the time of the competition, the open areas shown adjacent to the Hall were occupied with mature hardwoods, as represented in several of Fehn's drawings. © Sverre Fehn. Courtesy of National Museum, Architecture Collections	99
4.4	Tullinløkka, street-level plan. © Sverre Fehn. Courtesy of National Museum, Architecture Collections	100
4.5	Tullinløkka, sketch showing pedestrian street, looking north. One of the cafés is visible to the left, and the roof-garden-terrace is just visible at the upper right. © Sverre Fehn. Courtesy of National Museum, Architecture Collections	101

4.6	Tullinløkka, building section, looking north. © Sverre Fehn. Courtesy of National Museum, Architecture Collections	103
4.7	Tullinløkka, wooden model with resin roof removed, looking north. © Sverre Fehn. Courtesy of National Museum, Architecture Collections	105
4.8	Tullinløkka, long section drawing, looking west. The curved shells of Fehn's proposed museum addition are visible to the right (north). © Sverre Fehn. Courtesy of National Museum, Architecture Collections	105
4.9	Tullinløkka, image of model, gallery interior. © Sverre Fehn. Courtesy of National Museum, Architecture Collections	108
4.10	Royal Theater, image of model showing lobby entrance. © Sverre Fehn. Courtesy of National Museum, Architecture Collections	110
4.11	Royal Theater, site plan. © Sverre Fehn. Courtesy of National Museum, Architecture Collections	110
4.12	Royal Theater, view of Stærekassen, straddling street, looking east from square. © Susanne Nilsson	112
4.13	Royal Theater, view of Stærekassen from below. © Peter Mulligan	112
4.14	Royal Theater, full-scale mock-up of entry from Kongens Nytorv. © Ukjent. Courtesy of National Museum, Architecture Collections	113
4.15	Royal Theater, ground floor plan. © Sverre Fehn. Courtesy of National Museum, Architecture Collections	114
4.16	Royal Theater, west elevation, and cross-section looking west. © Sverre Fehn. Courtesy of National Museum, Architecture Collections	116
4.17	Royal Theater, model, south portion of enclosed street-lobby. Theater entrance at stairway. Restaurant was under winged-roof at upper right of image, with the new fly-space beyond. © Ukjent. Courtesy of National Museum, Architecture Collections	118
4.18	Royal Theater, perspective drawing of lobby, looking north, showing one of two elevated connecting walkways bisecting the main structural pier as it spans the space. © Ukjent. Courtesy of National Museum, Architecture Collections	119
4.19	Royal Theater, image of model showing lobby entry from the square, simulating nighttime. © Ukjent. Courtesy of National Museum, Architecture Collections	123
5.1	Architecture Museum, 1997 scheme, ground floor plan. Entrance at right. © Sverre Fehn. Courtesy of National Museum, Architecture Collections	134
5.2	Architecture Museum, 1997 scheme, south elevation. © Sverre Fehn. Courtesy of National Museum, Architecture Collections	134

xiv *Figures*

5.3 Architecture Museum, 1997 scheme, building section. © Sverre Fehn. Courtesy of National Museum, Architecture Collections 135
5.4 Architecture Museum, 2001 scheme, south elevation. © Sverre Fehn. Courtesy of National Museum, Architecture Collections 136
5.5 Architecture Museum, 2001 scheme, building section. © Sverre Fehn. Courtesy of National Museum, Architecture Collections 136
5.6 Architecture Museum, detail of exhibition area in existing building. Photo by author 137
5.7 Architecture Museum, 2008 scheme, main floor plan. © Sverre Fehn. Courtesy of National Museum, Architecture Collections 138
5.8 Architecture Museum, pavilion interior. © Ivan Brodey. 140
5.9 Architecture Museum, pavilion roof detail showing structural glass fins, glass louvers, mullion-less glass wall, skylight at inverted eave, concrete shell roof, and curtains. From construction drawings. © Sverre Fehn. Courtesy of National Museum, Architecture Collections 141
5.10 Norwegian Pavilion, Brussels, roof plan. Nine opaque extensions at perimeter depict roof-tarps. ©Sverre Fehn. Courtesy of National Museum, Architecture Collections 142
5.11 Norwegian Pavilion, Brussels, northwest corner, looking through Plexiglas wall to exterior perimeter zone. © Sverre Fehn. Courtesy of National Museum, Architecture Collections 143
5.12 Architecture Museum, view of perimeter zone between glass and concrete walls. Photo by author 144
5.13 Architecture Museum, 2001 scheme, plan detail showing proposed recessed hinged shutters at openings. Note also divisions in the floor surface of the perimeter zone, which represented the proposed glass-block system (not built) to provide light to basement. Pivoting display panels shown at interior. © Sverre Fehn. Courtesy of National Museum, Architecture Collections 145
5.14 Architecture Museum, view of exterior wall. Photo by author 146
5.15 Architecture Museum, view of rear corner. Photo by author 147
5.16 Architecture Museum, Architecture Museum, entry foyer. Glazed flooring area at bottom left reveals original flooring detail below. © Ivan Brodey 149
5.17 Architecture Museum, 2001 scheme, wooden model showing detail of cafe patio. © Sverre Fehn. Courtesy of National Museum, Architecture Collections 150

Acknowledgments

I want to thank Per Olaf Fjeld and Sophie Hochhäusl for their invaluable insights, attention, and patience in helping me prepare this manuscript, in all its iterations. Moreover, Per Olaf's writings on, and personal insights into, the works and life of Sverre Fehn form the basis of all that follows. Thanks also to Bente Solbakken and her staff at the National Museum's Architectural Archives for the assistance and direction on which I was utterly dependent. Likewise, thanks to Stephen Hillier and Robbie Terman for their assistance with their respective archives at Cooper Union and Cranbrook Academy. Many thanks to Mari Lending and Rolf Gerstlauer for helping me find my footing in Oslo. I am grateful for the help of Kristin Gjesdal and Espen Hammer with deciphering Fehn's handwritten passages, for suffering my lousy Norwegian, and also for their unflagging encouragement. Thanks to Anne Beate Christophersen for facilitating my visits to the Skådalen School—that material did not advance to the final version of this manuscript, but I look forward to making future use of it. I am especially appreciative of Emily Randall Fjeld's kindness and hospitality in accommodating me, and then my family, in Tønsberg—the water was icy but the house could not have been warmer. Thanks to Kenneth Frampton for his attention and early insights—I have perhaps never learned so much in the course of an afternoon; and further thanks for his thorough and thoughtful review of the late draft—an author could not hope for a more diligent reader. Similarly, thanks to Grahame Shane for his kindness, thoughts, and advice in the earliest stages of this work.

A special thank you, belatedly, to Dalibor Vesely. His extensive input in the development of my inquiry, his willingness to stick with me as I focused on those interests, his unequaled generosity in the sharing of ideas, and his companionship in Philadelphia, Kyoto, and London are treasured and will not be forgotten. Dalibor, you were wrong about Ricouer and children and Rossi, and right about most of the rest.

I am most of all indebted to David Leatherbarrow, for his generosity with his time and analysis, his endless patience and encouragement, his close counsel, and for his persistent and careful construction of the intellectual scaffold from which so many of us work. There is scarcely an idea in this book that is not founded on his insights and teachings.

And thanks of course to my parents and sisters, who never revealed a trace of skepticism; and to Zoë and Brigit, who grew up with both a house and a father cluttered with books and aspirations. And thanks most of all to Lynne, for everything she has given, and for all she has endured. Without my family, I am lost.

1 Fehn in the City
"What Makes This All So Alive"

> The tree which strikes its roots deep into the earth can still hope to drive its flowering crown to the sky, but thoughts which immediately separate themselves from nature at the outset are like plants without roots, or can at best be compared to those delicate threads which swim in the air in late summer, equally unable to reach the sky and touch the earth through their own weight.
>
> Friedrich Schelling

If you walk east along Karl Johans Gate from the heart of modern Oslo and then continue south on Kongens Gate toward the waterfront, the density of the city gives way to an assemblage of parks, ruins of fortifications, and public institutions. You are still unmistakably in the city, but, moving further south, air, room, sunlight, and flora become more prominent in the ambiance of the street, and the sea-air grows stronger. You have arrived in one of the oldest parts of Oslo, and traces of its maritime and military past, 12 centuries of it, are evident. The vicinity's present iteration might best be described as an emergent cultural and museum district, including the Opera House and Munch Museum a short walk further east. Closer by, several large buildings from various eras have been converted for the purposes of tourism and high-culture, and two such buildings from the 19th century, now museums, flank the street as you approach the intersection at Myntgata. Just around that corner to the west, nestled against the smaller of those buildings, is a fortress-like pavilion with canted, windowless concrete walls separated from the street by a wide band of grass, the unusual structure's contemporaneity announced by an array of greenish glass louvers crowning over its top (Figure 1.1). No entry through those walls is apparent—it is an addition to the Greek-revival building that stands behind it, and access to the newer portion requires passage through the old. The signage reads, "Nasjonalmuseet-Arkitektur."

The building is one of the last constructed works of Pritzker Laureate Sverre Fehn, and one of only a handful that he ever completed in a city. Most of Fehn's architecture stands on suburban and exurban sites, often

DOI: 10.4324/9781003343646-1

2 Fehn in the City: "What Makes This All So Alive"

Figure 1.1 Nasjonalmuseet-Arkitektur, looking west. Photograph by the author.

Figure 1.2 Glacier Museum, Fjærland, Norway. Photograph by Josh Mings.

set in dramatic Nordic landscapes. It is not surprising, then, that appraisal of Fehn's work has tended toward consideration of its relation to wilderness or nature, to horizon, to local building traditions and local character, and, perhaps inevitably, to notions of Nordic light and shadow. There is something severe in Fehn's architecture, and to go as far as suggesting that it in places embraces a form of primitivism would not exceed even Fehn's own theorization of his work. The sloped concrete walls and citadel-like perimeter of the strange addition to the museum recall an architectural vocabulary that Fehn deployed in some of the most remote of his projects—as at the Glacier Museum in Fjærland (Figure 1.2) and the Aasen Center in Ørsta (1991 and 2000, respectively).

In contrast to those settings, Oslo is a large, dense, contemporary city by Norwegian standards and urban by any definition. Making sense of the building poses challenges, then, for our understanding of Fehn's architecture. Is this walled pavilion an urban misfit, striking but detached, an emissary of a rugged and regional architecture out of place in its more worldly and urbane setting? Or, contrary to first appearances, might the building be understood as actively and effectively participating in its urban setting? Could this seemingly aloof building be informed first and foremost by attention to the city? How could that be? By what means and toward what ends?

Those questions provide an opening to a trove of lessons to be found in Fehn's work, lessons pertaining to the relation of architecture to urban life. Fehn's work may seem an unlikely place to turn for such lessons. One of the aims of this book is to correct that presumption by simply casting light on an urban dimension of Fehn's architecture that is, in fact, robust, and which has so far garnered inadequate attention. What follows, though, is neither a compendium of his urban efforts[1] nor a biography focusing on the provenance and chronological development of those aims. My interests are more specific with regard to Fehn's work, and more general with regard to the architecture of the city. Let me explain, in two parts.

Fehn's urban understanding, I will show, is marked by a profound concern for fit, continuity, and active participation within a setting—the very notion of participation will emerge as central to analysis of his work. Therein are the specific themes I hope to cull from Fehn's larger opus. Because my interests are thematic rather than encyclopedic, I have not attempted an exhaustive study of all of Fehn's work that might be categorized as urban, but, rather, have focused on a select subset that facilitates exploration of what I take to be Fehn's greatest preoccupations with urban architecture. Those concerns can be illuminated by Fehn's pronouncements, and I will refer to those as I proceed. But it is in the architecture itself that those ideas are most evident, most fully developed, and, in their engagement of the actual city, most complex. Consequently, though I will make appeals to Fehn's written and spoken statements, and while I have found it useful at points to depart from Fehn's buildings to examine parallel or contrasting architectural ideas, I have aimed to keep architectural configurations as the primary vehicle for understanding and exploring the intersection of architecture and urbanity in Fehn's work. This book is primarily an account of lessons embodied in those few architectural works of Fehn that I have selected for study, and the reader will not find much here useful to biography, hagiography even less.

Second, with regard to the applicability of Fehn's architecture to more general topics related to architecture and urbanity, Fehn's thinking on urban architecture, and also the work to which it led, exhibits characteristics that can seem exotic at times. His unorthodox narrative style, the consistently prominent role of mass and opacity in his designs, his eschewing of master-plan approaches to the city, and his persistent concern for the historical depth of settings all conspire to make Fehn's work difficult to fit within well-worn historical narratives of late modern architecture. Perhaps those narratives surrounding Team X come closest. Fehn was good friends with several architects working under that aegis; he knew those ideas well and was occasionally active in advancing their development. Early in Fehn's career, Reyner Banham thought it prudent to include him, if only briefly, with many Team X members in his, *The New Brutalism*.[2] Like most of his Team X colleagues, Fehn was at once student and critic of modernist architecture and its prevailing approaches to the city. But even as he was sympathetic to many of their central tenets, Fehn, never an official member of Team X, kept a distance.[3] In the course of the research presented here, I have often had occasion to wonder about that divide. As Per Olaf Fjeld put it, "The city was always on Sverre's mind—always."[4] But despite a deep concern for architecture's urban aspects, Fehn's use of the term *urbanism*, in contrast to that of his Team X colleagues, was remarkably spare. Fjeld characterized Fehn's general disposition to the urbanist work of his generation as "skeptical."[5] Much of that skepticism can be attributed to the way Fehn tended to align the term *urbanism* with what he took to be the deracinating effects of the ever-greater systemification of the city, an observation I will substantiate below. Such willingness to follow his intuitions away from prevailing dialogs contributes to the notion that, in the context of mid-to-late 20th-century urban attentions, Fehn's architecture was unorthodox even among those who had declared their unorthodoxy. And yet—and this, for me, is the pivotal point—if Fehn's work can feel oddly aloof from the prevailing stylistic and intellectual tropes and counter-tropes of his time, an examination of his urban work shows it to be decidedly not aloof from the topographical and cultural settings to which it belongs. That is, the peculiarity of Fehn's work does not stem from eschewing norms and givens in pursuit of novelty, but from an uncannily inventive attention to circumstance and habituation. Fehn's urban work, then, points beyond itself, in two senses. Locally, I will show, Fehn's sense of urbanity is founded on the architectural facilitation of dialog between the given conditions and the architectural project, where the given conditions include not only topographic and corporeal ones, but also patterns of movement, cultural habits, historical depth, and temporal rhythms. In this sense, Fehn's architecture can be understood as an instrument for multiplying connections between occupants and creative possibilities latent in the given conditions. Nowhere, for Fehn, are those possibilities richer and more multilayered than in the city, with each urban site offering its unique compilation of strata. Fehn's architecture, I will show, is designed to penetrate and engage those strata.

But if no two cities are the same, nor any one city the same from one moment to the next, there are also qualities that cities share and that make each one like all others. It is not surprising, as Fehn's work proceeds from one urban setting to the next, that the body of the work would collectively exhibit similarities. This is consistent with expectations regarding evidence of a designer's signature in the appearance of the project, and Fehn's work is no exception. But because, as I hope to show, Fehn's work is concerned with aspects of urbanity in which an architectural project can stage and participate but not itself suffice, the result is that the markers of consistency legible across his projects are not only signatory but also representative of a general relationship between architecture and urbanity. This is the second sense in which Fehn's architecture points beyond itself, in which the lessons of his urban works exceed relevance to their unique situations and emerge as generalizable to broader understanding of architecture's role in urban settings. If Fehn's thinking on urban architecture can seem to teeter between poetic and cryptic, if his approach to those architectural problems can seem unorthodox within his professional circumstance, then the urban attentions substantiated in his designs and the lessons derived therefrom are, nevertheless, imminently portable. In the following chapters, I will explore the relationship between these local and general urban attentions.

On Urbanity

I need to return to the term *urbanity*, because it is central to most of what follows, because my use of the term even to this point has already emerged as critical, and because its definition is neither obvious nor uncontested. Complicating matters, the term *urbanity* and its cognates appear in this text not only in relation to my thinking but also in citation of Fehn's thinking, and while the second has informed the first, they are not everywhere the same. An opening consideration of the term will help delineate its usage here and will help to further define my interests in Fehn's urban architecture. I will begin with a more general consideration of the term before proceeding to Fehn's usage.

In its simplest sense, the term *urbanity*[6] can be a mere category indicating association with the city: if it is found in a city, it can be said to belong to urbanity, a heading encompassing all things city. The term has also been used more narrowly to allude to a realm of sophistication, refinement, or high-culture, and in this sense can evoke, intentionally or otherwise, exclusivity and condescension. The usage I employ in this text is narrower than the first definition and distinct from the social stratification and exclusion implicit in the second. It is intended here, rather, to indicate something essential to urban life. Urbanity, in this sense, is expressed in the conditions and institutions we commonly associate with city, but is also the progenitor of those conditions, not merely their byproduct. A better understanding of the relationship between this ineffable phenomenon and the architecture of the physical city is among the primary goals of this book.

Corollary to this conceptual parsing of urbanity from the city—that the terms are neither synonymous nor coextensive—are the ideas that, one, urbanity belongs to a mode of living that might be found outside of cities as well as within them; and, two, that cities, at least conceptually, are not guarantors of urbanity, inasmuch as different urban configurations might variously sustain, augment, neglect, or diminish urbanity. My interest in this separation, especially with regard to Fehn's work, follows a rich history in the consideration of city and city-ness. One of the oldest formulations remains one of the clearest. Aristotle's *Politics* is almost entirely given to an explication of governance and its relation to the polis. In modern analyses of that text, scholars have largely tended to conflate the two things, routinely translating πόλις as *state*. But Aristotle, in a preamble to a section of his meditation, suggested that a political account of the city was subordinate to an account of what the city *is*, making clear his presumption of the difference. He then briefly but presciently framed the distinction as follows. Attempting in a few lines to consider what made a polis a polis, he posited that you might have a diverse population living harmoniously in light of a system of laws, that those people's needs might be met with a functioning economy, that the size of that population might be vast, their proximities dense, with provisions made to assure their safety, and, yet, he asserted, you might still not have a polis.[7] That is, Aristotle intuited that the polis in its essence was not to be found at a particular scale, nor in a system of laws, nor economies, nor even in the peaceful coexistence of large numbers of people. This suggests, in what first seems paradoxical, that the essence of city-ness—whatever that may be—can be decoupled from definitions of city: you might have one without the other, or both but to varying degrees.

If this line of thought long predates modernity, it is with the advent of the modern industrial city that the problem evolved from a theoretical to an empirical one. In his book, *Ethics and the Urban Ethos*, theologian Max Stackhouse argued that in the modern era, "the urban ethos" had spread far beyond the city, and that, paradoxically, city-dwellers were increasingly alienated from that ethos.[8] As the modern industrial city matured, it became plausible to doubt that cities were the guarantors of urbanity.[9] In the 20th century, modern theorists of urban life from diverse disciplines came to regard the fractured relation of urbanity and city as an emergent problem. While the antithesis of urban life had traditionally been embodied in the hinterlands or the exurban wilderness beyond, that antithesis might now, observers argued, be found not only in the suburbs but also in the city itself.[10] One of the most sustained arguments on this topic came from political and social theorist Murray Bookchin, who over the course of several decades developed the idea that modern "urbanization" is antithetical to the urbanity of the city. For Bookchin, the term *urbanization* referred to sprawl and globalization as driven by the modern nation-state and its economic codependent, the multinational corporation. Whereas cosmopolitanism had typically been pejoratively cast as antithetical to nationalist interests, Bookchin understood both phenomena—cosmopolitanism and nationalism—as parasitic to the city.[11] Developing arguments delineated by Lewis Mumford decades earlier[12] and (as he was surely aware) by Peter Kropotkin earlier still,[13] Bookchin argued that the paramount problems of injustice and ecological degradation were symptoms of urbanity's consequent diminishment, even as the technological, infrastructural metropolis proliferated—in fact, Bookchin argued, the hegemony of the technological and infrastructural dimensions of the modern city exacerbated the diminishment of its urbanity.

While I have no reason to believe that either of the two was even aware of the other's existence, Fehn and Bookchin were coconspirators in this critique. In an essay titled, "Urbanism," the only essay in which Fehn explicitly wrote under that heading, Fehn states the problem this way:

> The city as a convergence of thoughts cannot favor a production that is removed from thinking. When a city realizes that a production is rational, it rejects the fabrication. It gives no room, as it creates no 'room' around itself. The hydroturbine has no interest. When the steam produces energy the city leaves. The technique makes energy independent from thought. Its production is reduced to the boredom of mechanical perfection.[14]

A fuller understanding of this passage requires explication of what Fehn means here by "convergence of thoughts" and "room," a task I will take up when returning to the quote in Chapter 4. Clear for now, though, is that for Fehn there is something essential to city that is not consonant with an instrumental rationalism and its products. He writes as if the city, personified, were repulsed by it. Of course, the physical city does not and cannot "leave." But in Fehn's thinking, the city-ness of the city—echoing Stackhouse's "urban ethos," Bookchin's "city life," Aristotle's essence of the polis—might, nevertheless, be displaced or diminished: for Fehn, something essential to the city—urbanity—is put at risk when rational production is its end. Fehn's architecture, I will show, pursues several design strategies for countering those risks so that a more robust urbanity might be obtained in the contemporary city.

8 *Fehn in the City: "What Makes This All So Alive"*

Fehn, Romanticism, Cosmopolitanism, and the City

The previous quotation from Fehn is so reminiscent of an earlier one from Eric Gunnar Asplund that one cannot help but wonder if Fehn's was in response to it specifically. In any case, I want to use Asplund's quotation as entrance to consideration of another aspect of Fehn's urban approach that will be useful here at the outset, and which will help to further elucidate a concept of urbanity and its relation to architecture. In an essay from 1931, Asplund expounded on problems associated with Stockholm's phlegmatic modernization and the role of architecture therein. In a passage where he argues for replacing "the old good, that must disappear," with "the new good," he wrote:

> It is true that development is not always the same as improvement, and we do not know whether horsepower is better or worse for human life and happiness than the horse. But building-art cannot decide such questions; it is a servant that has to accept the prevailing culture and base what it does on it.[15]

If Asplund's quotation is representative of a progressivist approach to the architecture of the city, can Fehn's, 40 years later, be correctly understood as representative of a reactionary one? It seems an easy argument to make. As mentioned above, Fehn's work has typically been cast as regionalist. Adding to that conservative characterization, Fehn's works do not facilitate erasure of what Asplund referred to as "the old good." On the contrary, as I will show, orientation toward a setting's historical depths is among the primary concerns of Fehn's urban architecture. Fehn's statements about architecture can also exhibit a poetic, not to say mystical, quality that might hasten categorizing his approach as generally conservative. But if Fehn's architectural purview is seen to align with certain strains of Romanticism, that reading is complicated by other attentions evident in his work. A few biographical details will help found this point.[16]

The primary influence in Fehn's early architectural education was the Norwegian modernist master, Arne Korsmo, a key figure in the propagation of progressivist ideals in Norway and beyond (Fehn and his family would eventually live in the modernist Villa Dammann, designed by Korsmo in 1931). Early in his career, Fehn worked with Andre Shimmerling as an original contributor to the avant garde publication *Le Carré Bleu* (originally *International Folio of Architecture*). While Shimmerling was contributing to the Finnish branch of CIAM, Fehn joined the Norwegian one, PAGON, which had been established by Korsmo at the request of Sigfried Giedion in 1950. From 1953 to 1954, Fehn left Oslo to work for Jean Prouvé's atelier in Paris, a period in which that office's projects focused on the development of prototypes for deployable lightweight metal housing, including Maison des Jours Meilleurs (1954). While living in Paris, Fehn visited the studio of Corbusier during off-hours.[17] In this period, Fehn was also especially attentive to the works of Louis Kahn[18] and Carlo Scarpa. Fehn would eventually meet with Scarpa while working on the Nordic Pavilion in Venice, which I consider in Chapter 2. As mentioned above, Fehn was also friends with several key members of Team X—notably, Alison and Peter Smithson, Aldo Van Eyck, and Giancarlo De Carlo. It was perhaps those alignments that led Reyner Banham to mention, in *The New Brutalism* (1966), Fehn's pioneering work with Gier Grung (even if, as Banham himself understood, the relation of the works collected in that text was subject to scrutiny). In the late 1970s, Fehn was an early participant and lecturer in De Carlo's International Laboratory for Architecture and Urban Design (ILAUD), where he taught alongside Peter Smithson, Van Eyck, and Renzo Piano, among others. While Fehn's professional and academic careers were based in Oslo, his activities as both practitioner and academician led to significant stints abroad, including teaching appointments at Cooper Union in New York, Cranbrook Academy in Detroit (both 1980), and the AA in London (1981–1982). Fehn was also highly literate in diverse arts, frequently and unassumingly drawing on references to novels, poems, paintings, and music from many cultures and in several languages. His annotations in his sketchbooks (of which he amassed dozens) are multilingual, in places combining languages on the same page. In his essays, he was as likely to refer to Borges as Jacobsen (Pietro Belluschi lecture), Veronese as Munch ("Poetry of the Straight Line"), and Kubrick as Ibsen (Cooper Union lecture).

This strongly cosmopolitan disposition can also easily be traced in his architectural efforts. Rather than traditional forms and techniques, Fehn, from the beginnings of his career frequently deployed experimental structural systems and building components in his designs—see, for example, any of several systems deployed at the Norwegian Pavilion (Brussels, 1958) or his Ecological House prototype (Mauritzberg, Sweden, 1992; Kolding,

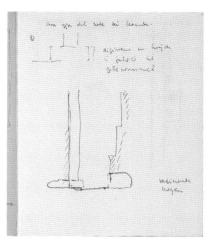

Figure 1.3 Sketch section of street in NYC, by Fehn, from sketchbook, 1977. Compare to Fehn's well-known sketches depicting caves as originary architecture. Fehn's handwriting is difficult to decipher but the top line seems to be, *hva gjør det hele så levende*: "what makes this all so alive." © Sverre Fehn/BONO. Courtesy of National Museum, Architecture Collections.

10 *Fehn in the City: "What Makes This All So Alive"*

Denmark, 1996). While most of his projects were located in Norway, Fehn pursued design work in at least 11 different countries. Even when working in Norway, his constructed projects eschewed strictly vernacular appearances, demonstrating a formal and material vocabulary consistent with subsets of mid-century modernism, sometimes drawing comparison to the buildings of Louis Kahn. It has often been remarked that the greatest esteem for Fehn's buildings came from *outside* of Norway, and Fehn himself puzzled over the hesitancy with which his countrymen—or at least its cultural critics—seemed to regard his buildings.

As a counter-thesis to the conservative cast discussed above, these cosmopolitan signals suggest the potential merit of a reappraisal of Fehn's architecture, one that would emphasize its more worldly characteristics as a check, or at least as complement, to assessments that have sought to emphasize a regionalist complexion. That endeavor is clearly within reach and would no doubt help expand our understanding of the scope of Fehn's architecture.

But if such an effort is forthcoming, we should not expect it to help us much with a better understanding of the urban dimensions of Fehn's works. If the antithesis of provincialism is cosmopolitanism, it is not clear that the causes of urbanity align with either. The two terms, *urban* and *cosmopolitan*, share notions of sophistication and complexity, and it has become common to conflate the concepts, as if the presence of one necessarily assured the other, or even to presume them to denote the same phenomena.[19] That mistake hampers our understanding of the architectural structure of urbanity. Returning to the pavilion in Oslo, for example, a scholar might reasonably highlight the project's obscured cosmopolitan traits—use of standardized components, a floor-to-ceiling glazing system, stylistic reference to mid-century Brutalism, no obvious engagement of vernacular traditions, hints of Miesian high-modernism—and yet still leave unexamined questions about the building's participation within, and co-structuring of, its urban milieu. Cast that work as conservatively regionalist or progressively cosmopolitan, either way, you are no closer to understanding its urbanity. Fehn's work indeed demonstrates connections to both local and global concern, but, I will show, those concerns are supplementary, not tantamount, to Fehn's interest in the architectural engagement of the city.

The preceding observation is not a point about the categorization or mischaracterization of the works of one architect, but rather how that architect's works illuminate a general characteristic of urbanity that such categorization fails to behold. As I will endeavor to elucidate in what follows, Fehn's successes in realizing richly urban configurations depend not on commitment to either edifying the past or overcoming it—the choice, I think, that Asplund's manifesto offers—but, rather, on a fluid, productively blurry relationship between creative attention to what has been and creative participation in what is emergent. Exposing simple conservative-progressive dichotomies as inadequate, this suggests that a definition of urbanity should include reference to the structure of movement from latent conditions to actual ones, that the degree of care and creativity brought to the regard of the existing condition, as an amalgam of pasts, prefigures the degree of creativity and vibrancy available to the unfolding present and its prospects.

In light of prevailing current cultural debates and their architectural intersections, I want to briefly pursue that last point, especially because the theme will recur in the ensuing explorations of Fehn's urban work. Fifteen years having now passed since his death, Fehn could not have anticipated the extent of the latest forms of environmental and social crises inflicted on urban life. Indeed, as a long-lived white European male weaned on mid-20th-century Modernism and hailing from a relatively conservative Norwegian culture, no doubt many would preemptively disqualify his work as pertinent to those contemporary crises. It would, indeed, be a mistake to gloss over certain conservative aspects of Fehn's work; but rather than regard those aspects as unfortunate, inconvenient, or anomalous, it is imperative to understand them as essential to the work's broader liberal aims. Amid a contemporary culture with a strong proclivity in arts, politics, and daily discourse to quickly delineate and harden liberal-conservative divides, this architectural understanding that interrogates supposed mutual exclusivity between conservative and liberal forces is both challenging and important to advance. It is abundantly clear that the city, generally, is a liberating and liberal force, and has been throughout history. It is perhaps owing to the overwhelming strength of this characteristic that we have yet to adequately account for those critical ingredients to urban life that do not cleanly conform to certain tenets of liberalism. As already argued, for example, the compatibility of urbanity and neoliberal pursuits cannot be presumed. As I will further explore in the next chapter and hope to clarify in all that follows, Fehn's architecture is especially instructive on this point, primarily in the ways it simultaneously marshals approaches typically allied with either end of the conservative-liberal spectrum and shows the two forces to be not antithetical but codependent, at least in the context of urban architecture, and mutually sustenant to urban life. Other than those who might dismiss Fehn's architecture as overly Romantic, not many would think of that work as overtly political, if by political we have in mind the intentional engagement and representation of contemporary political debates and broad political-historical themes. Yet Fehn's architecture, because of its intense interest in creating environments conducive to an active, diverse, contested, provocative, and dialogic urban life, and because of its carefully balanced intercourse with the natural world as given, and despite the circumstances of its author's personhood, and while that architecture significantly exceeds the sphere of politics, its political implications and political promise are profound, and have much to offer any who would seek a more equitable, tolerant, vibrant, city. These are among the most important ideas this book seeks to advance.

12　*Fehn in the City: "What Makes This All So Alive"*

Turning to Fehn's Urban Architecture

After dismissing key features associated with the city as summarized above, Aristotle never returned to the initial question with which he opened his chapter: "What is a city?" He does though, at the close of that chapter, turn to φιλία as essential, he says, to any polis "truly worthy of that name, and not only nominally so."[20] That is, Aristotle intuits that the essence of urbanity is a form of love, or at least inextricable from it. Some modern thinkers, too, have paralleled that line of thought—Alfonso Lingis, James Hillman, and Alberto Perez-Gomez; Hillman's thesis, arguing that that the city *is* the soul, may be the most encompassing.[21] No matter how compelling or truthful we may find them, such insights do not offer much of immediate use to those involved in the actual fabrication of the city: "make your buildings more loving, more soulful," might make a fine credo but it is not at all clear what it might indicate for architects, like Fehn, seeking to design buildings that meaningfully engage and realize a higher degree of urbanity. For them, a more specific question arises: "How do buildings materially manifest and promote the condition of urbanity?" How we answer that question will affect what we expect from our cities and, by extension, what we should expect from the buildings that constitute those cities and how we assess the architectural decisions that shape them. If novelty and density and efficiency and infrastructure and busy-ness and publicity and worldliness do not on their own nor together add up to urbanity, how, exactly, might an architect otherwise conceive, engage, and sustain configurations conducive to urbanity? What design habits might inadvertently render urbanity *less* probable? What, even, is the vocabulary for such a conversation? How might it be disseminated? Such is the conceptual topography I have in my sights as I explore Fehn's projects, though I do not pretend that I might satisfactorily exhaust those broad questions in the form of a single book. My aim, rather, is to find in Fehn's works a landing of sorts from which further explorations might be launched. If Fehn, like others before him, intuited the essence of the city to lie elsewhere than in its networks and systems and laws, where did that intuition lead him as a designer, and to what effect in his buildings? The formulation that I rely on throughout as I study Fehn's architectural works is, "What is the nature of this building's urbanity and how is that condition materially effected?"

Organization of the Work and Its Themes

Overall, the book is organized into five chapters, including this introductory one, comprising detailed consideration of ten select projects—six built, four proposed—with reference to several others. The chapters are organized thematically, as if in layers, each serving as substrate for the next. To explain the structure of the following text, it is helpful to further develop an idea I introduced above: the ways that Fehn's architecture can

Fehn in the City: "What Makes This All So Alive" 13

be understood to point away from itself. One way to refine that idea is by appealing to a concept of architectural *reach*. Fehn's architecture, I want to argue, is marked by three kinds of reach: chronological, circumstantial, and ethical-cultural (it might be easier to use the term *practical* here, if not for confusion about its definition). These categories, I will show, are mutually informing, and not intended to be distinct. Loosely, then, each category corresponds to each of the three chapters that compose the main body of the text.

By chronological reach, I mean the ways that Fehn's architecture seeks to marshal a site's historical vestiges for involvement in present, nascent conditions. For Fehn, the most essential concept in this kind of reach is *ground*. Chapter 2 examines the critical role of *ground* in his urban thinking and designs, where ground is not merely the primitive foil against which a sophisticated urban condition is measured, upon which it rests, but is also essential to the vibrancy and sustenance of those conditions, and actively so. In Fehn's thinking, ground, history, and the present were inseparable, a matrix in which the past's incorporation into contemporary daily life was, in his words, "the key to culture's birth," a phrase to which I will return. That thinking connects ground to urbanity in ways consistent with etymologies of *culture* and its cognates, in which a relationship is proposed between "the roots" and "the crown" of culture, using Schelling's terms.[22] But Fehn carries this idea beyond the realm of theory, directly to that of construction. This is not a case of architectural design aimed at the modeling of a philosophical construct. On the contrary, in Fehn's work it is the architecture that carries the most potent meaning while the supporting words, representations, and mental constructs float around them like aromas. In his designs, I will show, Fehn deploys excavation, surface treatment, form, and detailing to render the multilayered past, in differing scales of time, variously available to the unfolding present. The resulting extension of cultural possibility and continuity are, for Fehn, essential to a robust urbanity. I explore those ideas primarily through a consideration of three projects—the *Vasa* Museum, the Hedmark Museum, and the Trondheim Library.

With the idea of circumstantial reach, I have in mind engagement of, literally, "that which stands around," but also immaterial local conditions for which the word "standing" is only apt in the sense of something that is given and ongoing. The way a building engages its climate, for example, or its landscape, belongs in this category. So too, though, might ineffable qualities like a place's mood or character, as expressed in the idea of "ambiance," a word descriptive of phenomena straddling the threshold of physical and mental realities. While considering the philology of the term *ambiance* and the related term *milieu*, Leo Spitzer described that threshold as "an inexpressible harmony between men, things, and situations."[23] Pursuing that idea in an architectural context, Chapter 3 uses three of Fehn's constructed projects to explore three kinds of architectural engagement of

14   *Fehn in the City: "What Makes This All So Alive"*

urban ambiance. The first project considers how a small project typical to daily city life—a store-lined street, a busy sidewalk, a simple shop—creates an ambiance that relates the exotic and theatrical aspects of urban life to the mundane and practical ones. Exploring the previously introduced idea of how urbanity might be obtained in a setting detached from the city, the second of the projects shows Fehn working to establish an urban ambiance in a non-urban setting. Villa Norrköping demonstrates how a detached dwelling on a rural site might nevertheless be understood as embodying an urban character. The simplicity of the building's setting, relative to the city, permits a focus on how specific design decisions related to light, surface, and spatial modulation sustain practices that can be understood as essential to urbanity, even in an exurban environment. Having considered two projects at the limits of an urban spectrum—a small shop, a suburban house—I turn to a hybrid case in the third project, Fehn's Nordic Pavilion in Venice, a project at once in a garden and in a city. This is the best known and most considered of the projects I examine in this book. Against the backdrop of others' diverse approaches to this most famous of Fehn's projects, my goal is to better understand the building as a work of urban architecture, and to derive urban lessons from it that might be relevant beyond its immediate setting. Key here is not only the project's assertion of an urban ambiance but also its participation within an existing one.

Building on ideas explored in the previous sections, Chapter 4 focuses on the urban lessons of two unbuilt proposals that Fehn made for major public projects on dense, fully urban sites. There are rather obvious problems associated with constructing arguments entirely from examination of unconstructed designs. Chief among those, in this case at least, is that I am left to make arguments dependent on the primacy of spatial experience using two projects that only exist in the forms of drawings and models. But the two projects, a museum in Oslo and a theater in Copenhagen, both remarkably complex as urban interventions, reward deciphering even as proposals. Of the many architectural lessons held in these two designs, most significant is their engagement and augmentation of established urban patterns of movement and habituation. Fehn appeals to several urban concepts in these works, none more germane than what he calls "the floor of city," which, he says, "is known to all of its citizens." Fehn means more here than rehearsing the existing rhythms and textures of an identifiable urban meander. In both projects, he sets up conditions for various kinds of participation in their respective cities, participation that ranges from quotidian to extraordinary, and that puts the two modes into active relation. To develop that idea in relation to Fehn's architectural configurations, I appeal to notions of methexis, discord, and theatricality in urban settings.

In the final chapter, less conclusion than recapitulation, I return to the work introduced at the beginning, Fehn's Arkitektur Museet in Oslo, and bring one of his earliest constructed projects to that analysis—the Norwegian Pavilion for the 1958 Brussels World Fair. Making use of ideas

Fehn in the City: "What Makes This All So Alive" 15

developed in the preceding chapters and pursuing questions posed here at the beginning, Fehn's last project is finally examined as an urban work: "What is the nature of this building's urbanity?"

Notes

1 An encyclopedic effort would include Fehn's Bøler Community Center, the Skådalen School for Deaf Children, and his proposals for Oslo's Karl Johan Complex and Homansbyen Metro Station, to name four of the most significant that are not included here. Those are strong projects with important lessons in their own right, and were researched and documented in preparation for this book.
2 Reyner Banham, *The New Brutalism* (New York: Reinhold Publishing, 1966), 125, 137.
3 Mari Hvattum briefly considered this situation in her excellent essay on Fehn's Villa Schreiner. See, Mari Hvattum, *Villa Schreiner*, eds. Nina Berre and Mari Lending (Oslo: Pax Forlag, 2014), 29.
4 Per Olaf Fjeld, conversation with author, Tønsberg, August 7, 2010.
5 Per Olaf Fjeld, correspondence with author, March 21, 2020.
6 Etymology is of not much help here. The word's provenance is clear as far as Latin's *urbis*, but its deeper origins are contested. The Latin *urbanus* meant, "of a city," and also, "citified, cultivated." The word *urbanity* is attested from 1530. For an account of the concept in the classical era, see Edwin Ramage, *Urbanitas: Ancient Sophistication and Refinement* (Norman, OK: University of Oklahoma Press, 1973).
7 Aristotle, *Politics*, Book 3, Chapter 9, 1280b, 1281a.
8 Max L. Stackhouse, *Ethics and the Urban Ethos* (Boston, MA: Beacon Press, 1972). See especially Chapters 1–3.
9 Gertrude Stein's infamous quip about Oakland—"there is no *there* there"— comes to mind: her assertion was arguably wrong, but not inconceivable.
10 Documenting the history of that critique would be a book in itself. A much abbreviated list of key contributors from a cross-sampling of disciplines, each with useful and extensive bibliographies of their own, includes Lewis Mumford, Max Stackhouse, Murray Bookchin, Raymond Williams, Jane Jacobs, Stephen Toulmin, James Hillman, David Harvey, and Henri Lefebvre.
11 Murray Bookchin, *From Urbanization to Cities* (London: Cassell, 1992), Chapter 1. See also, Bookchin, *Limits of the City* (New York: Black Rose Books, 1986), especially Chapter 4.
12 Lewis Mumford, *The Culture of Cities* (New York: Harcourt, Brace, & Co., 1934).
13 Peter Kropotkin, "Mutual Aid in the Medieval City," *The Nineteenth Century: A Monthly Review* August (1894).
14 Sverre Fehn, "Urbanity," in *The Thought of Construction*, ed. P.O. Fjeld (New York: Rizzoli, 1983), 142.
15 Erik Gunnar Aslpund, et al., *Acceptera* (Stockholm: Tilden, 1931) collected in *Modern Swedish Design: Three Founding Texts*, eds. Mary Creagh, et al. (New York: Museum of Modern Art, 2008), 303.
16 Fehn characterized his relationship to modernist thinking in an interview in *Skala*, saying, "I have never thought of myself as being modernistic." Also:

> I have never thought of myself as modern, but I did absorb the anti-monumental and the pictorial world of LeCorbusier, as well as the

functionalism of the small villages of North Africa. You might say I came of age in the shadow of modernism.

See Mathilde Petri, "Sverre Fehn: An Interview." *Skala* 23 (1990): 12–17.
17 Many biographies of Fehn have variously emphasized the point—stating, for example, as Wikipedia's entry does, that Fehn "knew" Corbusier. In a personal conversation with the author, Per Olaf Fjeld recounted that Fehn attempted to visit Corbusier several times, but that he can attest with certainty only one meeting.
18 See Fjeld's book for how Korsmo's relationship with Kahn influenced Fehn. Per Olaf Fjeld, *Louis I. Kahn: The Nordic Latitudes* (Fayetteville, AR: University of Arkansas Press, 2019), Chapter 1.
19 The two words are frequently listed as synonyms in popular thesauri, and even appear in their respective definitions in some popular dictionaries.
20 Aristotle, *Politics*, Book 3, Chapter 9, 1280b, 1281a.
21 James Hillman, *City and Soul* (Putnam, CT: Spring Publications, 2008).
22 Friedrich Schelling, *On the History of Modern Philosophy*, trans. Andrew Bowie (Cambridge: Cambridge University Press, [1833] 1994), 173.
23 Leo Spitzer, "*Milieu* and *Ambiance*: An Essay in Historical Semantics." *Philosophy and Phenomenological Research Quarterly* 3, no. 1 (1942): 1. See Spitzer's further treatment in his, "Classical and Christian Ideas of World Harmony: Prolegomena to an Interpretation of the Word 'Stimmung.'" *Traditio* 2 (1944): 1–42.

2 Opened Ground

> Just, in fact, as the vessel is transportable place, so place is non-portable vessel.
>
> Aristotle. *Physics*, Book IV, part 4

Sverre Fehn wrote, "We must again find a dialogue with the earth."[1] Perhaps no consideration informed his work more than that of *ground*. During an interview in 1990, Fehn said, in a bit of understatement, "The physical ground means a lot to me." Regard of ground as something more than dirt and toil is common among architects, but some have given special attention to that set of ideas. Adolf Loos averred that the essence of architecture inhered in the experience of a grave-like mound of excavated soil.[2] Loos is germane here not just as a familiar example, but also because his thinking on culture and ground in the essay to which that quote belongs is aimed, ultimately, at a clearer understanding of the city. Fehn shared that concern. Exploration of connections between ground and city appears throughout his work. Engagement of ground pervades Fehn's projects, sketches, explications, and teachings, so that to give a full account of his understanding and use of ground—as concept, metaphor, and construction—would be to encompass much of his work, if not its entirety. Indeed, the pervasiveness of Fehn's attention to ground has perhaps contributed to difficulties in understanding his work's urban significance: if Fehn, like Loos, found synthesis in ground and urbanity, it is not immediately clear what the two terms might have to do with each other. It is easy, even, to construe the terms as opposed: the city enlightened, liberated from a constraining ground. In this chapter, I want to follow Fehn in suspending that opposition. When Fehn deploys the term *ground* (and related terms like *layer*, *floor*, and *earth*), it frequently appears with terms like *city* and *culture* and *urbanity*—not antithetically, but coactively. More important is Fehn's architecture, where it is precisely in his attentions to urban configurations that his engagement of ground is most elaborate. Understanding this relation is essential to understanding Fehn's urban thinking and work, and that is reason enough to explore it. There is more to be found here, though, than a better understanding of the

DOI: 10.4324/9781003343646-2

interests and design habits of a single talented architect. An examination of Fehn's work will direct us beyond it, to a set of points pertinent to urban architecture more generally, to architecture's capacity to engage ground in order to yield a greater urbanity.

Typically I might now introduce Fehn's essay on the urban aspects of ground, explicate that text, and then proceed to architectural details that support what was discovered in the writing. But no such essay exists, and in any event, that methodology would be backwards. What we have is clear evidence of the importance in Fehn's thinking of both city and ground (and their conceptual cognates), coupled with many written and spoken allusions—typically short and often apocryphal—to a relationship between them. A better understanding of Fehn's thinking on those connections requires careful examination of design decisions evident in his buildings and proposals, checked against the textual fragments as a set. That is what follows. I will then attempt to use an amalgam of those observations to attempt a summary of Fehn's connections between ground and urbanity. I require patience of the reader, then, on two counts. First, the relevance of some of the following analyses to the broader topic of architecture and urbanity will often not be immediately clear and will at times be left in a liminal state, so to speak, until further substantiation is amassed, substantiation that frequently requires sustained examination of architectural detail. And second, the broader, more coherent interpretations of the interconnections in Fehn's works between ground and urbanity which I eventually offer cannot be definitive, only interpretive. This, at the outset, can be said with certainty: an analysis of the urban aspects of Fehn's architecture that lacks an account of his thinking on ground is partial, at best; and an attempt—even a primarily hermeneutic one—to better understand the link between ground and urbanity in Fehn's work informs a better understanding of the architecture of urbanity in general.

As alluded, there are no shortage of projects that could stage a consideration of Fehn's understanding of ground, and almost as many that could further a consideration of ground's relation to urbanity specifically. I have selected three projects to explore in that context—a competition proposal for a museum, a constructed museum, and a competition proposal for a library, in that order, each particularly useful for understanding key components of Fehn's interrelation of ground and urbanity. The first project is the proposed *Vasa* Museum in Stockholm, wherein Fehn's engagement of urban concerns is less explicit than the following two projects, but which illuminates Fehn's thinking on *ground* as well as any of his designs. To understand how Fehn translates those ideas into a more specifically urban narrative and engages them in constructed material form, I turn to his Hedmark museum in Hamar. Despite its relatively isolated location, the Hedmark Museum demonstrates a subset of concerns related to ground and urbanity—as Fehn himself argued—that will be useful when turning to Fehn's projects in dense urban settings in this chapter and the ones that

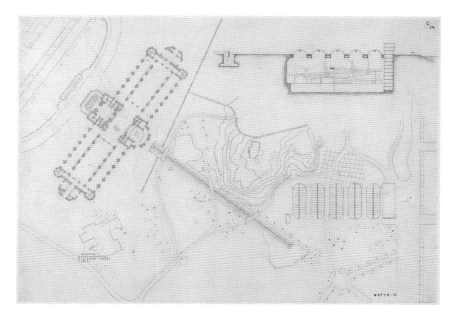

Figure 2.1 Vasa Museum, site plan and building section. © Sverre Fehn. Photo: Veiby, Jeanette. Courtesy of National Museum, Architecture Collections.

follow. Lastly, Fehn's proposal for the Trondheim Public Library, where Fehn's address of ground for the augmentation of urbanity found its most complex expression, will serve as a case-study of Fehn's implementation of these ideas in a fully urban setting. Chronologically, the two proposed projects were designed after the constructed one: I do not intend to show Fehn's sequential development as a designer here, but to better understand a way of designing that keeps ground and urbanity in close and active relation, and to consider what might be gained.

"Dance Round Dead Things"

Sverre Fehn wrote that the architect

> can establish places under the ground, and these become the new way to travel into the past, as the horizon faces a new journey. [...] The cultural artifacts that are uncovered are now placed on the surface of the earth, but where is each object's personal shadow? The problem is, where shall each object meet its new light? I think my projects penetrate this struggle. [At this point, Fehn lists six of his projects that he understands as pertaining to the topic.] But the idea culminated in the Vasa Ship Museum, where the entire museum was an underground journey.[3]

The project to which Fehn refers, perhaps the most widely cited of his unbuilt designs, one that Fehn himself frequently presented in his lectures, is his 1981 competition proposal to transform a disused 19th-century dry-dock in Stockholm into an exhibition complex for the ruins of the *Vasa* (often, *Wasa*), a hulking 160' tri-masted warship that had been salvaged in 1961 after 333 years at the bottom of the city's Saltsjön bay. Fehn did not win the competition, and, according to one account, the jury made no mention of his proposal. The winning entry, constructed in 1988, suspended the ship roughly at the water-level of the adjacent bay and enveloped it in a large, formally frenetic hangar dominating the waterfront. In striking contrast, in a move that must have seemed exotic to the competition jury, Fehn proposed that the deep dry-dock be *further* excavated so that the entirety of the salvaged vessel could be positioned in an underground chamber, in Fehn's words, "as if it was still at the bottom of the ocean."[4] Even with the truncated masts unrestored, this would have required excavating to a depth of 30m—and, as discussed below, Fehn's design required even more extensive earthwork. The proposal orchestrated a series of relationships between the site's existing local conditions, the ruins of the ship, the city's past, and the larger contemporary city. In all of these interconnections, Fehn's treatment of the ground is decisive.

The existing dry-dock was located on the city's Djurgården island, fortuitously adjacent to the Nordic Museum (designed by Isak Gustaf Clason, c.1899). Fehn proposed a long passageway incised into the surface of the park behind the existing museum, extending axially from the museum's basement, toward the bay, to a balcony-like entry point near the top of the cavernous underground chamber that was to be fashioned from the dry-dock: a linear subterranean passageway connecting the 19th-century building to the new exhibit (Figures 2.1 and 2.2). From there, a suspended helical catwalk descended into the chamber, diagonally between the masts, across and then adjacent to the ship, looping down, and finally arriving at the floor of the exhibition area positioned near the ship's waterline far below the actual surface of the harbor. Fehn's competition drawings and later commentary indicate that the base of the chamber was to consist of a pool to buoy, support, and protect the hull, and which would reflect the window-framed sky far above. The resultant up-lighting effect, characteristic of marine environments, would have been accentuated in this dim subterranean context, rather like sky reflected in the bottom of an artesian well, rehearsing at once the ship's brief existence on the sea, and also its long existence beneath it.

Light into the vestibular axial ramp and the exhibition chamber were accomplished through low, greenhouse-like roof structures roughly coplanar with grade (section, Figure 2.1). At the long passage, those skylights were supported by a thin concrete beam running the entire length of the subterranean corridor, bearing on a row of columns in the middle of that hall, and fit with trussed mullions above. The skylights at the dry-dock chamber were supported by a series of massive, shallowly curved concrete box-beams in clear spans.

Opened Ground 21

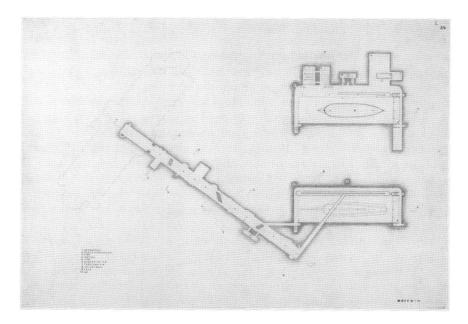

Figure 2.2 Vasa Museum, floor plans. North at left. © Sverre Fehn. Photo: Veiby, Jeanette. Courtesy of National Museum, Architecture Collections.

These glazed roof enclosures were to be the only grade-level presence of the new exhibit, treated more like components of a landscaping plan than pronouncements of a new building. Curiously, the proposed building had no facade, no physiognomy at all. It is a clear indication that Fehn's urban attentions and creative energies were directed somewhere other than formal expression: not many architects (or clients) afforded an opportunity to realize a major waterfront project in a large city would pursue a design so thoroughly incognito. But much was gained from this set of decisions. By connecting the new exhibit directly to the existing museum, the older building maintained its role as the primary architectural focus and singular point of entry, avoiding visual competition between old and new, and avoiding the logistical complications of detached venues: the new building would build upon and enhance the role of the old. On a larger scale, Fehn's decisions with regard to siting, both horizontally and vertically, reflect a concern for maintaining and complementing the character and visual connection between the existing museum and the harbor, and with the city's center across the harbor to the northwest (whereas the project that was actually constructed, frankly, makes a mess of those relationships).

Further developing the role of the almost entirely submerged museum as a participant in a landscape, the long cut of the sky-lit access-way linking the existing museum to the dry-dock chamber was to be flanked at grade by shallow reflecting pools along both sides of its entire length (Figure 2.1). At both ends of the long cut, that aqueous border opened into two proposed, irregularly shaped ponds to be set into the landscape between the older museum and the harbor, completing the liquid frame and making an island of the long rectangular excavated passage. Depth framed by sky. Or, rather, the cut was entirely framed by water and sky at once, rendering the geoposition of the passage strangely ambiguous, as if carved from nothingness.

This reflective water-frame was bridged at three points where the cut intersected proposed paths crossing the garden, interrupting the continuity of the glazed roof and affording views down into and along the linear cut from without where the project's relationship to the landscape would be best beheld. These proposed garden paths are significant. Fehn's drawings show them circumnavigating a small knoll near the site's center to reach a gate in an existing wall that extended from near the southern end of the Nordic Museum. Though Fehn's site plan gave no indication of what the gate led to, that wall defines the northwestern perimeter of Galärvarvskyrkogården—literally, "dry-dock graveyard"—an important naval cemetery dating to the 18th century. Its presence on the site, as Fehn received it, was strong, with an existing chapel and many of the gravestones literally lying within the shadow of the museum (Figure 2.3). Fehn's site plan, then, connected the graves of sailors, the wreckage of the *Vasa*, the existing Nordic Museum, and the *dromos*-like cut through the garden, bringing multiple layers, scales, and vantages of history into correspondence with each other and with the city.

Figure 2.3 Galärvarvskyrkogården. 100 m east of drydock, view toward Nordic Museum. Cemetery extends to within 5 m of museum. Photograph courtesy of First Morning travel blog, www.firstmorning.se.

That elaborate interweaving magnifies the subterranean passage's role in the project even as its presence on the site is subdued. What might have been merely instrumental—a hallway connecting exhibits—is instead marshaled to enhance the meaning and experience of the project as a whole. The passage is preparatory; it affords continuity to the existing conditions and also enframes those conditions, drawing what was initially circumstantial and fragmented into new and weak coherence. The literal connecting of the site's manifold histories, the emphasis of descent, the hall's constriction, and, for those preceding along the hall, the bracketing-out of middle-distance all predicate the ambiance of the main chamber.

For Fehn, these decisions concerning the linear passage are not only about staging a series of stimulating spatial experiences. He likened such excavations to surgical incisions that exposed the hidden innards of the body, and, for him, this earthen vivisection was the most primary step in all architecture:

> The grass is the skin of the earth. As a surgeon opens the body from breast to navel, so the architect opens the Earth from the Nordic Museum to the old dock where the ship will lie. This way you can make a journey where the objects can retreat to a quiet, shady world where they can continue their conversation.[5]

Cutting reveals what is hidden, that is clear. Less expected is how Fehn's observation ends in conversation: disclosure opens dialog, what was marginal is readmitted. Those are the two most important ideas conveyed in Fehn's statement; but there is another one, admittedly secondary, that arises from his choice of analogy. A surgeon's project is recuperative. It imagines and then endeavors, at some risk, to realize the patient's healthier future. This suggests that Fehn understood the *Vasa* proposal as surgical not only in its incising but also in its concern for well-being. The spatial sequences that Fehn orchestrates at *Vasa* are sensuous. Sensory stimulation, though, is not their end but rather a means of opening a space for dialog between past and present. Fehn's analogy suggests that the health of the present depends on that dialog.

Indeed, Fehn's design actively facilitates such dialog on multiple levels and at various scales, as if providing imaginative prompts for opening conversation. Small objects recovered from the wreckage were to be organized into displays in niches along the connecting passageway. The presentation of the largest of the museum's artifacts—the *Vasa* itself—was peculiar not only for its relationship to grade and sea but also for the perspective from which it was encountered: the visitor entered the chamber from near its top. Fehn wrote of the significance of this sequence, entering at the position of the sails, arguing that the essence of sailing is found where canvas, wind, and mast meet.[6] At the broadest cultural-ethical level, sea-faring and its milieu are foundational in Scandinavian cultures, and remain significant—a nautical heritage that, as many have observed, has historically characterized Scandinavian architecture and building practices.

Fehn was actively engaged in that heritage, and his thinking was often borne by a nautical predisposition.[7] His notebooks and lecture notes are replete with boat images, usually sailing vessels, in a range of scales, angles, details, and circumstances (Figure 2.4). When Fehn, at *Vasa*, established architectural conditions whereby a visitor might behold something essential to sailing, it was also an opening to consider connections between the exhibited relic and broader cultural themes. But the project's spatial sequences structure more than an exercise in historical cross-fertilization: its presentation of the ship is not pedantic but daring. The *Vasa* is presented so as to exceed its status as dry historical fragment, and to recover something of its originating audacity, ingenuity, and sublimity. One of Fehn's most succinct summaries of the intentional interfusing of past and present at *Vasa* came in a lecture he titled, "The Skin, the Cut, and the Bandage." Just after relating a story about the discovery of an ancient Greek tomb found with a child still holding his doll, and about the tragedy of separating them, Fehn said, speaking of his *Vasa* proposal in second person:

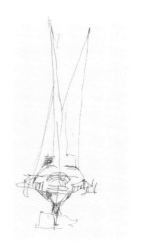

Figure 2.4 Sketch of sailing vessel from aft, by Fehn, from sketchbook, 1993. © Sverre Fehn. Courtesy of National Museum, Architecture Collections.

> Back to the museum, with this morality in your heart. You made a cut in the park, and in that cut you put a concrete beam, and resting on that concrete beam you have some wood construction that nearly touches the ground, but doesn't. You work with this philosophy that says you use the skin of the earth to preserve and exhibit an object that was on the boat 30m underground. Life has come here. You think about a knife, cutting with this concrete construction. Suddenly you get something, because when you think about boats, you think about life in the white sails, and the masts like columns.[8]

For Fehn, finding an architecture capable of opening up such an active and imaginative level of dialog between past and present involved calibration. In Fehn's estimation, success led to the re-animation of the past, brought to the present: amidst ruin, cemetery, and ground, "Life has come here."

It is an uncertain claim, given that the project was never realized, but I want to argue that Fehn's risky decision to position the boat in a subterranean chamber was part of that calibration. I have discussed how that decision was a weak move—productively weak—in the project's deference and accentuation of the existing conditions. But, below grade, that move had the effect of amplifying the presence of the ruined ship and rescuing the vessel from the more univocal existence it would have suffered (and has suffered) at the surface. I suspect the effect is two-fold. First, at the surface, the vessel would be more exposed to the contemporary city, in which it would appear as aberration or, worse, as a kitsch-like tourist destination. Fehn's design assumes greater control of circumstance, enabling a balance between detachment and select exposure, between discrete relic and an otherwise overwhelming contemporaneity. Second, the somber ambiance of the scheme is conducive to subverting the distances—dimensional and cognitive—between viewer and artifact. There is a high degree of reflectiveness—as Fjeld says, silence—evident in the design: not a tomb, but more tomb than diorama. The *dromos*-like access, the quietude, the bracketing of the world above and the light that filters down, the attention afforded the landscape and its given relationships, and the water at the chamber's base all advance the possibility that the ship-artifact might be met as something more than a chronological fragment utterly foreign to its now contemporary context, less an amusement than something akin to the neighboring cemetery—pensive, awesome, provocative. There is something humbling in this ambiance. This is possible because the overwhelming presence of the contemporary city has been partially checked, and the presence of the ship has been heightened, by the countervailing effect of the ship's interrupted interment.

It is in this sense that Fehn's design calibrates the weights of past and present, seeking a balance that will yield a more equal footing as a precondition for dialog. Fehn's design edifies the premise that architectural configurations can abet (or hamper) productive communication across eras, which is to say, reminiscent of Loos' mound, between the dead and the living, between the proxies of past cultures preserved in the ground and the actively unfolding culture of the city, understood as the same culture. Fehn's design thinking at *Vasa*, then, suggests a relationship between ground, dialog, and city, in which engagement of ground offers both historical extension and, counter to stasis, multiplication, through expanded dialog, of possibilities for divergence from existing conditions. This, I think, is the key interrelation of Fehn's dual concern with ground and urbanity. The various architectural engagements of ground that Fehn utilized at Vasa facilitated expanded dialog—not to enshrine nor summarize the past, but to enliven it, to render it available, effecting a more vibrant, more fecund, present.

Of Urbanity and Exhumation

Responding in an interview to a question about one of his most famous projects, Sverre Fehn said, "Someone without an urban sensibility in his or her subconscious could not have solved Hamar (Figure 2.5). One must understand the building as an urban reality. The exhibition became culture born again, new." This is a perplexing statement. As an entrance to foundational questions of urbanity, Sverre Fehn's Hedmark Museum[9] in Hamar makes an unlikely point of embarkment. As previously discussed, Fehn was not an urbanist in the mold of peers like de Carlo, Bakema, and Van Eyck, and even less so in comparison to urbanism's Post-Modern devotees. He knew those sets of ideas well, even participating at times in their dissemination, but he made no attempt to emulate that work nor ever presented himself as an urbanist. In fact, he explicitly distanced himself from the term, a position that likely factored in his reluctance to align with his colleagues (like Geir Grung) under the aegis of Team X, even though important pieces of his design thinking exhibited sympathy with their ideals. Second, modern Hamar is relatively small, and, while the town presents several urban lessons, the Hedmark project itself is peripheral to the town. The project site occupies part of a low promontory on the eastern shore of Lake Mjøsa, Norway's biggest, in a region largely characterized by the farms that populate the surrounding foothills, the distant arête, and the forests between. It is a topographical setting more accurately described as rural than urban, and at the threshold of wilderness: the Hedmark Museum is an isolated project on the outskirts of an isolated town in sparsely populated territory. Third, the project is a museum, a building type typically regarded as a

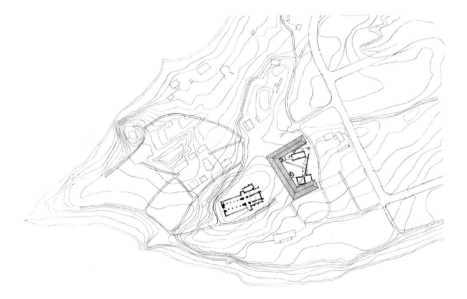

Figure 2.5 Hedmark Museum, site plan of peninsula (north at top). © Sverre Fehn. Photo: Ivarsøy, Dag Andre. Courtesy of National Museum, Architecture Collections.

symbol and agent of urbanity but almost always contrived, paradoxically, as a citadel apart from that context, often excising the exhibited objects from the context of the city within which they were derived. That critique has its own rich history. One of its most succinct expressions came from André Malraux:

> Indeed every work surviving from the past has been deprived of something – to begin with, the setting of its age. The work of sculpture used to lord it in a temple, a street, or reception-room. All these are lost to it. Even if the reception-room is 'reconstructed' in a museum, even if the statue has kept its place in the portal of its cathedral, the town which surrounded the reception-room or cathedral has changed.[10]

Fehn subscribed to this critique, echoing Malraux in asking, "Is there any greater loneliness than a catalogued mummy in foggy London, lying in the shadowless world of fluorescent lighting?"[11] Fehn's museum projects reflect a determination to break with those norms, for purposes I will discuss below. If urbanity is obtained in Fehn's Hedmark design, it is not by way of type.

Yet for all that, Fehn understood the Hedmark project to be essentially urban. An understanding of Fehn's link between the conditions of this project and, as he says, "urban reality" will help to fathom the urban dimension of other of his projects, and will inform a more general understanding of how architectural engagement of past and ground can contribute to the founding, perpetuation, and structure of urban settings. The Hedmark Museum presents Fehn's greatest realized effort to structure and incite a dialog between past and present, and to deploy this architecturally structured dialog in the founding of urban conditions.

A summary of the site's history will help make sense of the museum's purposes and of Fehn's design.[12] In the 11th century, the site became the new center of a nearby important farming network that had been operative in the Hedmark region of eastern Norway for several 100 years, formerly centered at Aker. The impetus for the shift to the new site may have been linked to the landholding interests and personal history of Harald Hardråde, the surprisingly cosmopolitan warrior traditionally regarded as the last of the Viking kings. A medieval village arose around the extensive new farm and emerged as a locus of trade and of Christianity as conversion from Germanic paganism falteringly advanced. During his service to the Catholic church in Norway, prior to his ascension as Pope Adrian IV, Nicholas Breakspear made Hamar the seat of a new bishopric, and, consequently, the construction of the Romanesque *Domkirke* there was underway by the middle of the 12th century. The medieval town thrived as a center of commerce, production, and political and religious power into the 14th century, but was then decimated by bubonic plague and subsequently began a long process of decline. The remnants of Hamar and its defining buildings were further diminished in the aftermath of the Reformation during which the vacated cathedral and bishop's house were converted to a sheriff's residence referred to as *Hamarhus* fortress, and then by war with Sweden, and then fell into complete disuse and ruin as the region's dwindling cultural and mercantile interests shifted south to the emergent city of Oslo. For all practical purposes, Hamar ceased to exist. Rural once again, the site was eventually converted to private property, and a farm known as *Storhammer*, comprising a handful of agrarian buildings adapted to the few remaining medieval ruins, was operated there from the mid-18th century. It was not until the middle of the 19th century, amid a zeitgeist of Romantic nationalism and economic expansion, that modern Hamar was founded from scratch just to the south of the medieval site, rising by the new millennium as a rail-connected tourist destination and minor lake port. Though almost all of medieval Hamar had vanished, the surviving ruins of the cathedral and of Storhammer were objects of curiosity, eventually attracting archaeologists to the site's 1,500 years of layered history, and gained recognition as a place of significant regional, national, and European heritage. In 1963, a project was initiated that would make a museum of the ruins, one that would allow for the archaeological work there to continue while making the findings of that work (and other regional artifacts) legible and available to the public. It would be named the Hedmark Museum. Fehn was charged with the project in 1967 through a bit of happenstance—a connection with a former student—and was periodically occupied with its design and realization until 1979 (Figure 2.6).[13]

Figure 2.6 Hedmark Museum, concrete ramp at courtyard. © Ukjent. Courtesy of National Museum, Architecture Collections.

Acknowledging that for no building are images and explications adequate substitutes for experience, the Hedmark Museum's ambiance is especially elusive to description. Before a summary of the constructed project, an anecdote may help convey something of its overall effect. When Australian architect, now Pritzker laureate, Glenn Murcutt was lecturing in Oslo in 1989 (he was 52), a student charged with filling Murcutt's afternoon drove him three hours north to Hamar. Murcutt enjoyed the scenic inland countryside along the way, but he had never heard of the Hedmark Museum before, and little of its designer, and so had no idea what to expect. Afterwards, in his diary entries from that day, Murcutt described the museum as "a great work by a great master—I wish to meet this man—what a joyous experience to be in such manmade work.... I cannot believe how good this work is," and would later refer to it as "the most significant architectural experience of my life."[14] In the following decades, he returned there several times. What is telling about Murcutt's enthusiasm is that the formal appearance of the Hedmark Museum is *not* dramatic—its architectural feats lie elsewhere (Figure 2.7).

The project was designed to reoccupy, stabilize, and largely enclose the existing ruins of the medieval bishop's estate, later fortress, and farm, as described above. The museum loosely comprises four interconnected areas—three sides of a "C" and the courtyard space they collectively bound (Figure 2.8). Starting at the north with the top of the "C" and proceeding counter-clockwise, those four parts house, respectively, (1) a series of exhibits featuring historical objects of daily farm-life aptly arranged in the ruins of a barn that had been appended to the remnants of the medieval defensive walls; (2) a series of exhibits focusing on the site's medieval history; (3) an area given mostly to administration, research, storage, and assembly; and (4) the middle of the "C"—a roughly three-sided courtyard that stages ongoing archeological work at the exterior. Running through all of these, in a design that might aptly be described as riparian, Fehn wound a viaduct of rough-shuttered concrete, variously configured, that in places narrows and accelerates, and at other points opens and slows, staging an array of proximities and perspectives between visitor, ruin, and the exhibited artifacts as the path winds, rises, and falls through the project's different zones and their associated epochs.

Figure 2.7 Hedmark Museum, view through aperture at southwest interior, looking north. © Helene Binet.

30 Opened Ground

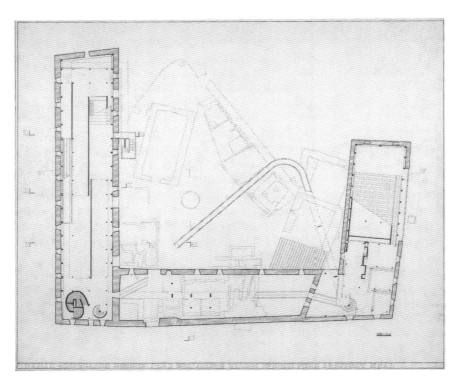

Figure 2.8 Hedmark Museum, plan of second level (north at left). Main entry into lobby area on the first level is below large opening shown here in west wall, with access to courtyard directly opposite. Three small rooms referred to in the text as "reliquaries" can be seen here, dotted-in to the south of the entrance. © Sverre Fehn. Photo: Ivarsøy, Dag Andre. Courtesy of National Museum, Architecture Collections.

Where in this history, site, and architectural configuration might the "urban sensibility" that Fehn professed be found? And what might it have to do with ground? Helpful to both questions is an elaboration of Fehn's understanding of the relation of ground and past, as initiated in the previous consideration of the *Vasa* Museum. Part of Fehn's general interest in ground could arguably be described as *primitivist*, though not in the typically reactionary sense of the term. In his writing and teaching, in an effort to emphasize humanity's fundamental relationship to and dependence on earth, Fehn frequently appealed to sketches of caves and holes. Sometimes, these appeared immediately adjacent to sketches of the planet, as if from space, sometimes dotted with indications of movement or the traces of movement, footprints, or paths (Figure 2.23). For Fehn, this was architecture at an originary level: digging a hole, adapting a cave, defining a path. Several of Fehn's designs exhibit this thinking, bringing highly sophisticated architectural settings into direct relation with their coarsest substrate. One of these is Fehn's design for Oslo's subway in 1997 (commissioned but not constructed), where the parabolic forms and canted piers suggested a cavern-like space. More direct is his 1994 winning competition proposal for the Museum of Hydraulic Energy in Sudal, where the building was embedded in the granite hillside and, in lieu of retaining walls, the exposed coarse bedrock was used as wall. Building on that idea, an existing fresh-water spring was incorporated into the design of the interior, making a grotto of the primary exhibition space. But this direct engagement of the earth's substance is not Fehn's only interest in ground. For Fehn, ground is also a liminal zone between past and present, holding in stasis remnants of the past that can be returned to the present through excavation.

Figure 2.9 Hedmark Museum, glazing detail at entry. Photo by author.

This idea informs one of Fehn's most recurrent dictums: "The earth is the great conservator."[15] Of the many variations of this idea that appear in his writings and lectures, this one is especially instructive:

> The largest museum is the earth itself. In its surface lost objects are preserved. The sea and the sand are the great conservationists and they make the voyage into eternity so slow that we find the key to culture's birth through the patterns left behind.[16]

In a slightly different iteration of that idea, Fehn wrote, with regard to the aforementioned pathways etched on the earth's surface:

> The traces of your footsteps lead the next man to follow the same route. The footsteps are a kind of architecture, because they mediate the walker's feeling for the landscape, telling the follower which view pleases him. It is like a letter addressed to the next walker.[17]

The two ideas—the originary ground, ground the museum—are related, but the second suggests a concept of ground that is both generative and receptive. Also significant here is the emphasis on "the traces" as media for communication between two "walkers" that are never co-present. That is the thinking that obtains at the Hedmark Museum, where Fehn's primary interest in ground was in establishing conditions conducive to dialog between that which was latent within it—primarily, in this case, excavated artifacts—and the museum's visitors. As at *Vasa*, Fehn sought not just to display the ruins and recovered artifacts but also to enlist them in dialog. In both projects, Fehn seems to be calibrating the relative volumes of the various components, as if in light of the observation that good conversation requires a balance of both careful listening and creative contributing. Unlike the *Vasa* proposal, though, the Hedmark Museum was constructed, and Fehn discovered opportunities for linking past and present as he addressed actual conditions and actual objects, with their inherent complexity and potential to surprise.

The pursuit of active engagement with the past and its artifacts is not strictly compatible with the causes of preservation, and this tension is prominent in the Hedmark Museum. Fehn once said that the responsibility of the architect at Hedmark was "to do as little as possible." It ended up, though, that that amounted to quite a bit. To be sure, as several observers have emphasized, there are many places in the Hedmark design where its structure is carefully withdrawn from the existing conditions. That point is well illustrated in the courtyard's sculptural ramp, where its monolithic section requires only four thin concrete piers to support its spans, minimizing the disturbance of the archeological site below (Figure 2.6). Passing into the project's interior, the ramp continues in this way, conducting visitors through the museum while mostly maintaining clear structural separation from the ruins. Another significant display of a strategy of "light touch" with regard to the past is found at the contemporary treatment of existing apertures, where tempered-glass enclosure meets medieval rubble walls (Figure 2.9). Using meticulously cut glass in a mullion-less design, Fehn preserves and presents the irregular jambs of the existing openings in sharp contrast to the precision of the contemporary fenestration, where the medieval walls maintain their mass while the contemporary fittings are, by comparison, almost atmospheric, with virtually no opaque components to interfere with the reading of the ruin.

The loads of the roof structure, too, are mostly resolved by introducing wood posts that pass to the ground immediately adjacent to the existing stone walls, with a gap clearly regulating their separation (Figure 2.10). But in some places, curiously, Fehn forgoes that separation, instead bringing posts to bear directly on the existing walls, using the artefactual remnants in a load-bearing capacity (Figure 2.11). In fact, if Fehn's architectural moves are in many places demure with regard to the existing conditions, there are many other places in the design where a different kind of thinking is evident. Take, for example, the three unusual rooms designed to display sets of smaller medieval artifacts. Kenneth Frampton referred to these as "treasuries."[18] *Reliquary* is also apt. These monolithic concrete rooms are each rather daringly balanced on a single concrete column, and their rough-shuttered masses collectively fill most of the space (Figure 2.12). It isn't that these assertions neglect their surrounds—despite their opacity, the surfaces

Figure 2.10 Hedmark Museum, roof support detail, by-passing medieval wall. Photo by author.

become sites for exhibit display, and their elevated position affords views onto the excavated floor beneath. But the vaults' presence in the space cannot be regarded as quiet, withdrawn, minimal, or deferent. If the ambiance of that space can be understood as an orchestrated chorus of differing eras, the voice of the present is made loud in the concrete vaults.

Returning, then, to the ramp and the apertures cited above, even in those cases, where structural span and transparency diminish the force of present intervention, the designs do not fall completely on that side of the ledger. The ramp, for instance, takes a circuitous route through the courtyard, a graceful arc that gestures to, and in place frames, the landscape. As much sculpture as viaduct, its presence in the courtyard and in the project as a whole is primary, not subordinate. Similarly, the

Figure 2.11 Hedmark Museum, roof support detail, bearing on medieval rubble wall. Photo by author.

treatment of the apertures can be understood as quiet and careful and withdrawn with regard to the existing condition, but then at points the glazing reads as figure, and sometimes as collections of figures, in which it is the existing walls that become background, secondary, or field (Figure 2.12). These details also suggest that the architectural balancing of what is existing and

34 *Opened Ground*

Figure 2.12 Hedmark Museum, view of three "vaults," looking south. Photo by author.

Figure 2.13 Hedmark Museum, view under ramp toward landscape. Photo by author.

what is new is not a zero-sum game. Fehn's artifices—the arcing ramp, the careful glazing—do not diminish the presence of the site's existing features but, on the contrary, draw out those qualities, and draw attention to them. For example, the smoothness of the glazing emphasizes by contrast the texture of the rubble wall. Similarly, as the ramp rises and curves, it draws attention to the landscape by framing what is distant and by affording a wider vantage of the setting for pedestrians circulating along and around the ramp (Figure 2.13).

As at *Vasa*, one of Fehn's strategies for setting up conditions for active engagement of the past, then, involves attunement: in places, some contributing voices are made quieter, some more vocal, until a resonating contrast is achieved. As I will explore below, Fehn's thoughts on harmony make it unlikely that that was the aim of these calibrations, but rather more like the balancing of opposing teams in pursuit of richer competition. Fehn's understanding of the role of architectural design in such attunement is perhaps best seen where the Hedmark Museum's architecture intersects with its artifacts. That is also where the link between the project's architectural structure of dialog and its "urban sensibility" is strongest.

Beyond Display

> One should go to the Museum the way painters go there, in the joy of dialogue, and not as we amateurs go, with our spurious reverence.
>
> Maurice Merleau-Ponty

It is typical in museum architecture for the building and its exhibits to be separately designed—frequently, even, designed by different offices. Fehn's approach could hardly have been more antithetical to that practice. When establishing his working relationship with the Hedmark Museum's curators, Fehn took the display design to belong to the design of the whole, and so he successfully negotiated access to the objects for which he was designing displays, often arranging them in his office as he worked. Fehn commented on this demand:

> Every single thing stolen from the depths of the earth has claims on the magic of history. The objects may be born again and find their "space" in their new context. So that the objects can find this space, the architect must take up residence in the objects, as words take up residence in the soul of the actor.[19]

Fehn had expressed a related line of thought in a lecture a couple of years earlier:

> And you must be the object yourself. You must feel it. Because the only story you can add to the object, as an architect, is how you place it.

You must be the object yourself. [...] In that particular way, you feel the material, you feel the ground. Then you begin to observe that the story itself is told by the hard thing.[20]

Fehn is advocating here for exhibit design that facilitates an unusual degree of intimacy between artifact and museum visitor, and he describes that relationship using analogies to theater and to narrative. As implemented at the Hedmark Museum, it is likely that the resulting displays do not entirely conform to museum visitors' expectations. First, there is a paucity of signage and description. There are a few placards, but even those are mostly relegated to the periphery, and so encounter between visitor and artifact is not presided over by the chaperoning annotations typical of museum culture. More unusual still, rather than develop a universal system of display adequate to the artifacts as a set, each presentation device—its frame or mount—is tailored to the unique artifact it displays. Some of those devices are simple and quiet, others more complex and unignorable, but in total, whereas museum-goers have been overwhelmingly accustomed to devices of display that tend toward passivity and transparency, Fehn's devices are active and present. It is a common trait of contemporary museums that their external appearances are exuberant while their displays are passive. At the Hedmark Museum, that relationship is thoroughly (though not completely) inverted. For those not familiar with Fehn's opus, it is worth mentioning that it is marked by the development of these ideas about exhibition, across many projects, over several decades—most notably at displays for the Norwegian Pavilion (Brussels, 1956), the Preus Photography Museum (Horten, 1997), and the Medieval Gallery (Oslo, 1979). Especially at Hedmark, these unexpectedly *involved* exhibition devices can be understood as belonging to Fehn's aforementioned "urban sensibility." Careful consideration of specific displays will help develop that idea. Two will suffice.

First is Fehn's design for the dual display of a medieval fragment of an ornately carved soapstone sepulcher lid and a relatively small crucifix, barely visible here in a small glass case fixed to the top left edge of the white stone (Figures 2.14 and 2.15). Fehn set the two artifacts within a field of two symmetrical polished slabs of sandstone joined by custom designed hardware insertions that minimally ornament the front surface. There are several striking features of this ensemble. By bringing the two artifacts into relation through such a device, manifold scalar relationships are created. The crucifix is diminutive and fragile compared to the mass and size of the 13th-century soapstone fragment positioned to its right. The first belongs to the scale of the hand and invites and structures very close inspection of its fine detail—perhaps inches of distance between the face of a curious viewer, leaning, and the cross, with its canted glass enclosure beautifully anticipating both that proximity and that bodily posture. The positioning of the stone fragment, itself weighty, suggests its relatively larger and unwieldy whole.

Opened Ground 37

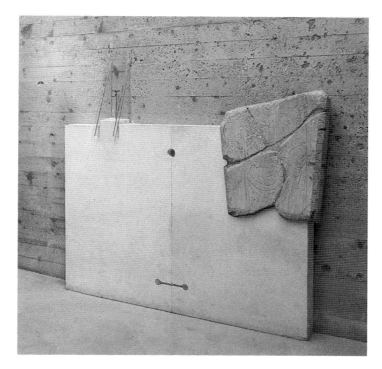

Figure 2.14 Hedmark Museum, display of crucifix and sepulcher fragment. Photo by author.

Yet the crucifix is mounted upright in a drilled hole along the top edge of the sandstone slab, suggesting—in a curious scalar inversion—horizon. If there were any doubt about that reading, it is cleared by two additional details. The stone surface into which the crucifix is mounted is slightly canted and rotated relative to the axes of the slab, and that portion of the slab's top edge is also slightly raised: the sandstone slab edge becomes landscape, the crucifix, topographically positioned, stands on a hill, and what is small relative to the stone fragment now dwarfs it. Or if this imagined landscape is expanded rightward to include the soapstone fragment in its ensemble, the soapstone's position between mass and air, spanning horizon and breaching the bounds of the sandstone's geometries, then the faint figure etched in its surface assumes an apparitional cast, augmented by the word carved into the medieval slab's edge centuries ago (Figure 2.16), made visible through its precise positioning within its sandstone setting: "GOD." Once that particular scale is apprehended, a third scale opens, as the polished sandstone setting can in that context be read as a section cut deep into the earth, inviting imaginative inquiry about the relationship between the crucifix, the events it is meant to commemorate, and the subterranean fissures and joints in the depths of the rock. Geological relationships are evoked: the sandstone *is* a section of deep earth, excavated, now finished and exposed to view, spurring speculation about the circumstances that had surrounded the quarrying, movement, and inscribing of both itself and also the contrasting soapstone. Scales of time and purpose layer up: the event of the Crucifixion, its rehearsal in totems and carved imagery centuries thereafter, the distance of Golgotha, the aeonic timescales of the sedimentary and metamorphic rocks, the labors of the cast of craftspeople involved in fabricating the various components of the ensemble, across ages, the lives of which the artifacts had been a part, the present appeal to the observer invited to bend closer, the silence of the tomb-like vault in which you stand. The implication of the viewer as participant in what Fehn has called "the shadow" of the artifacts is key. The display device does not make such connections per se—half of that work is achieved in the mind of the viewer and in any case is not inconceivable without the device. The device makes those interconnections more available and visceral, more present.

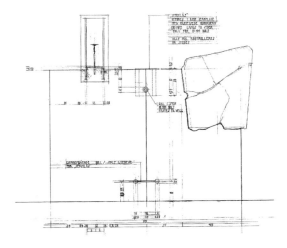

Figure 2.15 Hedmark Museum, construction drawing of display. © Sverre Fehn. Courtesy of National Museum, Architecture Collections.

In the second example, a plough, excavated from the archeological site's farming history, is mounted to a display device that is, in turn, mounted to a rough-shuttered concrete wall (Figure 2.17). That device is primarily composed of two metal plates welded along a diagonal edge, as if folded. The topmost of those two planes supports the artifact, and it is canted to restate the

Figure 2.16 Hedmark Museum, detail of sepulcher fragment. Photo by Geir Ove Andreassen, Anno Domkirkeodden.

Figure 2.17 Hedmark Museum, display of plow. Photo by author.

angle of the plough when ploughing, the lateral force of the ox's movement driving the wedge into the earth. The earth's upheaval is mimicked in the mounting apparatus, where the metal plate is torch-cut in a T-pattern with the resultant triangles folded upward like lapels. Those steel tabs do the work of holding and supporting the artifact, but they are also expressive, as if the mounting surface is sheared by the plough. That trope is further advanced by the deep rust finish of the metal plates, recalling rich, wet loam, and also by the second plate that folds behind and beneath the plough, suggesting earthen depth. The long slot-cuts in that second plate receive the two bolts that connect the ensemble to the wall beyond, but which clearly double as figures of some sort. Are these merely signature flourishes, in the spirit, say, of Scarpa's corbelled leitmotifs? I doubt it: conceptually rotated and in a scalar shift similar to what was effected in the previous example of the soapstone, the lower plate of the plough's mounting device can be read as a plan-view of a field—a long straight row cutting across the surface of a dark expansive plane.

There are many others like these two. A small boat, for example, hung unexpectedly high and adjacent to a partial wall, setting up a fish's-eye view from below; and then, having continued up the ramp to the mezzanine, the boat is encountered anew at a more familiar angle and set of distances—as if moored along a dock. In another example, a glass urn is positioned near a window where its imperfections and optical distortions are more discernible. It is a two-armed fixture—one holding, one stirring (Figure 2.18).

Collectively, Fehn's devices for display create a distinct atmosphere—if not entirely unfamiliar, certainly unfamiliar in the settings of museums. Like the larger scale architectural moves discussed above, these finer-scale designs are atypically active in the presentation of the artifacts. Where we are used to blank white walls, bright and even lighting, hidden hardware, and minimal framing, the displays at the Hedmark Museum are, on the contrary, designed to actively participate: the devices enlist surroundings, allusions, provocations to expose—to excavate—the objects' hidden complexity. The exhibiting devices, then, are not merely elaborate and artful, but configured to expand the field in which the viewer might imaginatively engage the presented object. Stated differently, Fehn's displays increase the conversant capacity of the artifacts. Fehn's devices assist in connecting the artifacts to their broader situation—the conditions of their use, the circumstances of their fabrication, their role in the lives to which they belonged—in a way that is not descriptive and detached, but immersive and immediate. Again, Malraux:

Figure 2.18 Hedmark Museum, exhibit of glassware. Photo by author.

> We have learned that if death cannot still the voice of genius, the reason is that genius triumphs over death not by reiterating its original language, but by constraining us to listen to a language constantly modified, sometimes forgotten—as it were an echo answering each passing century with its own voice—and what the masterpiece keeps up is not a monologue, however authoritative, but a *dialogue* indefeasible by Time.[21]

Fehn's designs at Hedmark advance such dialog, fostering a relationship between beholder and object that defies passivity—Fehn, through meticulous detailing and by making use of the immediate setting, invites active and imaginative engagement: the viewer is prompted to enter into dialog with the object. Unlike Malraux's formulation, the dialog that Fehn facilitates is not limited to "masterpieces," but includes the artifacts of everyday life, substantially expanding the scope of Malraux's observation.

It is worth briefly considering the broader implications of this approach, if only as a place-holder for later development. Fehn's concept of "earth as conservator" belongs to a set of ideas concerning the movement from latent conditions to active ones—from what is possible to what is present. It is a set of ideas germane to consideration of making in general, and so can be found in speculations about intentionality, mimesis, and technology. Fehn's Hedmark designs, though, emphasize a more quotidian aspect of this movement—that the imaginative reading of latent conditions is endemic to human experience and is not limited to the process of making. One way to think about the architecture at the Hedmark Museum is that its efforts to implicate and engage the viewer in imaginative dialog with the objects and their settings has the effect of expanding the scope of what is available in the latent condition. As in the more specialized case of a fabricator or artist (or architect), imagination is a key element, but in the case of the museum-goer, there is no purpose, per se, nothing is made—at least there is no immediate product—and the result of the expanded imaginative dialog between object and beholder is not readily apparent. What, then, is gained? And what is Fehn's role here? The second question may help with the first. If Fehn's excavations and frames can be understood as expanding the scope of the latent condition—that part of the latent condition made available to imagination—perhaps that is a function that can be more generally ascribed to architecture. Inasmuch as architecture frames world, it is necessarily a factor in the breadth (and, one might argue, quality) of that scope. An architecture that was especially successful at enlarging that scope might be recognizable as such. Is that what Murcutt and others have found at the Hedmark Museum? A surprisingly vibrant, expansive, and imaginative availing of latent conditions? Might that be the foundation for the "urban sensibility" that, Fehn insisted, obtains there? If so, "urban sensibility" makes an apt start to answering the first of the two questions, "What is gained?"

In his own analysis of the Hedmark Museum, Fehn alluded to such a connection. As argued above, the prevailing modes at Hamar are provocation and communication—novelty and continuity advancing as one. The exhibits are not *read* so much as *encountered*, each with its unique predisposition, but also inviting the visitor's imaginative rejoinder. The museum's widening and narrowing conveyances hold and disclose these encounters, presenting artifact as entity—not quite the same kind of entity as the other visitors wandering past or gathered on the steps, but neither entirely dissimilar. This spatial experience, where historical depth, personal memory, imaginative enticements, everyday life, chance encounter, and alterity all layer up, loosely organized along discrete linear segments that accommodate varying paces and which establish conditions conducive to discovery, meander, gathering, appropriation, and pause, is descriptive of the Hedmark Museum. But also, more generally, it is descriptive of *street*. Fehn:

> The path is no longer a ramp, but a street ... a marketplace for exhibition and display, a reflection of different personalities and ambitions. Here we can feel the dimension of the old barn and the sled gallery, a dimension mediated by the resistance of stone. The image is of people striving together to overcome privation and to fulfill their hopes and dreams.[22]

There's nothing particularly novel in observing that the street is a place of exhibition and display, nor that it is a place that puts diverse people and their aspirations into relation and makes them available for speculation; it's just that at the Hedmark Museum we are apart from any conventional definition of city, and many of the people with whom we are mingling, the ambitions of whom we are mulling and connecting to our own, the objects and strategies of whom we are now taking up, are not present except through the tokens and ruins that once structured their lives and through our ability to construct from those remains stories that bring them usefully, meaningfully into our experience. It is tempting, then, to regard the Hedmark Museum as *necropolis*, inasmuch as it feels populated even when no one else is there. But because Fehn's designs offer up the relics and ruins for direct, rather than detached, engagement, the street that is full with the presences of the past, made available by plumbing its temporal and terrestrial depths, also structures the possibility of a fuller present.

In this sense, Fehn's opening assertion about the Hedmark Museum and "urban sensibility" is not the non sequitur it first seemed. In the address of an isolated, unpopulated ruin, Fehn's designs posit a relationship between ground, past, architecture, and urbanity.

In 1977, Fehn brought these ideas to a contemporary project in a dense urban setting. Unlike at Hamar, Fehn's designs at Trondheim would never be constructed. But the drawings for that proposal show how Fehn's thinking regarding the ground of urbanity at the *Vasa* and Hedmark museums found their fullest expression in direct engagement of the city.

Revealing Trondheim

> And so you could put children in part of the library, because the thick walls held the silence. And this is the silence of the old churches, and so the library is a place of silence, and so are the ruins. And so we put these things together to make a story out of the letters, and there you are. This is an important thing. Because you really in Europe can open the ground, and there it is.
>
> Sverre Fehn, from unpublished lecture transcript (Cooper Union, March 19, 1980), 21.

Opened Ground 43

About 400km due north of Oslo, on a peninsula defined by the western fjords of Trøndelag and the Nidelva River, sits the city of Trondheim. Now the country's third most populous municipality, it had for many centuries been the largest and most important city in Norway, a thriving center of trade, and the seat of kings. The city's history and mythologies remain significant to Nordic heritage. In 1977, public officials in Trondheim staged a competition for a new civic library to be located near the banks of the river in the very oldest part of the city. It was an area where new construction often unearthed archaeological ruins, and the proposed library site included remnants of foundations of at least four stave churches layered atop each other, and several medieval vaults, the original purposes of which remained obscure. A section of a once-important ancient street, Krambugata (literally, "trading-post street"), also crossed the site, though by the 20th century it had been reduced to little more than a back-alley.[23]

One of the most distinctive features of Fehn's entry for the library competition was the carefully designed engagement of these historical remnants. It is one of several similarities between this proposal and the Hamar project, which was unfolding concurrently. As with the Hedmark artifacts, Fehn used the unique characteristics of each ruin on the Trondheim site as progenitors of the new architectural components that framed and engaged them. At the southern part of the site, Fehn made a sunken courtyard around the ruined foundations of one of the ruined churches, and spanned that exterior court with an elevated cast-concrete walkway at street level (Figure 2.19). Those particular ruins extend underneath one of the site's

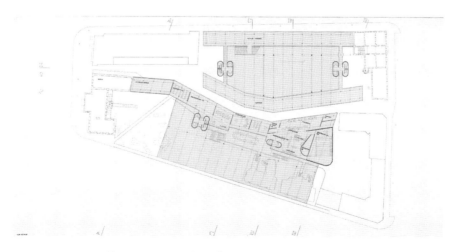

Figure 2.19 Trondheim Library, plan of second level, showing pedestrian street and connections to adjoining existing buildings. Exterior ruins at sunken court are visible to the left. Interior ruins, to be adapted as children's spaces, are visible in the main reading room at lower right. © Sverre Fehn. Courtesy of National Museum, Architecture Collections.

44 *Opened Ground*

defining existing buildings, Trondheim's former town hall, built in 1706. The library site backed up to that building, and Fehn's proposal extended the aforementioned sunken court *underneath* it by exposing and then replacing sections of its northern foundation walls with columns and I-beams, thereby incorporating the ruins beneath the building with the ruins of the sunken courtyard, reunifying what the baroque building's foundations had separated (Figure 2.20). Fehn substantially preserved the town hall in its given condition, except that he also proposed making the upper floor of it available for use by the library. This connection was accomplished through a bridge-like series of rooms that spanned several of the project's intersecting layers. The lower floor of the town hall, though, Fehn made into a museum of sorts. The plans at that location show a proposed 3m circular cut in the existing lower floor, opening a view—presumably glazed—down onto the archeological site connected to the courtyard by the elimination of the foundation wall.

North of the town hall, different ruins were differently engaged. Fehn located the library's main reading level and stacks at the level of the courtyard, and divided inside from outside with a glass curtainwall. In this way, the ruins in the court strongly contributed to the ambiance of the reading room (Figure 2.20). The town hall's clock-tower, visible for many blocks and standing at the back of the building to which it belonged, was also brought into this ensemble through the extensive glazed wall and excavated court. In an unusual move, that wall dividing exterior courtyard from interior reading-room directly straddled one group of architectural ruins, leaving them half-inside, half-outside the proposed project (Figure 2.20). Drawings of this detail were never completed, but it suggests the kind of carefully cut glasswork employed at the Hedmark Museum's new

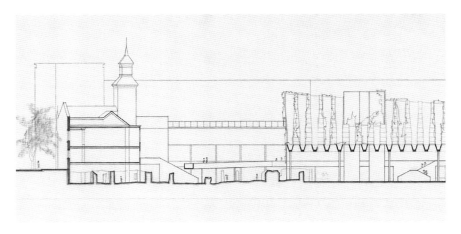

Figure 2.20 Trondheim Library, detail of building section. Existing town hall at left.
© Sverre Fehn. Courtesy of National Museum, Architecture Collections.

Opened Ground 45

enclosures. A similar "straddled" condition was designed for another set of ruins at the library's north line of enclosure. Just to the south of that location, two medieval vaults located entirely within the proposed interior were adapted as children's activity centers and children's reading rooms. In these cases, the ruins are not just reframed, but also repurposed, directly employed in the use of the library.

The library's main reading rooms are arranged around and amongst these now-interior ruins, all beneath a shed-like sloping roof that Fehn designed as a complex array of alternating concrete beams and lengths of skylight. Where the ceiling height increased to the west, landings and upper-floor levels looked down onto the reading room and the ruins it housed (Figure 2.21). This also set up a view out to the east through the glazed roofing, toward the river and the historic merchants' buildings along its banks. That latter view would have been partially obscured by proposed flora growing from planters integrated into the top exterior of each of the beams. The unusual planted roof also tied the building to the existing sloped park across Kjøpmannsgata, connecting the project to the street and to the riverbank. As Fehn put it, "The town's present floor is turned up like a lid and has become the roof of the new building, like an extension of the park down to the river."[24]

If Fehn had been solely concerned with the creation of a vibrant library connected to the city's historical vestiges in inventive and provocative ways, he might have stopped there. But his proposal also included an office building between the library and Søndre Gate to the west. This consisted of four floors of offices distributed in two parallel groups, above an additional level of small commercial shops at grade, organized around an enclosed court with a lecture hall suspended in its middle. The office building and the library appeared as a single complex in the drawings—they had similar roofs, supported by similar (and unorthodox) structural systems, and shared two levels of below-grade parking—but closer examination reveals that there was to be no interior connection between the two buildings. Compared to the rest of the proposal, the design of the office building was less developed—perhaps because Fehn understood the offices and shops as more flexible and variable participants in the project relative to the more

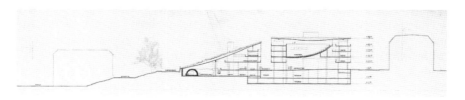

Figure 2.21 Trondheim Library, cross-section, looking south. River at far left. © Sverre Fehn. Courtesy of National Museum, Architecture Collections.

46 Opened Ground

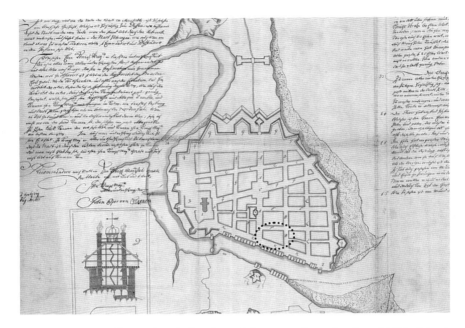

Figure 2.22 Trondheim, detail of Cicignon's Baroque plan, after fire of 1681. North at right. Modern library site highlighted by author with dotted oval. Remnant of medieval Krambugata visible as an alley at interior of adjacent blocks to north.

fixed status of the library. But Fehn seemed less focused on the new office building itself than on its contributions to the street it was intended to help redefine, bisecting the project site from north to south.

The historical record suggests that that street, Krambugata, is the city's oldest, originating in the Medieval era at a natural cove in the riverbank that was long-since infilled, then progressing along its bank, establishing an important market street and route to points further south. After the fire of 1681 decimated most of the city, Johan Cicignon's restoration plan led to the imposition of a baroque grid of wider streets, and to the establishment of a large market plaza several blocks to the west along Kongensgate (Figure 2.22). And, so, Krambugata's importance in the life of the city declined. By the time of the library competition three centuries later, the street was little more than a dead-ended alley, though its winding and cobbled form survived in broken segments at the interior of several blocks along the river, including that of the proposed library site. Fehn's design reclaimed some of the former life and status of Krambugata by reconfiguring it as a pedestrian street that wound through the block's interior for the length of the project and connected to the existing bounding streets. Toward that purpose, he allocated commercial shop space on the office building side of the narrow street, and, on the library side, proposed a café at the north end of the street and a bookstore on the south end, both within the building envelope of the library. Fehn located the main entrance to the library between these latter two venues, in the depth of the block along the rejuvenated Krambugata, rather than along the dominant street of Kjøpmannsgata to the east, thereby strengthening the vitality of the pedestrian street and creating a more intimate entry sequence for the library.

It is this renovation of the medieval street as a contemporary pedestrian one that emerges as the literal and conceptual core of the entire design. The street is the spine to which all the other elements, in plan and section, are keyed. To be clear, Fehn's treatment of the street is not scenographic: despite the design's attentions to circumstance, procession, and view, the configuration exhibits a preference for admixture and immediacy more than anything that might be understood as picturesque. Fehn's reiteration of the ancient street connected parking garage to church-ruin to library to office building to baroque hall, but seems less interested in unifying them than in establishing a stage where those various components, with all of their incongruities, might comingle. Fehn's street is an experiment in urban alchemy, in which the ruins are one critical set of components, but one among several. The distribution of the programmatic elements, the emphasis of the proposed pedestrian thoroughfare, and the openness of the project to the city's existing patterns and nodes check even the library's role as the central piece of the ensemble.

As Fehn's opening quote to this section emphasizes, the city's past exists in layers, and it is primarily through the design of the building section that those pasts are brought into dialog. Generally, the proposal's sections reveal remarkable variation in relation to the ground—for example, excavation beneath the town hall, excavation along the full length of Kjøpmannsgata and the associated vertical displacement of the sidewalk, the receding stacked mezzanines at the library's reading room, the office building's lecture hall completely suspended above a court, the interwoven lines of horizontal movement at different levels, the projection of enclosed rooms over open areas, and both interior and exterior walkways bridging open spaces below. Each of these sections brought differing programs and spaces into correspondence, as sections typically do. More unusual, though, are the sections' structuring of chronological correspondences. In several instances, Fehn designed the section to juxtapose ruin with contemporary city, not blending the two nor bracketing each, but availing one to the other.

One such example was at the south end of the reconstructed pedestrian street where the existing old town hall and fire stations (across the street to the west) combined to form a bit of a bottleneck. Fehn, counterintuitively, made the street at this location even narrower (Figure 2.19, left side of drawing). The narrowing resulted from the creation of a roughly 2m wide gap along the full length of the west facade of the old town hall, opening a view from street-level down into the archaeological site that the

48   *Opened Ground*

reconstructed street was to bridge. It is conceivable that Fehn anticipated the eventual modification or demolition of the fire station on the side of the street opposite this proposed gap, as might have occurred as more vibrant urban conditions materialized in this part of the city, conditions his design would foster.[25] If so, then the gap positioned the project in relation to the future as well as the past. But I think, rather, the "bottleneck" was more likely intentional. By opening up this slot along the street edge, the modified foundation at the corner of the old town hall is exposed to view, and the masonry building, separated from both ground and street, appears to hover. The effect emphasizes the depth of the site's chronology: the town hall is old compared to the library (to which it is connected overhead), but the ruins beneath it are older still. The narrowing of the throughway at this precise point has the effect of introducing an interruption in the continuity of the street (not unlike the surprising undulation of the viaduct in the Hedmark Museum): the ruins are interjected into the daily pattern, a juxtaposition of eras creating a hitch, a pause.[26] In this complex section, depth of ground and depth of past are shown to be depth of the present, related and made available to the nascent contemporary city.

This is analogous to Fehn's interfusion of past and present at Hamar. But at Trondheim, the comingling of eras goes further than the juxtaposition and co-framing of contemporary and medieval experience. The library project is connected, by design, to the life of an active city, and the scales and qualities of times that come into play are manifold. There is the time of the reading room, the time of the pedestrian street and the time of the vehicular ones, the time of the children's tomb-like activity rooms, the time of the shops, of the café, the time of the river, the times of the adjacent park, the time of the planted roof-deck and the life and decay, both, that it points to. Fehn's designs were attendant to each of these, maintaining their character while inventing ways to bring them into dialog. Fehn's mode was less an homage to the past than an experiment in sustaining the different qualities of time that urban life simultaneously presents, from which a heightened vitality might be realized. As described, he invented ways to juxtapose and interfuse those differing times, and to frame or present their overlap. Having now examined Fehn's Trondheim proposal, and looking back now at Hamar, it is reasonable to consider if even there, where the project's raison d'etre was archaeological, that Fehn might have been less concerned with the ruins themselves than with their contribution to the street that he threaded through them, and the urban living it was meant to structure.

I suppose not many would deny that Fehn's approach with regard to intermingling the various times of the site enriches the experience of the library. Fehn also understood the approach as enriching the city. Commenting specifically on his Trondheim proposal:

> If we are to reconquer symbols and find a past killed by rationalism, we must recreate the floor of the town. If we go down into it to the depth

of only three meters in some zones, a past will appear with the stories and symbols we have lost. The ruins of architecture which were part of the secrets of the earth will become the new voice we must listen to in order to find the key for a "different" urban solution. This is spoken by the design of a new library in Trondheim [...] a store of architecture of the past which is not just to be read, but in which the old volumes in a new history provide the town with its form.[27]

Fehn's Urban Ground

The descriptions I have set forth illustrate relationships Fehn posited between ground and culture, and the implementation of those ideas in his work. Peppered in those analyses are instances where Fehn connects, or suggests a connection, between ground and urban conditions specifically. In what follows, I attempt to summarize those allusions and what I have so far attempted to say about them, which, I admit, are among the most difficult concepts I have confronted in Fehn's work. I have sorted those ideas into four categories, though I hope I have made clear in the preceding analyses that Fehn's various appeals to ground are not distinct. In light of those summaries, in this section I will briefly consider part of the larger philosophical terrain to which those ideas belong, in four subsections, before circling back to Fehn's projects for a few concluding thoughts.

Ground as substrate of pre-rational experience. Heightened attunement to what is latent in the existing conditions, resulting in increased creativity and vibrancy in the present situation, may be regarded as a set of interrelated concepts belonging to urbanity. Fehn's architecture, by recognizing and establishing conditions conducive to pre-rational forms of attunement, multiplies (in excess of the rational forms) the latent content available to present use. Fehn wrote, "Every person has within themselves a function based on rational thought and at the same time a spirit undefined and irrational. [...]. The rational thought is not enough."[28] It is in this sense of ground, I believe, that Fehn's architecture and architectural thinking appeals to subterranean places that invoke pre-rational psychological dispositions—cellars, caves, tomb-like spaces—like Loos' mound of earth. In the projects explored in this chapter, such places are designed not to indulge a reactionary primitivism, but, on the contrary, to expand dialog with history, artifact, and city—all of which are, ultimately, dialog with others. It is primarily in this connection to dialog expanded in openness to pre-rational characteristics of place that this sense of ground pertains to urbanity.

Ground as historical medium. As cited above, Fehn iterated many versions of the statement, "the earth is the greatest museum." Corollary to that concept is chronological layered-ness, and the possibility of restoring interred historical fragments to positions of participation in the unfolding present. As Fehn demonstrated in the Hamar Museum, this is a form of restoration that prioritizes appropriation and reassignment over preservation and historical reconstruction. This has the effect of transgressing the typical separation of historical fragments from present circumstance, rather like Brecht's penetration of theater's "fourth wall." Pursuing that analogy further, the structured participation of the object in the setting is reciprocated in the participation of the viewer, now actor: the historical fragment is made available to, and involved in, the urban actor's improvisations. This is one of two senses in which Fehn's availing of historical fragments can be understood as contributing to a heightened urbanity. The other has to do with cultural continuity and narrative. Here, theatrical analogies remain useful but become more complicated, because Fehn's availing of historical fragments is not tantamount to the provision of props, as Fehn's historical fragments carry their own narrative—the narrative of their making, use, subsequent demise, and involvement and former value in the lives of others not present, for which the historical fragment functions as proxy. This idea helps make sense of Fehn's repeated appeal to *the story* of the historical fragments which his designs excavate and reframe: the historical fragment is a narrative fragment, now extended, continued, and modified, as it is woven into the narrative of the present, brought to new life. Fehn's relation of those ideas to the city is strongest in his Trondheim proposal, where he brings the excavated ruins not only to the life of the library, but also, as discussed above, to the daily life of the pedestrian street. For Fehn, the urban nature of this historical inclusivity resided in its capacity to establish conditions conducive to the expansion and multiplication of dialog, including dialog across eras, as discussed above in regard to Fehn's *Vasa* proposal.

Common ground and the city. As reflected in many of his lectures and sketchbooks, Fehn found commonality in our retracing of paths of movement across the surface of the earth (Figure 2.23). Ground, in this sense, is the receptor of those paths, traces, and patterns of movement—a field which we share, and across which we collectively navigate. Fehn said, remember, "The footsteps are a kind of architecture." While Fehn often presented that idea in the context of global exploration or more abstract circumstances, he also expounded those ideas in regard to urban settings. Fehn, for example, said that "every citizen knows the floor of the city."[29] He also wrote that, "The city has a rhythm, each beat reflecting the temperament of

Figure 2.23 Sketch of globe, featuring Villa Rotonda. © Sverre Fehn. Courtesy of National Museum, Architecture Collections.

its individuals. The path the citizen selects marks his association with the city." *Street* belongs to this surficial ground, and, Fehn continued, "A street has many names—corridor, stair, landing, are each a part of our street vocabulary."[30] This palimpsest of movement suggests an intimate relation between those patterns and, as Fehn said, the citizen: the patterns are read, so to speak, by the body that directly retraces them and that familiarizes their rhythms. It also suggests an intimate relation between citizen and citizen, inasmuch as your movement within the established order rehearses and precedes the movement of others—as Fehn noted, this is what makes a path a path.[31] Further, Fehn says the patterns are known to every citizen. That is, it takes no special ability or knowledge or status, only repeated movement, navigation, and habituation, which is to recognize "the floor of the city" as something its citizens hold in common. Aristotle posited a shared identity as essential to establishing a *polis* "worthy of the name." Fehn suggested that that identity is embodied in the physical urban configuration and the patterns of movement that interweave it (Figure 2.24).

Ground, Death, and the City. As described above, Fehn understood the involvement of historical fragments as catalytic to the unfolding of present narratives. But this provident nature of ground was, for Fehn, attended by an antagonistic relationship to construction. Fehn's elaboration of the concept of "the cut," as discussed above in regard to the *Vasa* project, reflects his emphasis of building's inherent violence[32] against the world as given—cutting, in the broadest sense, understood as endemic to fabrication. That Fehn, when discussing construction, consistently appealed to concepts of death shows that he understood the antagonism as mutual,

Figure 2.24 Sketch, Sverre Fehn. Text reads: "That is architecture." The image includes symbols of Fehn's Vasa and Hedmark projects, a pyramid, a jar, with various relationships to a ground plane. © Sverre Fehn. Courtesy of National Museum, Architecture Collections.

a struggle inevitably lost—ground as both source and end of all things. Fehn's most sustained consideration of the connection between those concepts and urbanity appeared in his essay, "Disappearance," in which he found something essentially urban in the confrontation of death:

> The places created by the spirit under the sign of death are where people gather. No other structure reveals society as a totality. Here man feels free and at ease. The unity of urbanism can be accepted. Death has a myth that is constant and possesses everyone. It is the 'room' around the mystery that creates peace and togetherness.[33]

Here, commonality in mortality is embodied in place—a sign, a room—where it becomes constitutive of community. The counterpart to this embodied recognition of a shared mortality is the confrontation of "nature's death" and its connection to urbanity. In another passage from the previously cited essay titled "Urbanism," Fehn wrote, "Nature's death is the city's merchandise. A field of grapes imprisoned in a bottle sits on the rack waiting. The bottle once opened bursts into life."[34] Here, the abundance of the city is exacted at a cost; and the abundance of nature is concentrated in a glass of wine. Considering the two quotes together—mortality embodied, the city sustained by nature's death—Fehn offers a picture of urban settings as sites of negotiation between what the city takes from the ground and what the ground finally reclaims. Further, Fehn suggests that an orientation toward death founds an orientation toward each other. As for the role of that concept in the design of urban settings, it is more difficult to surmise what Fehn had in mind, and the meanings of the phrases "the unity of urbanism" and "free and at ease" are unknowable in any decisive way. They suggest, though, that, in confrontation and recognition of death, qualities of solemnity and humility are to be found in the basest levels of urbanity, and that the places that engage those qualities and that render them legible in the built environment are "those where people gather."

Of Ground, Diegesis, and Urbanity

> The past recalled through the present is the key to urbanism. Architecture is the only means that can accomplish this unity. [...] The architectural landscape is not keyed into any particular time. [...] An urban solution finds its freedom through the past.[35]
>
> Sverre Fehn

As stated at the outset, Fehn did not coalesce his connections between ground and urbanity into a unified theory, and the above attempt to coadunate those ideas cannot be conclusive. Some of Fehn's concepts, though, belong to a broader philosophical terrain of which a brief consideration may serve to better inform what Fehn had intuited. Also, philosophies of phenomenology have been frequently cited in analyses of Fehn's work, and what follows may help evaluate the merits (and shortcomings) of those appeals. I want to consider two sets of ideas that made repeated appearance in Fehn's thinking: the relationship of ground to the present, and how that relationship might be connected to urbanity through the roles of dialog and imagination.

Typically for architects and builders, ground means the ground—that is, all construction requires address of the ground, and even the most highly conceptual projects must, if built, reckon with earth quite directly. In this sense, terms like *ground*, *strata*, *hiddenness*, and *excavation* assume their most literal and unsophisticated meanings. This is, of course, in contrast to most philosophical usage, where *ground* assumes meanings far more abstract. And yet, these attenuated levels of meaning can be connected in a graduated continuum of articulated strata, so that the ground in which we dig is not just a convenient metaphor for the ground of existence and sense and experience (as reflected in terms like *erdboden*, *sinneboden*, and *erfahrungsboden*), but is, rather, only the most basic articulation of a common, given, ground at the deepest substrates of experience, meaning, and continuity. Inversely, actions that engage earth at more basic and direct levels—like digging, cultivating, or disclosing what is hidden in the surface—can be vertically connected to higher levels of articulation such as myth and ritual. This idea was strong in early phenomenological philosophy (though modern philosophy has never really dispensed with it); Friedrich Schelling's thinking remains helpful in describing the relationship:

> The rule-less still lies in the ground as if it could break through once again, and nowhere does it appear as though order and form were original but rather as if something initially rule-less had been brought to order. This is the incomprehensible basis of reality in things, the indivisible remainder, that which with the greatest exertion cannot be resolved but remains entirely in the ground.[36]

Over a century later, Maurice Merleau-Ponty, among others, continued consideration of how those concepts might fit within modern culture, writing that "we must again learn of a mode of being the idea of which we have lost, the being of the "ground" (Boden), and that of the Earth first of all—the earth where we live...[37]" Common to these formulations, and generally in the parlance of phenomenology, earth and world are differentiated in the sense that earth is understood to be primordial and *vorgegeben*, in contrast to world, which is articulated to varying degrees of abstraction and complexity, built out of, upon, and up from, earth. As those adverbs indicate, the concept has a distinctly vertical character, with earth at the base. This implicit vertical hierarchy, though, is not *only* conceptual, not only a trope useful to philosophy—it is also descriptive of vertical differentiation essential to human experience: the difference between depth and height is more than a matter of vectors, and ultimately everything in our *world* connects to *earth*, not just conceptually, but actually. This proposed earth-world hierarchy, then, is a layered one, with the lowest strata being the most stable, the most foundational, and with the upper strata being the most highly articulated and ephemeral but still connected, tracing down through layers, to the earth.

A previously cited quote links Fehn's thinking to that set of ideas, where he said that "we find the key to culture's birth through the patterns left behind." Like so many of Fehn's pronouncements, the succinctness of the phrase is deceptive. Prima facie, it seems to understand culture as being birthed from an ur-ground, the lowest of the vertical strata—similar to the ancient Greek *apieron,* from Anaximander,[38] and consonant with tropes like "mother earth." This familiar concept—culture birthed from earth—appeared in Martin Heidegger's thinking as the difference between earth and world, where earth unapportioned (or *indefinity*, in Eric Voegelin's thinking) founds all latent possibilities, and where world, on the other hand, is essentially historical and inseparable from culture.[39] Heidegger's formulation, though, alluded to but did not explicate a third term, which positions the work of art at the functional juncture between earth and world. His particular interest here in the work of art per se, though, leaves the focus narrow and, despite his example of the Greek temple, Heidegger does not go on to build up (or down) from artwork to place. Edward Casey, ruminating on this missing fertile and active limen (generally missing, he argues, from modern thinking), proposed that *land* fills this gap, a term, he believes, that makes local conditions primary in movement from earth to world.[40] Similarly, though emphasizing slightly different facets of the problem, Pierre Bourdieu posits *habitus* as that operative middle condition between, in his vocabulary, nature and culture.

I am not sure what to call this in architecture, nor indeed in any parlance. T. S. Eliot, attempting to find a vocabulary to explain how innovative work depended on its precedence and simultaneously engaged and altered that precedence, offered the phrase "the mind of Europe," suggesting a collective consciousness that was conversant, shapeable, fecund. He described this as "a mind which changes, and that this change is a development which abandons nothing *en route*."[41] Eliot then proceeds to describe what he called, tentatively, *the historical sense*, "which is a sense of the timeless as well as of the temporal and of the timeless and of the temporal together," involving "a perception, not only of the pastness of the past, but of its presence," and concludes that "the past should be altered by the present as much as the present is directed by the past."[42] It seems unlikely that Fehn would have agreed with Eliot's assertion that *nothing* is abandoned, but Eliot's concept of past and present, as mutually informing and pliant, mirrors that of Fehn who wrote, "A new form is born from a person who discovers things that are ungathered. [...] The moment a new form is recognized it becomes culture; the past as a presence is envisioned anew."[43]

Opened Ground 55

Like his compatriots in phenomenology, Fehn's formulation also pivoted on a critical middle operation between earth and world. For Fehn (like Casey, whereas Eliot was mute on topography) that middle operation involved place, in which architecture is critical in constituting. Returning, then, to Fehn's "culture's birth" statement, there are at least two pertinent concepts. First is the idea that traces of the past recovered to the surface help to make past and present cohere. Second, those traces do not themselves birth culture, like seeds planted in the ground. Rather, the patterns are a "key" to be found. Here lies another component of Fehn's middle operation: the roles of discovery, imagination, and appropriation. This is an important amendment of the term *culture*, which, in both its agricultural and urban senses, might otherwise remain organic, systematic. In Fehn's understanding of the relation between ground and culture, the imaginative and communicative elements are essential, and they introduce uncertainty, which helps explain his use of the phrase "culture's birth:" culture, in this sense, is nascent and undetermined, while at the same time its "key" lies in engagement of what is given.

For Fehn (and for many of the thinkers cited above), this movement from latent earth to culture's birth appears somewhat mysterious, and involves operations at or beyond the threshold of rationality—there is a psychic, imaginative element—the "envisioning" to which his above quote refers. "Architecture," Fehn said, "is not a question of rationalism, but an irrational idea needs to be supported by a rational structure."[44] Fehn is not *against* the modes of rationality, reductivism, and systemification—his work relies on and makes creative use of architectural means derived from

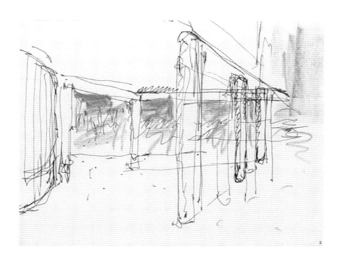

Figure 2.25 Sketch, Sverre Fehn. Sketch of Villa Savoye, from under main floor, looking out toward the landscape. © Sverre Fehn. Courtesy of National Museum, Architecture Collections.

those modes—but he is aware of their limits and sees less rational forms of understanding as their necessary complement (Figure 2.25).

Fehn once further expressed this tension between rational and irrational modes in an odd critique of Corbusier's Villa Savoye. Before turning to that quote, it needs to be noted that Fehn was a great admirer and student of Corbusier's architecture. As noted in Chapter 1, Fehn worked in Jean Prouve's studio in Paris in 1953–1954, and, while there, was a frequent visitor to Corbusier's atelier. One of Fjeld's books features a photograph of Fehn standing at Maison La Roche, sketching.[45] Fehn often used a rhetorical device in which he imagined conversations with deceased architects, in which Palladio and Corbusier were recurring characters. Fehn's sketchbooks feature many drawings of Corbusier's works, including several of Villa Savoye at different scales and perspectives (Figure 2.25). Keeping in mind that outline of Fehn's careful attentions to Corbusier's works, "In Villa Savoye," Fehn said, Corbusier "gave us a house that no longer had a mystery: no attic and no cellar."[46] In this critique, the attic and the cellar are places that refer to, maintain, engage, or evoke irrationality, and modernism effectively eradicates those places. Fehn was mistaken: the Villa Savoye *does* have a cellar, per its original design. Not only might we forgive Fehn for this oversight based on the observation that its cellar is almost always omitted from published drawings of Corbusier's project, it rather helps to prove Fehn's point: it is likely that the cellar's rare appearance in representations of Villa Savoye stems from its perceived incompatibility with the house's modernist tenets. Cellars are earthen places: excavated, dirty, cluttered, dark, damp, earth-bound, even superstitious—qualities typically understood as antithetical to modernism. Fehn's critique, then, was aimed not at disparaging Corbusier, but at maintaining a more expansive, extrarational engagement of habitation than a too-narrowly defined modernism permitted. For Fehn, ground, generally, had the capacity to evoke that irrational dimension—reflecting not an antirational stance, but an expansion into, or maintenance of, extra-rational forms of understanding.

Returning to consideration of the movement from what is given to what is emergent, a movement understood to involve a psychical, imaginative component, and looking carefully at these projects in which Fehn explores what he takes to be fundamental relationships between ground and urbanity, and considering his words and sketches that float about those projects, the concepts that repeatedly surface, that Fehn repeatedly directs us to, involve consideration of architecture's relation to narrative and dialog. At the *Vasa* Museum it appeared as a dialog between an ancient ship, a cemetery, a city, the sea, and the visitor. At the Hedmark Museum, it was the way the project seemed to present series of stories, at least their beginnings, offered up to the museum-goer whose status as audience or player was uncertain, but seemed in either case to be caught up in an improvised, unfolding dialog between past and present. And at Trondheim, the historical remnants were interjected into the life of the project and into the daily life of the street in a way that admitted them into the fold of the present and rendered them conversant in that daily life. As we've already seen, Fehn's commentary on the projects fuels that consideration of dialog. Another prime example, perhaps the most potent, comes from a lecture in 1980, where he was describing the Hedmark Museum:

> But then the dialogue between the concrete and the stone happens to be very beautiful, because it's two centuries I mean. I'm so tired of [designers] merely following history, without making a manifestation of the present. How can you have a dialog that way? It's impossible. You must have a manifestation of the present. Then the past will talk to you.[47]

As various quotes of his cited in this chapter have shown, Fehn often thought of his designs as engaging or structuring *stories*. But, as with his use of the word *room*, Fehn's concept of *story* in his architectural thinking was unorthodox, not least because it was so thoroughly contingent, suggesting a strange form of diegesis, between narrative and dialog, in which narration derives from multiple sources communicating in real time. Again, Fehn was not alone in making the connection between the actively imaginative engagement of what is given and the expansion, through dialog, of what is possible. As James Hillman put it, "The discipline of imagination asks 'where'; and by asking 'where' and fantasizing in terms of place, the psyche enlarges its interiority, the space by which it carries meaning." Hillman continues:

> Let us imagine the *anima mundi* neither above the world encircling it as a divine and remote emanation of spirit, a world of powers, archetypes, and principals transcendent to things, nor within the material world as its unifying pan-psychic life principle. Rather, let us imagine the *anima mundi* as that particular soul-spark, that seminal image, which offers itself through each thing in its visible form. Then *anima mundi* indicates the animated possibilities presented by each event as it is, its sensuous presentation as a face bespeaking its interior image—in short, its availability to imagination, its presence as a *psychic* reality. Not only animals and plants ensouled as in the Romantic vision, but soul is given with each thing, God-given things of nature and manmade things of the street.[48]

Hillman, like Loos, like Fehn, begins with the earth and ends at the street. Fehn's work shows that architecture has the capacity to facilitate that connection. Further, as the opening quote to this section shows, he asserts that such connections are essential to the life of the city, and dependent on architectural configurations.

This spatially and chronologically expanded concept of dialog, though, if essential, is neither synonymous with nor sufficient for urbanity, and the facilitation of dialog is not the limit of architecture's role in its structure. Fehn's architecture, again, can help us press further.

Notes

1 Sverre Fehn, "Has a Doll Life," *Perspecta* no. 24 (1988): 48.
2 Adolf Loos, "Architektur." *Der Sturm* no. 15 (December 1910): 98. Original German: "Wenn wir im walde einen hügel finden, sechs schuh lang und drei schuh breit, mit der schaufel pyramidenförmig aufgerichtet, dann werden wir ernst und es sagt etwas in uns: hier liegt jemand begraben. *Das ist architektur.*" Omission of capital letters original.
3 Per Olaf Fjeld, *The Pattern of Thoughts* (New York: Monacelli Press, 2009), 108. The other six projects that Fehn lists are Spiraltoppen Restaurant (1961), Voksenkollen Conference Center (1978), the Nordic Museum, the Hedmark Museum, the Røros Mining Museum (1979), and Tullinløkka Square.
4 Sverre Fehn, "Wasa Ship Museum," in *Intuition, Reflection, Construction*, eds. Marianne Yvennes and Eva Madhus (Oslo: National Museum, 2009), 98.
5 Sverre Fehn, "Wasa Ship Museum," in *Intuition, Reflection, Construction*, eds. Marianne Yvennes and Eva Madhus (Oslo: National Museum, 2009), 98.
6 Sverre Fehn, "The Skin, the Cut, and the Bandage," in *The Pietro Belluschi Lectures 1994–1995*, ed. Stanford Anderson (Cambridge: MIT Press, 1997), 22.
7 See, for example, Dal Co's development of this idea in his introductory essay to Norberg-Schulz's monograph on Fehn. Dal Co, Francesco, "Beneath Earth and Sea," introduction to *Sverre Fehn: Works, Projects, Writings 1949–1996*, eds. Norberg-Schulz and Pastiglione (New York: Monacelli Press, 1997), 7–17.
8 Fehn, "The Skin, the Cut, and the Bandage," 22.
9 Various sources alternately refer to the project as Beispegaard Museum, Bishopric Museum, Archbishop Museum, Hamar Museum, Hamar Cathedral Museum, Domkirkeodden, or Storhamar Museum. The project's official name is Hedmarkmuseet (there are no definite articles in Norsk).
10 André Malraux, "Museum Without Walls," in *Voices of Silence* (Garden City, NY: Doubleday, 1953), 65.
11 Sverre Fehn, "Fragments of a Museum and Two Exhibitions," *Byggekunst* no.4 (1982): 165.
12 Eyvind Lillevold, *Hamars Historie* (Hamar: Trykt i Hamar Stiftstidendes Trykkeri, 1949).
13 Fehn's office eventually designed two additional, smaller structures for archaeological work at the eastern part of the site, completed in 2005. Those works are not considered here. Also note that, despite several confused assertions to the contrary, the scope of Fehn's work did not include the adjacent cathedral ruins—the enclosure of those ruins was realized by architect Kjell Lund in 1988. That greenhouse-like project is visible in the background of some of the images included here.
14 Glenn Murcutt, interviewed by Ingerid Helsing Almaas in "Birds of a Feather: An interview with Glenn Murcutt, remembering Sverre Fehn," *Arkitektur N*, no. 7 (2009): 36.
15 Some form of this phrase, like, "the earth is the greatest museum," occurs in virtually all of his public lectures.
16 Sverre Fehn, "Fragments."
17 Sverre Fehn, *Poetry of the Straight Line*, 48.

18 Kenneth Frampton, foreword to *The Thought of Construction*, by P.O.Fjeld (New York: Rizzoli, 1983), 17.
19 Fehn, "Fragments of a Museum," 168.
20 Sverre Fehn, from untitled lecture transcript (Cooper Union, March 19, 1980), not published, 15–16.
21 Malraux, "Museum Without Walls," 69. Emphasis original.
22 Sverre Fehn, in Fjeld, *The Thought of Construction*, 130.
23 At the time of the library competition, the full significance and extent of the ruins was not yet known—a curiosity, but not the national treasure they would become in 2016 as ongoing archaeological work revealed the most recent ruins to be those of St. Clement's Church, where Viking king St. Olav was interred in 1031.
24 Sverre Fehn, "Trondheim Library," *Byggekunst* no.1 (1979): 77.
25 Indeed, while Fehn's project was never built, the fire station would eventually be transformed into a museum and gallery.
26 I think of this as an architectural instance of what Maurice Merleau-Ponty calls "a catch." See his use of the term in his *Prose of the World*.
27 Sverre Fehn, *Poetry of the Straight Line* (Helsinki: Museum of Finnish Architecture, 1992), 51.
28 Sverre Fehn, in Fjeld, *The Thought of Construction*, 150.
29 Sverre Fehn, from untitled lecture transcript (Cooper Union, March 19, 1980), not published, 14.
30 Sverre Fehn, in Fjeld, *The Thought of Construction*, 124.
31 On this idea, see also Simmel's comments on the archetypal path. Simmel, Georg. "The Bridge and the Door." *Qualitative Sociology* 17 (1994 [1909]): 407–413.
32 I consider the topic of violence more broadly in Chapter 4.
33 Sverre Fehn, in Fjeld, *The Thought of Construction*, 150.
34 Sverre Fehn, in Fjeld, *The Thought of Construction*, 142.
35 Sverre Fehn, in Fjeld, *The Thought of Construction*, 133.
36 Friedrich Schelling. *Philosophical Investigations into the Essence of Human Freedom* (La Salle, IL: Open Court Press, 1936. First published 1809).
37 Maurice Merleau-Ponty, *Husserl at the Limits of Phenomenology*, ed. Leonard Lawlor (Chicago: Northwestern University Press, 2002). Edmund Husserl, following Schelling, was among the first to launch a sustained pursuit of these points in the context of philosophy. Merleau-Ponty's explications of Husserl advanced those ideas, which can be traced through the 20th century to the contemporary work of philosophers like Jeffery Malpas and Edward Casey. Alfred Schutz, Georg Simmel before him, and others have explored this set of ideas in the context of sociology. See, Edmund Husserl, "The Earth, the Original Ark, Does Not Move," in *Husserl: Shorter Works*, eds. Peter McCormick and Frederick Elliston (South Bend, IA: University of Notre Dame Press, 1981) 222–223; Georg Simmel, "Brücke und Tür," *Der Tag*, September 15, 1909, 216; Alfred Schutz, *On Phenomenology and Social Relations: Selected Writings*, ed. Helmut Wagner (Chicago: University of Chicago Press, 1970); J.E. Malpas, *Place and Experience: a Philosophical Topography* (London: Cambridge University Press, 2007); Edward S. Casey, "Earth, World, and Land: The Story of the Missing Term," in *Adventures in Phenomenology: Bachelard*, eds. E. Rizo-Patron, and E. Casey, J. Wirth (New York: SUNY Press, 2017), 225–236.
38 The term *apeiron* has been taken up by many modern philosophers, including, famously, Friedrich Nietzche and Martin Heidegger. See Friedrich Nietzche, *Philosophy in the Age of the Greeks*, trans. Marianne Cowan (Washington, DC: Regnery Publishing, 1962). For a more general account of its meaning in

various Greek contexts, see, C.M. Bowra, *The Greek Experience* (New York: World Publishing Company, 1957).
39 Martin Heidegger, "On the Origin of the Work of Art," in *Basic Writings*, ed. David Farrell Krell (New York: HarperCollins, 2008): 143–212.
40 Edward S. Casey, "Earth, World, and Land: the Story of the Missing Term," in *Adventures in Phenomenology: Bachelard,* eds. E. Rizo-Patron, E. Casey, and J. Wirth (New York: SUNY Press, 2017), 227–235.
41 T.S. Eliot, "Tradition and the Individual Talent," in *The Sacred Wood: Essays on Poetry and Criticism* (London: Dover Books, 1920, 1997).
42 Parenthetically, Eliot adds that "the poet who is aware of this will be aware of great difficulties and responsibilities."
43 Sverre Fehn, in Fjeld, *The Thought of Construction*, 97.
44 Fehn, *Poetry of the Straight Line*, 47.
45 Sverre Fehn, quoted in *Pattern of Thoughts*, Fjeld, 34.
46 Sverre Fehn, quoted in *Pattern of Thoughts*, Fjeld, 139.
47 Sverre Fehn, from untitled lecture transcript (Cooper Union, March 19, 1980), not published, 14.
48 James Hillman, *City & Soul* (Putnam, CT: Spring Publications, 2006), 33.

3 Sverre Fehn's Ambient Urbanity

> With regard to architecture, naturalism cannot posit the requirement of truth, in the sense of a formal equality with something that is externally given. In a more obvious way, architecture claims an inner truth, namely, that the forces it bears should be sufficient for the loads, that ornaments find a place that gives full expression to their inner movement, and that details are not unfaithful to the style conveyed by the whole. However, more mysterious is that harmony or contradiction in which a building relates to the spiritual significance or meaning of life which is connected with it, and which shines forth from it, but only as a demand that it makes but does not always fulfil.
>
> Georg Simmel. *Venice.* 1907

We know from the preceding study of the Hedmark Museum that Fehn did not hesitate to describe even a remote, relatively isolated project as "urban." In that project, the criteria were met, for Fehn, in the facilitation of dialog with historical fragments, provoking an array of encounters and discoveries that implicated the visitor in the setting, which Fehn likened to a city street. In drawing that connection, Fehn emphasized the roles of imagination and active engagement, suggesting the importance of spontaneity and improvisation in urban settings, and showing how architecture can structure and prefigure those qualities. It is a way of thinking that identifies urban conditions with productive uncertainty: the setting is open, contingent, not self-defined. At Hedmark, that nascent condition and its associated dialogs depended primarily on an openness to historical depth. In Chapter 1, I described that openness as a kind of architectural *reach*. In this chapter, I want to explore other kinds of architectural reach in Fehn's work, and to explore, as at Hamar, how those pertain to Fehn's sense of urbanity and how he embodied those concerns in his designs. I visit three projects: the *Foto Huset* camera shop, in Oslo; Villa Norrköping, on the outskirts of its eponymous city; and the Nordic Pavilion, in Venice.

Camera

Fehn's *Foto Huset* project is the most difficult of the three to explore in relation to Fehn's urban thinking because it has been demolished, and because the record of what Fehn had to say about it is thin. I was drawn to attempt a better understanding of the project, nevertheless, partly because it is one of only a handful of projects that Fehn ever realized in a dense urban setting, and so I thought it prudent to scour it for connections to urban concerns. I found there a set of ideas I was not anticipating, and which, for the reasons I have given, can only tentatively be connected to Fehn's stated intentions with regard to urbanity. Instead, I primarily appeal to what might be surmised from the surviving record of the constructed project itself.

Before its demolition, the *Foto Huset* camera shop in Oslo stood in part of the first floor (Figure 3.1) and basement of a preexisting building on the south side of Prinsensgate, a dense commercial corridor in the heart of the city. It was a tiny project—less than 85m²—with a simple but elegant layout. The street-level was for the display and sale of camera equipment, while the bottom floor, accessible via an elaborate staircase (Figure 3.2), accommodated a small gallery space, storage, and service requirements.

Given the nature of the enterprise, an emphasis of light in the project was fitting. To achieve that emphasis, Fehn limited the roles of form, materiality,

Figure 3.1 Foto Huset, interior at night, view toward street, with back of store reflected in storefront. Entrance at right. © Tiegens/DEXTRA Photo. Courtesy of Norsk Teknisk Museum.

and detailing. These aspects of the design were not neglected—they were critical to the design—but were made subordinate, so that the role of light emerged as primary. Period photographs show that the lighting was easily adequate for the pragmatic tasks the store required—the display and examination of merchandise, review of documents, and monetary exchange. But the project's attentions to lighting dramatically exceeded those demands. Understanding the nature of that excess requires connecting Fehn's decisions about light to his broader atmospheric intentions.

Throughout his career, and in contrast to his consistently careful consideration of daylighting, Fehn's general approach to electric lighting in his architecture could be described as minimal, though it is perhaps not going too far to describe it as unaffected. He typically used inexpensive, nondescript fixtures in surprisingly

Figure 3.2 Foto Huset, detail of staircase, looking up. © Tiegens/ DEXTRA Photo. Courtesy of Norsk Teknisk Museum.

unceremonious ways: while the fit of Fehn's architecture within Banham's Brutalist canon is debatable, his approach to electric lighting undeniably exhibited an anti-aesthetic quality. At the camera shop, though, Fehn afforded atypical consideration to the electric lighting. Almost all of that was hidden in coves or cleverly integrated within casework, but a series of fixtures that resembled studio spotlights (and which may have been actual Klieg lights) featured prominently in the setting of the shop's central space. Those fixtures were concentrated in two locations. The first set was at the back of the store, lighting the crystalline staircase to the gallery area in the basement, and casting light on the photograph that spanned the entirety of the rear wall (Figure 3.3). That photo, *Grass in Frost*, was by Olso's Carl Nesjar, most famous for his work as Pablo Picasso's longtime fabricator and collaborator. Nesjar had exhibited photos in Fehn's Norwegian Pavilion in Brussels in 1958.[1]

The other group of fixtures was arranged in a row directly above another of the limited cast of components that vied for dominance in the project—a long display case made entirely of structural tempered glass. The glass case was positioned so that its last 53cm penetrated the shop's mullion-less glass facade, protruding into an exterior foreground Fehn created by insetting the wall from the property line about one meter (Figures 3.4 and 3.5). Fehn established the regular interval for the spacing of the hanging lights so that the last in the row was positioned on the exterior side of the glass wall and centered directly above the cantilevered protrusion of the glass case.

64 *Sverre Fehn's Ambient Urbanity*

Figure 3.3 Foto Huset, view from curb, looking through to back of shop. © Tiegens/DEXTRA Photo. Courtesy of Norsk Teknisk Museum.

This fixture, its light, the case below, and the glass wall occupied a threshold condition further defined by Claire Blanche marble panels on the flanking walls and soffit. Notably, the floor in this specific location, too, was of marble, before transitioning to travertine beyond the distended entry threshold. Especially given the slope that had to be negotiated between sidewalk and floor-level, this turn toward marble flooring was not a pragmatic choice: for Fehn, some other end governed its selection. Rather than simply extend the concrete of the sidewalk to the threshold of the door, Fehn, at some effort and expense, extended the floor of the shop into the floor of the city. The whiteness of the marble and its polished surfaces reflected light, presented images of the surrounding conditions, and received shadow patterns—especially those of the case and its objects. The chosen marble, though, was not *only* white—it was also streaked with light-gray veins so that the surfaces, unlike a purer whiteness that could have been easily achieved with plaster or paint, were variegated and imbued with depth—more like fog, with its textures, than a reductive blankness.

The orchestrated array of design decisions for fixture, light, glass, shadow, and marble created a space marked, I think, by two primary qualities. The first can be described as theatrical. The storefront and central interior made a stage for the objects offered for purchase, lit with stage lights and set against a photographic backdrop. Both allusion to and structure of theatrical conditions in urban situations were recurrent in Fehn's work, an idea I will return to. The second quality, which I trust is evident in the project photographs, can be described as atmospheric, or ambient. Those terms are philologically related but bear different nuances in common usage, where *ambiance* cleaves closer to mood (as with the German *stimmung*), while *atmosphere* carries slightly more empirical connotations. Generally

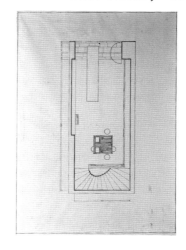

Figure 3.4 Foto Huset, main floorplan. © Tiegens/DEXTRA Photo. Courtesy of Norsk Teknisk Museum.

Figure 3.5 Foto Huset, glass display case projecting into sidewalk. © Tiegens/DEXTRA Photo. Courtesy of Norsk Teknisk Museum.

though, both words, as with their related terms,[2] describe a condition that exists as an interfusion of mind and place: when we speak of the mood of the room, we are describing conditions that are, at once, in that place and in our minds (Figure 3.6).[3]

Fehn's designs at Foto Huset were highly attentive to both mundane and spectacular ends. The mundane aspect of that atmosphere is further shown by Fehn's endeavor to add ambient temperature to the array: the exterior zone around the protruding case was heated by radiant circuits cast into the concrete beneath the marble, so that window-shoppers drawn to the display were afforded relief from the cold and the surface at grade was kept dry and free of ice. These twin concerns—the wonder of the project and its accommodation of mundane needs—are reflected in some of Fehn's only surviving remarks on the project. He wrote, "For the modern person the camera has become a kind of necklace,"

Figure 3.6 Foto Huset, entry and glass display case, looking east. © Tiegens/DEXTRA Photo. Courtesy of Norsk Teknisk Museum.

and also that the project enabled patrons to "engage the mysteries of the cut glass."[4] This indicates two different aspects of the relationship between patron and camera that informed the above sets of design decisions. First, the polished stainless-steel, glass, and black enameled devices displayed in the case were, in 1962, increasingly familiar, becoming part of the everyday apparatus of sophisticated modern life and no more extraordinary than, say, the act of wandering along a city street. Second, the camera as an instrument in a process for documentation and discovery was then, and remains now, nevertheless mysterious, marvelous, spectacular—as provocative and open to possibility as wandering along a city street. Fehn's design recognized and sustained both modes—the simple and familiar practices easily anticipated in the workings of a commercial camera shop, and also the oneiric and provocative qualities of photography's processes and ends.

While photographs and drawings make those observations evident, there is no archival text in which Fehn explicitly addressed the project's urban engagements, and I am left to tentatively reflect—I trust the reader will not take the following reflections as either definitive or exhaustive. What I think Fehn's design demonstrates is a project that is receptive to—designed to receive—what the city offers. The city offers daily life (shopping, navigating a sidewalk, negotiating the weather) and wonders (alluring objects, works of art, surprising interiors). The project accepts and sustains both. Further, I firmly believe, the project is especially attuned to those urban offerings. Fehn did not invent the busy sidewalk, but his project was opened to it, made use of and amplified its properties—the accommodation of the quotidian act of window shopping and purchasing a camera, and the staging of the unexpected wonder of window shopping and purchasing a camera. While I again want to emphasize that Fehn did not say it, I suggest, tentatively, that the effect can be understood as urban in three ways. First, receptiveness of, and reach toward, existing circumstance and conditions, making those more available to present daily life, may itself be regarded as movement along the spectrum toward urbanity, as similar to earlier consideration of Fehn's architectural engagement of artifact[5] and ruin. Second, the project's simultaneous accommodation of expectations typical to the setting of a small shop, and orchestration of conditions aimed at disturbing those expectations (an unexpectedly empty and luminous space; an unusually large photograph, of wilderness, at an unusual scale and distance; a unique and levitating display case) is at once confirming and provocative, a condition that may also be understood as reinforcing and renewing urban conditions. I will return to that tension, understood to be productive, in Chapter 4.[6] And third, the project's receptiveness to the city allows its participation in the city, which facilitates the participation of the inhabitants of the city. Put differently, the project opens up to and participates in what the city offers so that its citizens may do the same (Figure 3.7).

Figure 3.7 Foto Huset, glass display case, from interior. © Tiegens/DEXTRA Photo. Courtesy of Norsk Teknisk Museum.

68 Sverre Fehn's Ambient Urbanity

If urbanity has to do, at least in part, with the acceptance and architectural reification of cultural practices, and with structured departures therefrom, effecting the likelihood of more sophisticated, imaginative engagements of other, of world, and of possibility, then that condition is almost certainly more often available, more varied, and more complex in cities, but is not unique to them. An exploration of Fehn's Villa Norrkopping, and consideration of his explications of it, will help inform that idea.

Ex-Urban Urbanity

> Whence came the best culture, if not from the burgher?
> Johann Wolfgang von Goethe

Fehn's Villa Norrköping originated in 1963 as part of an exhibition of modern dwelling, *NU-64* (Norrköpingsutställningen 1964). The exhibition was intended to aid in the rejuvenation of the region's economy in the wake of the mid-century collapse of its textile industry.[7] The housing part of that program, the "Nordic Villaparad," comprised eight single-family houses designed by various Scandinavian architects from four countries. Fehn's design, Nordengatan 15, is the most widely recognized of the set[8], and has since been known simply as Villa Norrköping. The houses, constructed together on a parcel of gently rolling, disused farmland at the southwest fringe of the city of Norrköping in southern Sweden, were intended to be prototypical, and, accordingly, specific parcels were assigned only after the designs had been submitted.[9] At 150m², Fehn's design was the smallest of the eight, a single-story slab-on-grade house suitable for a small family. Fehn's plan, concentric and bilaterally symmetrical, has typically been described as a nine-square Greek-cross form, though it is more helpful to read it as a 6×6 form (Figure 3.8). The center of the plan is most dense, comprising the kitchen, baths, storage, and services, while the roomier perimeter is opaque at its sides but open to the rural landscape at its corners. The house's main living spaces are arranged between this core and perimeter, each flowing into the next. The fluidity of that circular movement could be modulated by a series of operable wooden partitions that slid from pockets in the brick cavity-walls, thereby allowing for varying degrees of privacy, spaciousness, and light, modulated at the inhabitants' discretion. There were seven such panels, symmetrically distributed—the would-be eighth was omitted to accommodate the main entry sequence, discussed below.[10] Alongside the central zone at the kitchen, Fehn designed a connecting hallway that provided access to the baths and allowed communication between rooms during times when the sliding partitions otherwise blocked passage.

Given the stated programmatic intentions in general, and Fehn's highly symmetrical design in particular, it is understandable that much of the existing analysis of Fehn's Norrköping design has emphasized its rationality

Sverre Fehn's Ambient Urbanity 69

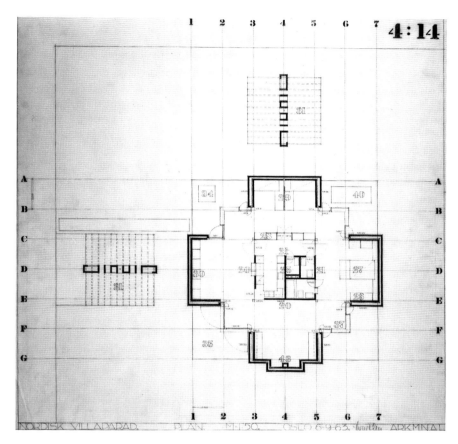

Figure 3.8 Villa Norrköping, plan. © Tiegens/DEXTRA Photo. Courtesy of Norsk Teknisk Museum.

and portability, its site-less-ness—certainly a quick look at the plan gives no indication of concern with the specifics of site. And yet, despite its prevailing symmetries and duplicate visages, the house does have a front and a back: there is a front walk, a front door, an entryway, and an interior vestibule. These are not mere labels—the symmetry of the plan is modified to accommodate these functions as specialized spaces within the overall order. For example, the main door is framed within a wall that in the other seven corresponding locations is brick, but here that wall is shortened by the entry door's width and substituted for wooden casework. The front door's location in plan assures its presentation to the main street, Nordengatan, mitigating any confusion about how to enter the unusual house. Also indicative of attention to site, a pair of outbuildings were constructed to the northeast and northwest of the main house, respectively, each with a cantilevered translucent roof springing from a brick linear core that housed storage compartments. Published plans of the project frequently omit at least one of these structures, fewer show both, but they were constructed at the same time as the main house. These outbuildings, rather like *barchessa*, were positioned on the two sides of the house closest to the two bounding roads, providing additional buffering for site margins that lacked substantial flora at the time of construction. The most active of these outbuildings in the daily use of the house—the carport—was located to the northwest, connected to the rudimentary side-street by a short driveway, and connected to the house by a short gravel path. Fehn's attentions to both site and use belie the project's supposed site-less-ness and abstraction (Figure 3.9).

Somewhat parenthetically, the intended pragmatic function of the shed to the northeast, nearly identical in its form to the one that serves as carport, is less clear. But at least one image taken immediately after construction shows a boat stored there. One wonders about both the boat and, given the house's transformable room plan, especially about the convertible automobile featured in those images, parked beneath the carport, top down, an urban cousin to the Jeep in Peter Smithson's Hunstanton photos (Figure 3.10). Props were placed for the interior photos as well: books, flowers, fish (reminiscent of Corbusier's photograph of the kitchen at Villa Stein), root-vegetables, cosmetics, and other staged objects are visible in the period images. While it is not known if Sverre Fehn worked with the photographer on those stagings, Per Olaf Fjeld recounts not only that many

Figure 3.9 Villa Norrköping, view from southwest. © Ukjent. Courtesy of Norsk Teknisk Museum.

Sverre Fehn's Ambient Urbanity 71

Figure 3.10 Villa Norrköping, view from street. Front door is visible to right of glazing at center of lower image. Photos from *Bauen + Wohnen* article on the project, 1964.

of the objects featured in the photographs belonged to Ingrid Fehn, but also that she lived there for more than two months before the house was eventually sold.[11]

As even a cursory look at the plan will justify, Fehn's Norrköping design inevitably provoked a comparison to Palladio's Villa Almerico. While the Renaissance project is several times larger than its 20th-century cousin, its perimeter delineation and proportions are nearly identical. In both cases, a concentric geometry fit within a rural landscape confers a sense of *axis mundi*. That sense is not much lessened by Villa Norrköping's comparatively modest claims on the landscape. Fehn once declared that Palladio was not on his mind when he designed the house,[12] and perhaps the statement was not disingenuous—a designer might proceed parallel to some precedent but only become cognizant of it afterward. Elsewhere, though, Fehn explicitly elaborated on the apparent correspondence between the two projects, 400 years apart. The comparisons he drew were not merely geometric. In an essay in 1979,[13] rehearsing a version of one of his favorite rhetorical tropes, Fehn connected Palladio to the Norrköping house:

In this house I met Palladio. He was tired, but all the same he spoke, "You have put all the utilities in the center of the house. I made a large room out of it, you know, and the dome with the opening was without glass. When I planned the house it was a challenge towards nature – rain, air, heat and cold could fill the room."

"And the four directions," I replied.

"Oh yes, you know," and he became smaller, "at that time we were about to lose the horizon. You have opened the corners," he stopped a little. "You are on your way to losing the globe."

"Tell me more," I said.

His voice began to weaken, but he whispered, "All constructed thoughts are related to death."

And then he was gone.

The ending of Fehn's parable is dramatic, but it is the preceding part that is most pertinent. Whether or not Fehn was correct about Palladio's intentions to omit the lantern that now shelters the house's oculus so that rain and cold would penetrate into its center, that this was where Fehn drew connections between the two projects is revealing: the house's admission, or readmission, of what it had ostensibly expelled was understood as essential to its design, and, further, the Norrköping house's open corners were implicated in that operation. I will develop that idea below. As Fehn's imagined dialog alludes, at the center of the roughly Greek-cross layout of both houses are lofting spaces that emphasize verticality. These spaces connect sky and light to the centers of their houses, and in both cases that center is wet—the presumed open oculus in Palladio's design, the pitched-to-center roof construction, and clustered plumbing fixtures in Fehn's—as if the recognition of water, of our mastery both of it and by it were foundational to dwelling and, perhaps, civility: "a challenge toward nature," where the stakes include "losing the globe."

There is one other set of connecting points to be drawn between the two projects that will help advance the present thesis. In an intelligent essay on Fehn's Villa Schreiner, Mari Hvattum noted that the house was "hardly a villa in any traditional sense of the term."[14] Palladio, similarly, made an issue of the categorization of the Almerico Capra house (now popularly titled "Villa Rotonda"), deciding to call it not a villa, but a palazzo, because of its proximity to Vicenza.[15] It is true that the house did stand not far from Vicenza—scarcely 2km. Even so, its setting was decidedly rural. While the house may not have been originally designed to function as a working farmhouse (in contrast to many of Palladio's villa designs), it is certain that the house was surrounded by farmlands, vineyards, and orchards, and that its primary orientation was not to the city, but to the agricultural countryside and the views onto it that the hilltop provided. The regional political culture and the emergent geo-political culture to which the house belonged, and which it so alluringly represented, have figured prominently in the rich history of writings on the villa as a type and on the Almerico house especially, part of a discourse that has rendered the project one of the most recognizable icons in architectural history.[16] That status as icon and convenient symbol of a nascent modernity has perhaps made it more difficult to keep in mind that the house was also a house—that is, it proposed and effected the setting for a way of domestic living, one explicitly balanced between rural and urban concerns. *Explicitly*, because arguably that duality is obtained in any domicile but is concentrated in the villa as a type, and it is especially concentrated at Villa Almerico. James Ackerman asserted that villas are subcategorized as either "a foil to the natural environment, standing off from it in polar opposition," or, rather, as an "integrative...open-extended type...embracing the ground, assuming natural colors and textures."[17] Villa Almerico, though, defies that taxonomy as it strongly exhibits both modes. The rational geometries, ecclesiastic character, the highly sophisticated interior and classical refinements firmly establish the house as "foil," as figure on the shore of Rhodes. But for the dweller in the house, that form, those pronaoses, switch from four fronts to four *frontings*, from impositions on the landscape to devices that order the landscape, reaching, bringing the landscape up to and into the house. If the appearance of the house sets it apart from the landscape, the experience that the house structures for the inhabitant, its relation to circumstance, is, conversely, integrative. I believe both the duality and the ambiguity were intentional and productive.[18]

To be clear, I am not much concerned here with how either house—Norrköping or Almerico—is labeled or categorized per se. What interests me is how both projects conflate urban and rural understandings of house. In his chapter, "On the Designs of Town-Houses," Palladio himself described the four loggia of Villa Almerico as addressing four contrasting landscapes, "which look like a very great theatre."[19] The phrase brings together urban and rural concepts. The house is not simply an oasis of urbanity in an otherwise extensive rural setting, but is designed to be open to, and to open onto, the circumstance upon which it depends and against which it must stand. The contrast results in theater. The house's urbanity is not so much checked by that admission as heightened by it, wild land and sophisticated house each enframed, staged, in the other.

The parts of Villa Norrköping that open the experience of the house to circumstance are easily identified. The vertical openness of the house's central zone was previously mentioned. The glazed corners, though, are the most important devices. Freed of load-bearing structure by cantilevered laminated wooden headers, the open corners present four different landscapes and day-lighting conditions—the street to the east, the berm bracketing the neighboring house to the north, the gently sloping terrain to the south and west. Despite their symmetries in plan, each of these corners includes details unique to their specialized roles within the use of the house and in relation to the landscapes they avail. The divergence from

74 *Sverre Fehn's Ambient Urbanity*

Figure 3.11 Villa Norrköping, east corner.

Figure 3.12 Villa Norrköping, west corner. © Sverre Fehn. Courtesy of National Museum, Architecture Collections.

symmetrical conditions at the entry corner to the north, for instance, was introduced above, and further variation can be found at the other three corners. The eastern one (Figure 3.11), designated a play-space for the children, accommodated an appropriately low table designed by Fehn, and is flanked by a pair of glass doors leading immediately into an outdoor area that was originally to include a large sandbox, as noted on the plans. The western corner, between the dining area and living room, trades the stepped glazing configuration of the other three corners for two floor-to-ceiling pivoting

Sverre Fehn's Ambient Urbanity

panels that, when opened, effectively remove division between the interior and a modest patio with its landscape beyond (Figure 3.12). The operation of these large panels likely assumed a seasonal rhythm. At the opposite vertex of this western corner, the interior casework was fitted with a corresponding smaller pair of sliding panels at counter-height that, when open, established a view into the yard (and of anyone gathered there) from the kitchen. The remaining southern corner near the parents' bedroom is similar to the eastern one, except that it offers the most daylight and the most distant horizon. Because each of these large window bays are situated symmetrically across the width of the house, its main spaces are unusually open to the exterior and always delimited by contrasting lighting conditions and views when the interior sliding partitions are fully retracted (Figure 3.13).

Material choices in the house, too, introduce qualities of wilderness and exposure, most notably in the brickwork. Because the perimeter walls are insulated cavity-walls and large enough to accommodate the sliding panels, Fehn could easily have used brick for the exterior wall alone, but he chose brick for the heated side as well. That brick is fair-faced, with a light sheen,

Figure 3.13 Villa Norrköping, view from carport through living area to landscape beyond. Note coarseness of brickwork. © Tiegens/DEXTRA Photo. Courtesy of Norsk Teknisk Museum.

and the mortar joints are thick and not deeply struck. Considering such treatment of brickwork and its use as an interior finish, and echoing Reyner Banham's connections between Fehn and Brutalism, Kenneth Frampton stated, "It is amazing how this house synthesizes in one consummate work traditions as far apart as Palladio, Rietveld, Brutalism and the tight brick vernacular of The Netherlands, not to mention the timber architecture of Japan."[20] In other contexts, Fehn expressed caution about architecture becoming, in his words, "too pretty," and it should be assumed that the coarseness here was thoroughly intentional. Further evidence is found at the interior doorways, which are all swinging pivot doors, and none of which are cased, not even at the bathrooms: the jambs of the single-wythe brick walls are left exposed at the door openings (Figure 3.16).

The degree of exposure effected by the fenestrated corners described above is dramatically countered by the degree of enclosure afforded by the four elongated C-shaped brick walls that inscribe the main living spaces arranged between the corners. These walls are strikingly devoid of aperture and ornamental detail, inside and out. At the interior, the result is a darkness amplified by the contrasting expanses of daylit windows beyond, and by the light filtering in from the central clerestory of the house's core. Rather than relieving that contrast with ample electric light, Fehn leaves the lighting spare, inverting expectations: light is concentrated in the depth of the house and at its corners, while the darkest zones are found at its perimeter and the center of its elevations. Commenting on this aspect of the project, Fehn wrote, "The house in Norrköping is based on a continuous rhythm of day and night. [....] Each room's moment is an expression, a religion of light."[21] The pronounced contrast of light and dark in the house emphasizes those diurnal rhythms, a luminous complement to the contrasts of openness and closed-ness to the landscape.

As previously cited, Fehn thought that architecture used rational means to structure irrational purposes. If the house's highly rational order is open to and enframes primitive circumstance—the landscape, materials in a coarse condition, daylight and darkness—it also presents a countervailing degree of sophistication manifest in the staging of typical quotidian enactments, and in the devices that augment them. At Villa Norrköping, the light and the darkness, the fluidity of air and of body circulating between interior and exterior and room to room, are modulated by the operation of the windows, sliding partitions, carefully designed side-vents, and adjustable caseworks. The design admits circumstantial elements, but it does not *fully* admit them nor cede to them sole determination of the ambient qualities of the living spaces (as might have been the case if asceticism had been Fehn's goal or aesthetic predilection). The devices that regulate that admission primarily belong to what David Leatherbarrow has described as "dwelling equipment,"[22] emphasizing that their modulation of circumstance is given to the attunement of ambient conditions for the staging of everyday practices. Fehn echoed that thinking while describing the dwelling equipment at Villa Norrköping (Figure 3.14):

> The sliding walls transform the interior space. Where the house of isolated rooms is restricted to a singular mood, the house at Norrköping displays, through its openings and changing enclosures, shifts in mood and patterns of behavior.[23]

The array of such ready devices at Villa Norrköping implicates the inhabitants in establishing conditions conducive to the performance of daily life, implication that calls for vision, judgment, and readjustment. The inhabitants are given the means of participating in the attunement of the interior ambiance for whatever their present purposes or mood.

Dwelling equipment available for the staging of everyday enactments need not be mechanically operable nor even necessarily aimed at regulating circumstantial conditions—a dining table or bookshelf, for instance, can be understood as dwelling equipment in this sense. Villa Norrköping makes provisions for daily enactments through the incorporation of such select casework and furnishings. Fehn designed specialized cabinetry at the kitchen, baths, and vestibule; three desks integrated into the design of each of the three built-in platform beds; built-in dual sofas flanking the hearth in the living room; and several less prominent devices accessory to the main living areas. The casework dividing and connecting the kitchen and the dining area includes both operable and fixed equipment. One previously mentioned component of that particular casework are the sliding counter-height panels that can be opened to connect kitchen to dining area to yard. That device also includes shelving so that, when opened, the aperture sets up the aforementioned visual connectedness while also framing and presenting the objects stored within the cabinet's depth (Figure 3.15). Just to the north of those panels along that same wall is an unusual piece of casework. Fehn's drawings label that shelf as the designated site for the telephone, and it is surprisingly elaborate (Figure 3.15, protruding at right side). The shelf-space penetrates the brick wall, allowing access to the phone also from the kitchen, and, because the kitchen is washed in light from the clerestory, the phone is backlit when viewed from the

Figure 3.14 Villa Norrköping, corner cabinet, one of two panels open, view into kitchen. © Tiegens/DEXTRA Photo. Courtesy of Norsk Teknisk Museum.

78 *Sverre Fehn's Ambient Urbanity*

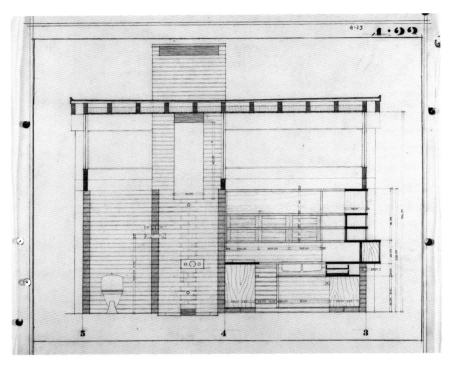

Figure 3.15 Villa Norrköping, cross-section and detail at kitchen. Casework at right adjoins dining area. © Tiegens/DEXTRA Photo. Courtesy of Norsk Teknisk Museum.

darker dining area. The shelf is also cantilevered—it is the only casework protruding from that wall. Why draw attention to the phone? The location is certainly appropriate, convenient to kitchen, dining, and vestibule. But projecting into the room? On display? And there, I think, is a critical point: there is at least a whiff of theatricality mixed in here with the practicality, a form of theatricality endemic to, as Fehn put it, the house's display of moods and patterns of behavior: they are not merely accommodated but presented. In an odd way, the relation of the phone to the house may be similar to that of the carport to the house. At various points in his career, Fehn vocalized and demonstrated, even romanticized, a concern for punctuating the internal coherence of his designs with the possibility of distant connections. Telephone service was not yet taken for granted in rural Sweden in 1964, and, consequently, a simple telephone might be understood as a new point of embarkment or viaduct to the larger world. More certain is the display of the phone as an artifact. If this were the only instance of such display, the point could be more easily dismissed, but the house features several similar moves to frame and display, to lend dramatic cast to otherwise unremarkable domestic objects and activities. Already noted was the display function of the operable corner cabinet in the kitchen. Another example is a shallow cabinet built into a wall dividing the parent's bathroom from the adjoining hallway. As with the phone, the location is pragmatic—it is helpful in bathrooms to have eye-level storage for small things. But this cabinet has doors on *both* sides of the wall (Figures 3.16, closed; and 3.17, open). This double-front is not about gaining additional light for a dark room—remember that the bathrooms, grouped with the kitchen beneath the clerestory, all with white marble-chip terrazzo floors[24] are among the brightest rooms in the house. Nor is it easy to make a case for convenience. Its design seems, again, driven by an interest in the display of the cabinet's objects, again, backlit. Elsewhere, the hot water heater—a decidedly rudimentary domestic device that could hardly be regarded as an artifact—is designed to protrude from the brick enclosure of the mechanical stack so that its stainless-steel sides are presented and symmetrically framed high within the wall where the polished surfaces catch direct sunlight from the clerestory (Figure 3.15—the tall blank rectangle in the middle of the stack is the water heater). Most prominent, though, is the stepped shelving integral to the large window configurations at three of the house's four corners. Predictably, the house's occupants—the same family has lived in the house since just after the end of the expo—make use of those shelves for houseplants and collected objects. As with previous instances, nothing could be more mundane than a domestic shelf filled with a family's collected objects. And yet, the lighting conditions and position of the shelves within their respective places give the objects a vaguely theatrical cast, slightly undermining their familiarity and amplifying their presence, their availability, to the daily performances they help to stage.

This raises another point. When Fehn wrote that at Villa Norrköping, "Each room erases itself as it combines with the rest to constitute the whole,"[25] he described a concept that is not only spatial but also chronological, a timeline unfolding as a series of daily enactments that are staged but not scripted, a narrative that dispenses with its beginnings as it adds to its ends. The description also presents an image of a room dissolving, itself disappearing, not just the enactments it has staged. Fehn's anticipation of various practices and associated settings, and his design of dwelling equipment in support of those, proceeds to a point, but the architecture's definition is

Figure 3.16 Villa Norrköping, casework at bath, view from hall, outer door closed. © Per Berntsen.

decidedly partial, at times ephemeral or, as Fehn said, self-erasing. Because his designs are set-like, they remain latent until the enactments they are meant to stage unfold. Fehn does not take on the design of all of the house's furnishings but selects a few to imbue with greater fixity and identity. And even where Fehn does give attention to the provision of dwelling equipment, those furnishings have a quality that might be described as infrastructural or provisional: there is something empty or unfinished about them. Until, that is, the rooms and their caseworks are inhabited. Without the objects placed by the inhabitants, in absence of occupation in general, the house is incomplete, indecipherable, or, at least, readings of the unoccupied house will skew toward its rational configurations— erroneously so. As noted, Fehn often commented on these two related points—the importance of the irrational elements of habitation, and the dependence of those irrational elements on rational configu-

Figure 3.17 Villa Norrköping, casework at bath, view from hall, both doors open. © Tiegens/DEXTRA Photo. Courtesy of Norsk Teknisk Museum.

rations. The second demands precision and control, but, if excessive, the first is jeopardized. Fehn's casework designs at Villa Norrköping suggest an attempt to set a productive proportion between provocation (props and cues) and recession (backdrop) in the mise-en-scène of architectural settings. At Villa Norrköping, the casework is aimed not so much at finishing the space as, on the contrary, extending its unfinished-ness, setting conditions conducive to the space's habitation, at once prefigured (anticipated) and open (improvised). It is helpful here to recall the theatricality evident at the Foto Huset camera shop. At Norrköping, there is no bustling sidewalk, no city, no public. But Fehn's decisions about enclosure, framing, surfaces, lighting, its modulation, the uncanniness of the spatial configurations, bestow a similar theatrical cast to otherwise mundane objects and tasks. In both cases, inhabitants are afforded an opportunity to more imaginatively engage their settings, to conduct themselves with a degree of reflection and self-awareness beyond routine.

Fehn openly discussed this theatrical cast generally in his work— introducing it here will help make sense of observations presented in Chapter 4. Reminiscent of Palladio's allusion to theater in his description of his Almerico project, Fehn described Villa Norrköping as "a stage play with light."[26] In both descriptions, the theatricality emerges from the respective house's openness to circumstance—in the design of the presentation of the landscape, and in the design of the admission of light. As the ambiguity of Fehn's phrase suggests, it is not just that the light is on stage, but that the light contributes to a stage play in which the house's dwellers are actors—not "a play of light," but light lending a theatrical cast to otherwise mundane enactments. Returning to an observation introduced above, if this pronounced, emphasized openness to circumstance does indeed add dramatic effect to the daily living that the house stages, introducing elements of unexpected delight, delight does not seem to be its end—at least, not its sole end. As shown above, the house stages a series of oppositions that defy notions of tranquility. The balancing of those differences feels not settled, not in stasis, but active, potent, in flux. I believe that is the sense Fehn had in mind when he further described the house as "a discourse of illumination,"[27] the sense of something in the course of negotiation, an unfolding dialog, an issue not yet settled.

The simultaneous accommodation of, and departure from, expectation and quotidian practices, with the effect of expanding awareness, possibility, and dialog, can be added to the sense of urbanity that Fehn's work offers. Openness to circumstance, and a concomitant theatricality, are key. Villa Norrkoping shows that those conditions can be achieved in settings apart from the city. But their fullest potential is found within cities, where they are multiplied and interconnected, and where their architectural engagement assumes greater complexity. Fehn left us an example further along the spectrum toward full-fledged city-ness, in Venice.

Figure 3.18 Nordic Pavilion, looking east. © Tiegens/DEXTRA Photo. Courtesy of Norsk Teknisk Museum.

But Not Yet Greater Than the City

> The building has nothing to do with Norway.
>
> Sverre Fehn, commenting on
> the Nordic Pavilion in 2001[28]

In 1962, Sverre Fehn realized what was perhaps his most recognized work of architecture, the Nordic Pavilion for Venice's Biennale (Figure 3.18). Endeavoring to understand the significance of Fehn's design in consideration of urbanity is a complicated task, but its physical layout can be described in a few sentences. The project is sited along a main east-west promenade in the Giardini (itself peripheral to the city proper), immediately adjacent to the preexisting American and Danish pavilions, and across the promenade from the Japanese, Soviet, and Venezuelan pavilions—the last of those designed by Carlo Scarpa a few years earlier. Situated almost entirely on one level near grade, the project nests in the side of a preexisting berm, an insertion made possible by a roughly 30m-long cast-concrete retaining wall that runs along the project's entire southern side. [29] At a right angle to that wall, the 22m-long east wall separating the pavilion from its American neighbor is treated similarly, making a solid L-configuration of those two sides. In sharp contrast, the remaining sides of the rectangle are almost completely open, marked only by sliding glazed panels that hang from the roof structure near the perimeter, set back a few meters to effectively create porch-like zones along the project's north and west edges. The space encompassed by those four sides is completely devoid of load-bearing structure, except for a massive composite pier at the northwest corner that carries the correspondingly massive concrete beam that makes the open plan and perimeter possible. The roof structure, discussed in more detail below, consists of a two-tiered lattice of thin concrete beams suspended a clear 4.3m above the floor, the top-most layer covered in translucent fiberglass, and the composite system modified in a few locations to allow for several existing trees to extend through the roof. The floor was made of a simple grid of roughly 52cm square slates which corresponded dimensionally to the grid of the roof structure above, and which was similarly modified in a few locations to accommodate the existing trees. Lastly, a steep exterior staircase marks the southwest corner, facilitating movement up the berm to points further south, with a storage and maintenance area constructed beneath its upper landing.

It does not take more than a glance to understand that the roof is the project's dominant architectural feature, and that that component is given to the modulation of light, to the careful integration of mature trees into the center of the project (Figure 3.19), and to the openness of the ground plane. Much of the architectural discourse on the project has understandably emphasized the first of these characteristics—the remarkable luminous condition effected by Fehn's two-way lattice of deep, thin, concrete beams. Those fin-like 100cm x 6cm structural members are spaced to assure that no direct sunlight is admitted; that intention is made explicit in Fehn's section drawings, which diagram how the interval and depth of the beams were determined by local sun angles. The surfaces of these unusual beams are not smooth—the formwork was rough-shuttered, and the imprint of the knotted, un-planed softwood is legible in the casts. The concrete was formulated with fines of white sand and chips of marble[30] so that, while retaining the imprint of the wood upon which their casting depended, the surfaces reflect light but limit glare. It is a striking effect. The question of *what* it effects requires closer consideration of the project's purposes and situation.

Figure 3.19 Nordic Pavilion, interior.

As mentioned, modulation of light is not the roof's only role in the project. The structural redundancy provided by the two-way matrix of deep beams enabled Fehn to interrupt that grid at select points in order to accommodate the trunks of existing trees rooted within the pavilion. As mentioned, the southeastern half of the site as given was defined by a low hill—an oddity in Venice, created as part of the modifications to the eastern portion of the city that Giannantonio Selva conducted under Napoleon's rule[31]—which was populated with a variety of deciduous trees. Fehn would later describe the project as being "of the sun and the trees,"[32] and it is difficult to overstate the importance of the pavilion's arboreal character: the trees are not merely decorative nor peripheral, but essential to the project as a whole. Fehn understood the trees as both bridging, and bringing into opposition, earth and sky:

> [In trees] is the dramatic confrontation between earth and sky. The point of intersection, the horizon, is where the tree gathers all its strength and reaches its maximum constructive size. From that point, it branches out in both directions towards minimal expression, stretching its roots down into the darkness and its branches up towards the light.[33]

Various plans drawn between the original competition entry and the start of construction called for the preservation of differing numbers of trees, but the final construction documents accommodated 16 within the pavilion's perimeter, with several more trees outside of that perimeter consistently appearing in the drawings—even some that were inconveniently close to the primary foundation walls, indicating that Fehn regarded their retention also as important. Most of the "inside" trees were grouped in a two-part strip of planting-bed running the length of the space (Figure 3.20), with the final version including one outlier along the pavilion's porch-like north edge where the accommodation of several trees had originally been envisioned. The resulting contrast between the orthogonal light-washed roof structure and the darker, canted trunks was dramatic. The relationship, though, between flora and structure was not completely dichotomizing. Details like the impression of woodgrain so visible in the concrete that framed the trees, and similar decisions related to the flooring, contributed to a more nuanced contrast, a point I develop below.

Standing out amongst these living components of the architecture is the largest of the trees, located at the northwest corner of the pavilion near where the project's dominant structural beam, the one that makes possible the openness of the plan, bears on its associated composite pier. This tree was a remnant of an old allée of *planes* that demarked one of the Giardini's original promenades. It occupied a special role in Fehn's thinking from the beginning, a role that grew more prominent as the design progressed. As evident in Fehn's early drawings from 1959, where the cantilevered end of the massive 30m beam approaches the tree, it was first conceived as passing alongside it, with the deep cantilevered lattice to be notched at the perimeter to allow the tree's preservation. By the time of construction, the

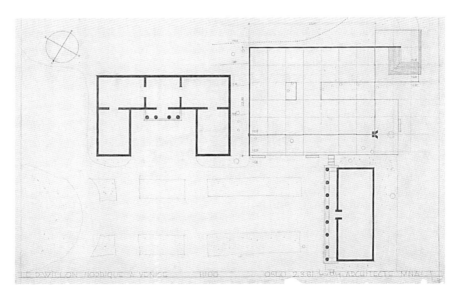

Figure 3.20 Nordic Pavilion, plan, final version, with American and Danish pavilions to west and north, with courtyard penciled in. Primary promenade at right-most edge of drawing. © Sverre Fehn. Courtesy of National Museum, Architecture Collections.

proportions of the floor plan, the location of the beam, and the design of the pier and roof had all been meticulously adjusted so that the beam would now approach the tree directly on center, requiring subtle recalibration of virtually all of the project's modules and ratios. Then, where the beam approached the tree, in a design move defying pragmatism and structural efficiency, it was designed to fork around it (Figure 3.18). The result is that, in this more developed design, the tree is not just accommodated; it is now afforded the central role in determining the form, structure, and imagery of the entire pavilion. Forked beam embraces forked tree. The cantilevered latticed roof, extended tree-ward in the final version, completes the tree's enframement. In this sense, the tree is made artifact, the building its frame.

As mentioned, the concrete beam described above is the primary provider of the remarkable openness that characterizes the pavilion, serving to eliminate the need for any structural supports within the enclosure. The effected emptiness has drawn comparisons to the pavilion architecture of Mies van der Rohe, but Fehn's pavilion is decidedly more *earthen*, not only with regard to its arboreal character but also, as Fehn described, in its relationship to the ground plane. The relative openness of Fehn's plan and the gridded character of both ceiling and floor might lead one to wonder if the scheme was intended to suggest boundlessness, but Fehn was diligent in his attention to the various boundary conditions, even as (or especially as) some of those boundaries exhibited an intentional weakness. Fehn's aim, the building's details strongly suggest, was not an ever-greater luminosity and boundlessness, but a calibration of shadow and light, ground and sky, fixity and flexibility, openness and enclosure, room and space.

That observation offers a way beyond an implicit provincialism that has often hindered a fuller consideration of the pavilion. The atmosphere achieved there has typically been called shadowless and, the logic goes, therefore essentially Nordic; and the pavilion's openness and arboreal attentions have been seen as a communion with the "natural" Nordic world of air and light and flora. Restated, the question posed above—what does the roof effect?—has generally been answered by understanding the project as reproducing in Venice an allochthonous distillation of a uniquely Scandinavian atmosphere. While Fehn's own descriptions of the project sometimes intimated such connections, the quote that opens this section suggests that such readings should not be understood as exhausting the pavilion's meaning. Fehn, in a gentler elaboration, said that he "was not thinking of Nordic light, but when the building was finished the Italians said that there was a sense of Nordic light in this building. I was glad about that, especially as I wasn't thinking about it."[34]

Similarly, in a city where the predominant character of the urban fabric remains essentially medieval, the Nordic pavilion presents an unmistakably modern image. Even within the context of the Giardini, notorious for the eclecticism of its mélange of international pavilions constructed over a century, Fehn's project stands out as especially bold, and boldly minimal.

It is tempting, then, to regard the pavilion, invoking Mies again, like one might regard the German Pavilion in Barcelona—as a masterful avant-garde experiment, a hybrid of building and sculpture designed to stand out and to primarily present as an object for artistic consideration: a museum of itself. But, just as the building cannot be accurately summed as invocation of a distant landscape, neither does a closer examination support casting the building as a detached modern art object. There are two key points. First, as at Villa Nörrkoping, the building admits what it must resist, and dramatically stages those oppositions. Second, as at Foto Huset, the building actively participates in its urban milieu, in ways that in some instances reinforce the existing conditions and associated expectations, while in other instances interjecting surprising departures from those conditions. Here again, difference and dialog emerge as critical.

Starting simply, consider the pavilion's floor. As it exists today, its white marble pavers multiply the light-reflecting properties of the latticed roof-beams, abetting the contrast between building and flora, and enlisting the floor-plane in effecting the pavilion's defining ambient lighting condition: in an imaginary ledger reconciling natural world with architectural abstraction, the floor would mostly belong on the former side. These bright pavers, however, owing to a regrettable decision in the early 1980s, replaced a floor that had been significantly different and original to Fehn's design. Made of Fåvang slate (as specified in construction drawings and as visible in early photographs), that original floor was a very dark gray (Figure 3.19). Rather than extending the distinction between the pavilion's surfaces and the flora that it framed, the slate embodied an ambiguous territory between the artifice of the roof and the earthen-ness of the trees and their garden areas. Decisions pertaining to the extent of the slate flooring structured a further kind of productive ambiguity. Fehn's competition drawings had proposed a single step down at the line of enclosure along the northern edge of the pavilion, emphasizing the portico-like qualities of that peripheral zone. As the design progressed toward construction, the step was eliminated in preference for a continuous floor surface spanning inside and outside, but still corresponding with the limits of the roof above. Also like the roof, the continuity of the floor was interrupted by the beds that framed and provided for the flora, and in one instance at the western edge, the bed spans a threshold condition. This is reminiscent of Fehn's understanding of Villa Rotunda, and of Fehn's own decisions at Villa Norrköping: the Nordic pavilion has a wet, vertical core that reintroduces into the building's center what its envelope must foreclose. As with the relation of the building's structural members and the site's existing trees, the effect is more than a juxtaposition of opposites: a correspondence, or dialog, between the design's parts is opened. As discussed above in regard of several of his projects, here, too, Fehn sought to calibrate that dialog in form, material, and detail. The pavilion's floor was implicated in several oppositions—inside/outside, artifice/wilderness, earth/sky, room/space, building/flora. Decisions pertaining to the floor's materiality, color, limits, and configuration at times strengthen the role of the floor in the context of those oppositions, and at other times permit participating components or concerns to productively weaken that role. This is what the allusion above to an intentionally weak boundary condition refers, and it belongs to a larger pattern of proportional adjustments evident in Fehn's design where definition of parts and their identity is maintained, but weakly so. Before venturing consideration of what the urban implications of such balancing might be, it is helpful to first pursue an understanding of how the pavilion is designed to participate in its urban surrounds (Figure 3.21).

Kenneth Frampton, also wondering about what might be missed in general over-attention to the ostensibly Nordic aspects of the Nordic Pavilion, wrote, "And yet paradoxically for Fehn, the building was also a subtle homage to the corner structure of the Doge's Palace…"[35] In a similar vein, I cannot walk through Fehn's pavilion on a bright day without thinking of the project just across the basin, one which Fehn repeatedly sketched from near the pavilion site—San Giorgio Maggiore (Figure 3.22). It seems unlikely that Fehn was pursuing direct allusions to either project. But the idea that Fehn had on his mind an expanded notion of site, that the pavilion is less foreign to its setting than has been commonly presumed, opens further consideration. More of Fehn's own commentary on his design supports that effort:

> The pavilion carries the ingredients of Venice. The city belongs to the water from which came its inspiration. The areas of green contrast with the water. The park with its landscape of grass and trees is very precious and scarce. Every existing tree grows unhindered inside the building, finding a total freedom through the roof.[36]

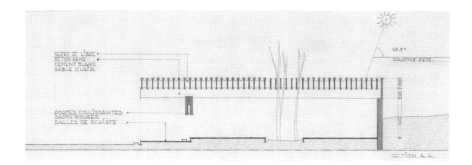

Figure 3.21 Nordic Pavilion, competition drawing, section. © Sverre Fehn. Courtesy of National Museum, Architecture Collections.

Figure 3.22 San Giorgio Maggiore from the Giardini. Sketch, Sverre Fehn, 1993. © Sverre Fehn. Courtesy of National Museum, Architecture Collections.

If the project's correspondences with iconic and distant projects like the palace and the church are debatable, its attentions to its immediate situation are indisputable.

In the project's current state, the ziggurat-like staircase at the southern corner, leading nowhere (Figure 3.18, on the far right), is not readily explainable beyond its role as a figure in the composition of the primary facade, in which the stair-form is contraposed to the large plane tree. Not insignificantly, the riser-tread ratio that makes the stairway somewhat difficult to navigate also makes it well-suited for seating, and the stairs can often be found to structure a kind of impromptu amphitheater for small groups. Period photographs and Fehn's site drawings reveal a third concern. There was an existing pathway on the site that moved along the edge of the allée and up the low hill, connecting to the furthermost group of pavilions beyond. Fehn's stairway maintained, modified, and reified that path, originally conducting pedestrians up the steps beneath the cantilevered roof and deeper into the park.

Also recurring in Fehn's line-drawings and sketches are the two existing neighboring pavilions—he almost never omitted them, and their presence in those drawings serves not merely to contextualize the location of the proposed project, but to directly inform its design. The zone along the long northern edge of the building, for example, is strikingly open, and at first glance may seem indifferent about perimeter definition along that edge—even more so when the large wood and glass panels are slid to the side. In preceding paragraphs, that long peripheral area was described as portico-like. Despite its lack of columns or arcuation, the latter term is apt because it is a long-roofed space open to the site on one long side, and because it structures movement both along and across its sheltered length. Like the hillside path, that longitudinal movement retraces a line of circulation that predates the project—a pedestrian easement of sorts linking the main thoroughfare of the promenade to the garden court around which the American and Danish pavilions were arranged. The Danish pavilion, oriented at right angle to that line of movement, has a more classically styled portico that fronts that court; which is to say, faced with choosing between a front presenting to the allée and a front presenting to the courtyard, the Danish pavilion was designed to decidedly turn its back on the promenade. Fehn's plan, in contrast, presents two fronts: the primary one to the west along the allée (which is the image most prominently featured in descriptions of the project, as in Figure 3.18), and a secondary front to the north along the courtyard. Fehn's design can be usefully understood as a joint between those two spatial conditions. In a small corresponding detail that appeared early in the design, Fehn further engaged the Danish portico by extending the lateral axis delineating its porch as a modest connecting walkway of simple stone pavers that anticipated movement between the existing pavilion and Fehn's proposed one (Figure 3.23). Fehn's development of the project's perimeter, then, sustained an existing line of pedestrian movement while anticipating a new one; and recognized, further defined, and bridged the two main public spaces—a court and a promenade—that the project dually fronted. The portico-like zone weakly differentiates between inside and outside, not as an assertion of extensivity, but as if balancing its role as a throughway with its role as threshold.

Figure 3.23 Nordic Pavilion, view from portico of Danish pavilion, looking south. © Ferruzzi, 1962. Courtesy of National Museum, Architecture Collections.

The Nordic pavilion's engagement of this part of its setting is not limited to a concern with circulation, sequence, and margin. The court on which that facade faces was only loosely defined before the Nordic pavilion's construction. Examination of Fehn's drawings shows that several decisions about the height and scale of the building's parts were made in consideration of preexisting dimensions in the neighboring facades and their collective definition of the garden court. The elevation drawings strongly suggest a relationship in dimension and character between the triglyphed entablature of the American pavilion and the line of structure above the Nordic

90 *Sverre Fehn's Ambient Urbanity*

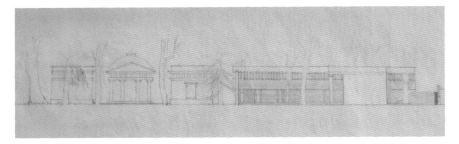

Figure 3.24 Nordic Pavilion, north elevation, American pavilion to the left, Danish pavilion and its portico drawn in cross-section to the right. © Sverre Fehn. Courtesy of National Museum, Architecture Collections.

Figure 3.25 Nordic Pavilion, looking south from garden court, Danish pavilion just out of frame to the right. © Ferruzzi, 1962. Courtesy of National Museum, Architecture Collections.

pavilion's portico, which, in turn, typologically echoes the portico of its Danish neighbor as it appears in the section drawing (Figure 3.24). The effect strengthens the coherence of the courtyard that had been only partially realized by the two earlier buildings. It also emphasizes the notion that the Nordic pavilion *has* facades; that is, the design's fronts attend an antecedent public realm.

There is an additional effect in the portico's configuration that pertains to the topic of architectural attunement, though for Fehn to have anticipated it would indicate an almost inconceivable degree of foresight. Still, as Fehn himself noted, it is characteristic of well-designed buildings to exceed their designer's conscious intentions. The fin-like roof structure coextensive with the portico is achieved by cantilever, so that the narrow beam-ends collectively create a surface-like datum within the upper reaches of the northern facade (Figure 3.25). At the cantilevered portion of the roof structure, the previously noted effect of the vertical diffusion and reflection of sunlight exhibit here also horizontally. Looking at any north-facing building elevation in the northern hemisphere is typically an exercise in looking into shadow. This backlit condition appears in landscapes in general, but is often more pronounced in buildings where their height, expanse, and opacity bring them into greater contrast with the lighted sky beyond. In Fehn's design, that darkened condition becomes a foil: the sunlight captured by the system of fins is conducted horizontally to the building's shadowed face, setting aglow what is typically dark. I believe this is what Fehn had in mind when he wrote, "The ceiling lowers the sky to a surface that belongs to the building."[37] Conforming to the established building heights, nestled at an inside corner, partially cloaked in foliage and partially obscured by the preexisting pavilions, the Nordic pavilion, in fulfilling its role in the co-formation of the courtyard, risks passivity and marginalization. But the improbable illumination of the upper facade under fortuitous light conditions effectually amplifies its participation in the court.

Given the primary purpose of the building, it may seem puzzling that the project's interior does not include nor offer many clues about partition, furnishing, or equipment. There are some weak indications of interior differentiation, like the position of the long planting bed and its bridging of inside and out, or the aforementioned loosely defined paths of circulation. But, when not in use, and especially when cloudy, the pavilion decidedly recedes, as if it has been turned off. Fehn did design a typical chair and table as part of his work for the pavilion, but these were only realized later elsewhere (the chair reappeared at Villa Norrköping), and scarcely any idea of how those particular furnishings were to have been placed or deployed in the pavilion is evident in the drawings he made of them. As already made clear, Fehn had a strong interest and formidable talent for furnishing, casework, and exhibit design. This had been established even at this point in his career, evident in his earlier pavilion for the Brussels World's Fair in 1958, which I return to in Chapter 5. As shown at Villa Norrköping, relationships between device, object, and body would emerge as among the most important of Fehn's architectural attentions. But unlike Brussels, where he had carefully designed displays specific to the artifacts they presented and composed them within a building conceived as deployable and temporary, the

92 *Sverre Fehn's Ambient Urbanity*

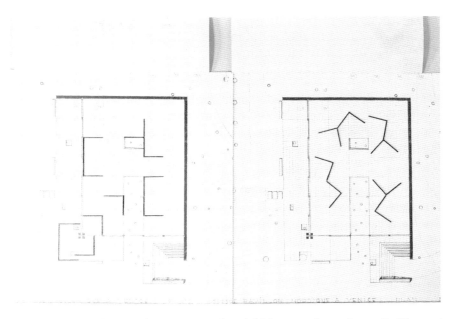

Figure 3.26 Nordic Pavilion, proposed exhibition configurations. © Tiegens/ DEXTRA Photo. Courtesy of Norsk Teknisk Museum.

Venice pavilion, Fehn understood, would be an enduring site for the periodic presentation of objects and installations not yet imagined. Accordingly, Fehn's design work included plan and perspective drawings of possibilities for different kinds of exhibition that the pavilion might accommodate (Figure 3.26). Those provisional schemes engaged the project's more permanent components in suggestive ways, but, developed no further than diagram, they remained only suggestive. In this sense, the luminous ambiance of the project is provisional—it undergirds the staging of actions unknown but nevertheless prequalifies those actions by setting them before circumstance in specific ways (e.g., the building's accommodation of flora, or its admission of rain and light), and by participating in, and co-sustaining, its urban milieu.

The title of this chapter is a reference from Palladio. In considering the design of a church in relationship to the city to which it belongs, he advised that the building should be great, "but not yet greater than the greatness of the city requires."[38] The two architects shared a concern for calibrating not only a building's intrinsic coherence, but also for its circumstantial, urban correspondence.

In the preceding consideration of the urban dimensions of Fehn's Nordic Pavilion, the word *participation* was mostly used in relation to the way that buildings can be said to participate in their settings. But as the chapter's first two projects showed, there is a relationship between a building's participation and the kinds and qualities of participation that it facilitates for its occupants, users, or citizens. In the next chapter, the topic of participation and its meaning with regard to urbanity are explored in two of Fehn's most complexly urban projects.

Notes

1 The photo might have been part of Nesjar's *Ice and Mud* series from the 1950s, which featured "mikrolandskap" photos, presumably from Larvik, but archival information, if it exists, is not readily available. The image was almost certainly black and white. See, Hanne Holm-Johnsen, "Photography," in Sylvia Antoniou, ed., *Carl Nesjar: Linking Art, Nature, and Technology* (Oslo: Labyrinth Press, 2008). Nesjar was in Paris while Fehn was working there in the 1950s, but I have found no indication that they met in that earlier period.
2 See especially Leo Spitzer, "Milieu and Ambiance: An Essay in Historical Semantics." *Philosophy and Phenomenological Research Quarterly*, 3, no. 1 (1942), 1–42. Also, Spitzer, "Classical and Christian Ideas of World Harmony: Prolegomena to an Interpretation of the Word "Stimmung." *Traditio*, 2 (1944), 409–464.
3 For an unforgettable consideration of that overlap in the genre of short fiction, see Sims' horror story. Sims, Bennett. "House-Sitting." In *White Dialogues* (Columbus: Two Dollar Radio Press, 2017).
4 Sverre Fehn, "Fotoforretning I Oslo." "For der moderne menneske der fotografi-apparatet blitt et slags smykke." An ambiguity is presented in the phrase, "mysteries in the cut [or polished] glass"—referring at once to the glass case that holds the "pricy trinkets [kostbar liten gjenstand]" but also the glass lenses that enable photography.
5 For my more detailed consideration of this idea in relation to one of Fehn's earliest projects, see Anderson, Stephen. "Of Artifact, Urbanity, and the City: Sverre Fehn's Norwegian Pavilion and the Structure of Urbanity." In *Projecting Urbanity: Architecture For and Against the City*, ed. David Leatherbarrow, Chapter 6 (London: Artifice Press, 2023).
6 Thinking through this concept, I cannot help but be reminded of a passage from Maurice Merleau-Ponty, where he describes a similar duality essential, he believes, to genuine dialog. I include it here only as an extended footnote because, despite its illumination of dialog, it takes us further from Fehn, and because its connection to spatial settings is, at this point, only tentative: "Speech endlessly renews the mediation of the same and the other. Speech perpetually verifies that there is no signification without a movement, at first violent, that surpasses all signification. […] if the other person is really another, at a certain stage I must be surprised, disoriented. […] Then I catch up from behind…" See, Maurice Merleau-Ponty, *Prose of the World* (Evanston: Northwest University Press, 1973), 142–143.
7 Thord Strömberg, "Sakta vi går genom stan," in *New logo. Industristaden byter skinn*, ed. Mats Berglund (Stads och kommunhistoriska institutet, 2005). [In Swedish].
8 Most notably, Jørgen Bo and Vilhelm Wohlert, Danish architects renowned for their work at the Louisiana Museum, designed two of the houses, Nordengatan 5 and 7, to the south of Fehn's site.
9 Per Olaf Fjeld, *The Pattern of Thoughts* (New York: Monacelli Press, 2009), 80.
10 There is an anomalous eighth panel that can be slid from an interior partition to subdivide the children's bedroom.

11 Per Olaf Fjeld, personal correspondence with author, 2020.
12 Sverre Fehn, *Poetry of the Straight Line* (Helsinki: Museum of Finnish Architecture, 1992), 11.
13 Sverre Fehn, "Tree of Life," in *Signs and Insights*, ed. Giancarlo De Carlo (Urbino: ILAUD, 1980), 99.
14 Mari Hvattum, "Sverre Fehn's Villa Schreiner," in *asBuilt 10 Classic*, eds. N. Berre and M. Lending (Poland: Pax Forlag, 2014), 18.
15 Palladio, *Four Books of Architecture*, book 2, Chapter 3. Some historians have argued that another factor, probably, was the client's intention to use the house not as a periodic retreat from the city, but as a full-time residence.
16 On the nuances and political dimensions of the typological distinctions between villa, palazzo, villa urbanus, and villa rustica, in addition to the many classic texts such as Ackerman and Wittkower, see also Paul Holberton, *Palladio's Villas* (London: John Murray Publishers, 1990), and Pier Aureli, "The Geo-Politics of the Ideal Villa," in *Possibility of an Absolute Architecture* (Cambridge: MIT Press, 2011), 47–84.
17 James Ackerman, *The Villa* (Princeton: Princeton University Press, 1985), 22.
18 David Leatherbarrow and Richard Wesley have developed related facets of these points. See, D. Leatherbarrow and R. Wesley, *Three Cultural Ecologies* (New York: Routledge, 2018), 29–33.
19 Palladio, *Four Books*.
20 Kenneth Frampton, "The Tectonic Form of Sverre Fehn," *Area* 116, September 2014. Retrieved from https://www.area-arch.it/en/.
21 Fjeld, *Pattern of Thoughts*, 64.
22 David Leatherbarrow, *Uncommon Ground* (Cambridge: MIT Press, 2000), Chapter 4. Especially pertinent to Fehn's thinking, see paragraph beginning "At night…" on page 160.
23 Per Olaf Fjeld, *Sverre Fehn: the Thought of Construction* (New York: Rizzoli, 1983), 64–67.
24 The floors at the core of the house were terrazzo; remaining floors were carpeted in woven matting.
25 Sverre Fehn, in Fjeld, *The Thought of Construction*, 67.
26 Sverre Fehn, in Fjeld, *Pattern of Thoughts*, 80.
27 Sverre Fehn, in Fjeld, *Pattern of Thoughts*, 64.
28 Hans Ulrich Obrist, "Interview with Sverre Fehn," in *Arbitare*, January, 2001.
29 The project is rotated about 20 degrees from cardinal points in conformance to the given promenades. For the sake of simplification, I describe the pavilion using the closest cardinal directions.
30 As specified in the construction drawings.
31 See, John Dixon Hunt, *The Venetian City Garden* (Berlin: Birkhäuser, 2009), 136–146. Also, Vittoria Martini, *Just Another Exhibition: Histories and Politics of Biennials* (Florence: Postmedia Books, 2011).
32 Sverre Fehn, in *Sverre Fehn: Works, Projects, Writings 1949–1996*, eds. Norberg-Schulz and Pastiglione (New York: Monacelli Press, 1997), 82.
33 Sverre Fehn, *Poetry*, 34.
34 Obrist, 2001.
35 Kenneth Frampton, in Fjeld, *The Thought of Construction*, foreword.
36 Sverre Fehn, in Frampton, "The Tectonic Form of Sverre Fehn," *Area* 116, September, 2014.
37 Fjeld, *Construction*, 112.
38 Palladio, *I quattro libri dell'architettura*, Book 4, Chapter 2. Original Italian: *Magnifici, ma non però maggiori di quello, che ricerchi la grandezza della Città*. Various English translations substitute "bigness" for "greatness," or use both.

4 Sverre Fehn, the City, and the Architecture of Participation

> To assure the citizen a meaningful existence is to strive for a construction that will complement the established rhythm by giving the past a new function. This structure will reveal the thought of generations. The key to this unity is within the existing order of movement. [...] The project is a continuation of the existing street. The construction participates with the city as it opens up to its many levels.
>
> Sverre Fehn

In previous chapters, one of the architectural ideas I have tried to better understand in Fehn's work is the relationship between cultural and topographic stratification. To be clear, the phrase "cultural stratification" could understandably be read as pertaining to elitist hierarchies, whereas in the context of the structure of urbanity, as I have approached the concept, it alludes to differing levels of permanence and sophistication and their interrelation. Nowhere are those relationships more pervasive and complex as in the city, and, as already seen at Fehn's Trondheim Library proposal, nowhere are there greater opportunities for creatively exploiting them. Dalibor Vesely wrote:

> The reference to the city as a reflection of the universe may appear today as a lost distant memory as long as we do not realise that the reality of the city is not homogenous, but stratified, that the surface levels (strata) are more open to change than the deeper ones which show a high degree of continuity and identity with the archaic past. This can be seen very well in the history of the main element of the city, the street, in its changing character, but at the same time in a surprising continuity of its presence and relative lack of change. It is perhaps not an overstatement to see *street* as the main structuring element in the development of cities.[1]

Like Fehn, Vesely intentionally conflates cultural and topographic stratification; both men cite the street as the fundamental stratum of the city.

DOI: 10.4324/9781003343646-4

Perhaps it is implicit in the very definition of street, but Fehn explicitly emphasized the role of movement in rehearsing the order of the city—in Fehn's quote here, those observations are general to cities; elsewhere, as I will describe below, Fehn also recognized specific patterns as belonging to a city.

While Sverre Fehn was able to realize only a handful of architectural works in dense urban areas, he maintained a robust engagement of architectural problems related to the city through the pursuit of several architectural competitions. The most significant and complex were the museum expansion at Tullinløkka square in Oslo (1972), and the expansion of the Royal Danish Theater in Copenhagen (1996). Fehn did not win the Oslo competition, and while his Copenhagen design was selected for construction, the project did not survive the intensely partisan debate that unfolded in the wake of the competition. Still, the two projects initiated much speculation among architects, and Fehn was asked to reflect on those designs in many interviews long after it was clear that the proposals would not advance. Together, the two projects present a set of issues regarding the relationship of the architectural project to the city, some that are more

Figure 4.1 Tullinløkka, looking north, 1906. The square is visible as a grassy square right of the center of image; a diagonal path is barely discernible; university buildings in foreground. A small portion of the street-park axis that defines the heart of the city can be seen at bottom left. Photo by Narve Skarpmoen.

complex versions of ideas already introduced, some that are specific to large scales of urban culture, and which directly involve consideration of street and urban patterns of culture and movement. I will consider each project in turn, then further develop the themes that they share.

Strata, Structure, Street

While the project in Hamar was unfolding, Fehn turned his attention to a museum proposal for a very different setting. In the heart of Oslo, Tullinløkka square is a plaza of sorts with a history that dates to when the city was gaining more formal definition and increasing density in the 19th century (Figure 4.1). The site had once been part of the privately held Tullin estate, which was acquired by the city as it expanded.[2] Situated just north of the city's most prominent public center, period photos show the roughly 100m square to be well defined by the end of the 19th century. By 1930, the square was essentially enclosed by the perimeter facades of the National Gallery of Art to the east (c.1880, wings added in c.1905 and c.1920), the National History Museum to the west (c.1901), Oslo University's Domus Media building (c.1852, with "the Aula" addition in 1911) just across Kristian den IV's Gate to the south, and, across Kristian Augusts Gate from the open northern edge, the frontage of a dense commercial block. The open area within that perimeter had been modified on several occasions, and the plot had seen a wide variety of uses in its history—playground, ice skating rink, sports field, an 1883 manufacturing expo, demonstration grounds, cycling track, and landscaped park. During the Nazi occupation, the square was commandeered for vehicular parking, eventually including a petrol station. Once converted to automobile usage, it had remained that way until increasing cognizance of the square's underperformance in the life of the city led to a competition for the design of its reconfiguration in 1972. The competition brief was the impetus for Fehn's proposal.[3]

The scope of the competition included goals beyond the rehabilitation of the open square. The two facing museums—the Historical Museum and the National Gallery—had been posing some problems for the museums' administrators, not least of which was a need for more exhibition space. Fehn brought further complexity to the problem. As his proposal makes clear, he had in mind not only the institutions of the square and its museums, but also the university building to the south, as well as the less formal but nonetheless urban institutions of assembly, performance, meeting, and wandering. Fehn's approach, then, was attentive not only to programmatic concerns typical of a museum expansion—assuring ample gallery space, connective circulation, parking, services, etc.—but also to broader and less quantifiable aims, such as engaging the existing life of the city and facilitating its growth.

Understanding how Fehn manifested those concerns in the proposed project requires moving between a variety of his design explorations, no one

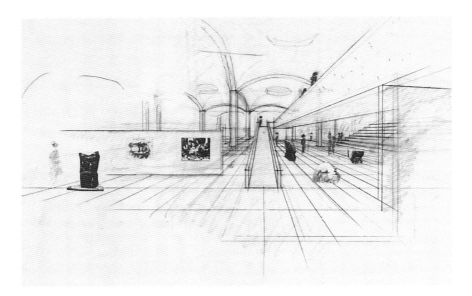

Figure 4.2 Tullinløkka, interior perspective, mixed media. © Sverre Fehn. Courtesy of National Museum, Architecture Collections.

of which presents the full scheme. The multiple approaches to the design's development indicate a working process that served an exploration of multiple roles for architecture within an urban setting. The design work included at least three different models—one in plaster, one of balsawood combined with molded-plastic composite, and a third in balsa and Styrofoam—each respectively examining the massing, structure, and luminosity of the design. Photographs of these models were featured in Fehn's competition boards. Of the several kinds of drawings that Fehn used to develop the project, the most striking was a series of constructed perspectives that incorporated montage—a method he had deployed in his earlier entry for the Norwegian Pavilion in Brussels in 1958. These drawings did not show the project as a whole, but instead depicted the occupation of discrete places or rooms within the proposed project, including printed reductions of would-be artworks displayed in the several gallery spaces (Figure 4.2). Reductions of these drawings, too, were featured on the competition boards, along with orthographic drawings and diagrams.

Fractured Geometries, An Urban Cut

Taken together, the various explorations present what first seems like a straightforward column grid distributed across the site in pavilion-like fashion and roofed with an array of shallow domes, somewhat reminiscent of Aldo van Eyck's roof design for the Amsterdam Orphanage (1960). Closer inspection reveals the project's organization to be more complex. To start, unlike Van Eyck's design, Fehn's domes transitioned to their columns by means of pendentives, making a lighter, airier structural system.[4] Each pier was actually a composite of four columns, one for each of the four adjoining domes. Piers were intended to double as chases for services and rainwater collection. The most significant departure from the apparent rationality of the gridded layout, though, is that the grid itself is irregular: the field of column-clusters is divided diagonally and shifted east-west by an odd interval, opening a gap in the grid that accommodated a pedestrian through-street (though Fehn's building sections label it only "gate": street).

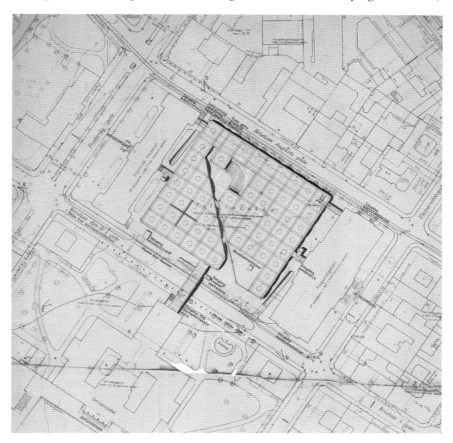

Figure 4.3 Tullinløkka, site plan featuring diagonal pedestrian street and amphitheater. Note over-street walkway at Kristian IV Gate connecting University Hall to proposed museum addition. At the time of the competition, the open areas shown adjacent to the Hall were occupied with mature hardwoods, as represented in several of Fehn's drawings. © Sverre Fehn. Courtesy of National Museum, Architecture Collections.

100 *Sverre Fehn, the City, and the Architecture of Participation*

At grade, this rift and shift were most easily legible along the north edge of the design where the pedestrian street intersects Kristians Augusts Street and registers the odd bay size in the plan and north elevation. In the roof plan, the pedestrian street reads as a diagonal cut (Figure 4.3). The photographic history shows that this southeast-northwest path had been traced across the site several times in the past—a habitual route between the heart of the city and points to the northwest. Whether or not Fehn was aware of that history, the urban configuration continued to suggest the usefulness of such a diagonal pedestrian throughway, as Fehn noted in the text for his competition boards where he described the pedestrian street as a *snarvei*, or "shortcut," connecting institutions and hotels to the north with Karl Johans Gate, the city's axial center two blocks to the south.[5]

Fehn's pedestrian street was mostly open to the sky and intended to connect one existing public street to another, passing through the museum without providing any entrance into it. The pedestrian street was public, then, in the sense that it was available for use as a throughway and access to it was not controlled. Fehn's design, though, advanced a more complex understanding of *public*. While there was no way to enter the museum from the proposed pedestrian street, this did not mean that it was entirely separated from the museum's interior. It would be more accurate to say that the street was separated from the museum *only* with regard to bodily access. Galleries at the ground and upper floors were arranged so that the

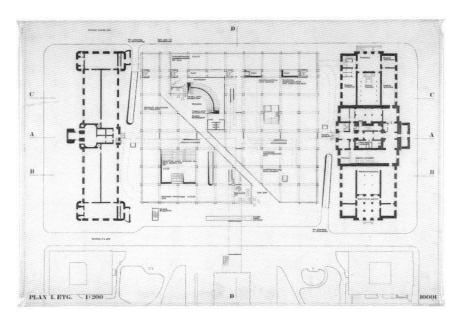

Figure 4.4 Tullinløkka, street-level plan. © Sverre Fehn. Courtesy of National Museum, Architecture Collections.

Sverre Fehn, the City, and the Architecture of Participation 101

street's meandering and storefront-like design would bring the museum and its artifacts directly into the experience of people simply passing through the site en route to further destinations without ever actually entering the museum proper, at least not in the typical sense of *entering*. The division between those places that are open to the general public for everyday use and navigation, and those places where accessibility and climate are regulated, appears ambiguous in most of the models and drawings but is clearly delineated in the orthographic plans, which locate the large glass-paneled frames that were to cordon the pedestrian street from the museum's interior (Figure 4.4).

Plans and vignettes show two cafés (Figures 4.4 and 4.5) that were to anchor each end of the pedestrian street. While the omission of any indication of doors in the design proposal leaves ambiguous the question of accessibility to the cafés, Fehn's drawings show tables both inside and outside, indicating that he envisioned the glass partitions separating museum from street at those locations to be somehow operable. Absent graphic depiction, Fehn's competition text described a two-tiered glazing system in which the lower portion could be raised so that the cafés would straddle the division between museum and street, separating the two while serving both.[6]

Along this route connecting the two cafés, opening like a pool in the middle of the museum, was a small amphitheater, complete with supporting

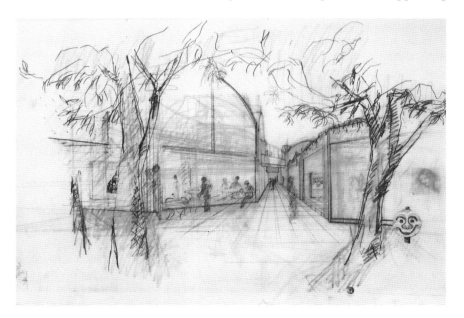

Figure 4.5 Tullinløkka, sketch showing pedestrian street, looking north. One of the cafés is visible to the left, and the roof-garden-terrace is just visible at the upper right. © Sverre Fehn. Courtesy of National Museum, Architecture Collections.

spaces for use during performances. Labeled "amphitheater" on the plans, Fehn's text also referred to this space as "a small plaza." In the building's section, the amphitheater vertically dovetailed with a lecture hall immediately below, but, unlike the lecture hall, the amphitheater and its support spaces were not to be accessible from the museum but, rather, accessible to only the street. The amphitheater, then, would be available to double as a lunch-spot or meeting place when not deployed for performance or lecture. Analogous to the museum's conferral of its interiors to the experience of the street, the amphitheater is separated from but visually available to the experience of the museum, especially from the exhibit area to the west.

Considered as a whole, the opening of this circulatory gap and its ancillary spaces in the middle of the museum sets up an equivalency or kind of exchange: the street is given some of the curiosity and provocation of the museum exhibits, and the museum is lent something of the daily life and theatricality of the city. Where most museums are designed to keep those two worlds separate, Fehn's design goes to great lengths to interfuse them, addressing his general critique of museums as discussed in Chapter 2. Given the inclusion of the amphitheater, and given the provocation that Fehn placed in the lower right corner of one of his competition drawings (Figure 4.5), further consideration of the role of "theatricality" in the design is warranted. For reasons that will become obvious, that exploration will be delayed until later in this chapter, after explication of the Copenhagen project.

There is another set of design decisions germane to the Tullinløkka project's urban orientation that can be found in a second deformation of the governing grid layout. Though it doesn't appear in the earlier renditions, the more fully developed scheme shows another odd interval, in this case running east-west for the full length of the grid, creating a very narrow irregular bay that separated the northernmost bay along Kristian Augusts street from the remainder of the project to the south (Figure 4.4, near top). While it does not show well in the building sections (owing to the depiction of the vertical circulation), the plans indicate a double-height atrium-like slot in that narrowed bay, which accommodated stairways and which featured a continuous skylight that ran most of its length. Thereby effectively culled from the rest of the project, the full bay along the street housed administrative suites on the upper floor where it was connected to existing administrative spaces in the adjoining museums and accommodated a curating/restoration workshop at street level. Separating uses in such a manner makes practical sense for the museum, but why allocate such perfunctory pieces of the program to the project's most public facade, especially a project concerned with the integration of the museum and its mission into the daily life of the city?

As previously discussed with regard to several of his designs, Fehn repeatedly demonstrated a concern for balancing a building's assertiveness with deference, novelty with normality. In this case, for all the spectacle and

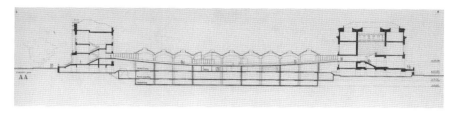

Figure 4.6 Tullinløkka, building section, looking north. © Sverre Fehn. Courtesy of National Museum, Architecture Collections.

energy of the proposed design, many of its features are configured so that the existing buildings' identities are maintained, their priority reconfirmed. Except for three select bridge-like connectors, all above grade, Fehn's proposed gallery addition remains detached from the existing buildings. Also, approaching the project from a distance, the upper datum of Fehn's domes was set well below the rooflines of the adjoining buildings, establishing a clear hierarchy (Figure 4.6). The two existing museums also maintain their preexisting internal organization, including, most importantly, their entry sequences: Fehn proposed no new entrance at the most visible facade along Kristian Augusts street; in fact, there was no new public museum entrance *anywhere* in Fehn's design—the existing building entrances retained their regulative and projective purposes.

These decisions that preserved the existing museums' primacy were well served by Fehn's decisions regarding the location of the offices and workshop, since it avoids interjecting a new museum facade that would have competed with the original buildings, and because a more monumental facade might have falsely suggested entry. There is another consideration here that may have contributed to the end-bay's relative detachment. By locating the offices and restoration lab along the sidewalk, the work of the museum—its daily, work-a-day life—was aligned with the daily life of the city street. For the administrators, curators, and technicians conducting their work in those spaces, on one side they were afforded overview of the museum's galleries, on the other side they were connected to the mundane activities of the street. In a sense, then, the fusing of city and museum was furthered in this set of design decisions, not between citizen and museum, but between the workings of the museum and the working city. As with the insertion of the pedestrian street and its storefront-like elevations, Fehn advanced the cause of making the museum part of the daily life of the city, not apart from it.

Walking City

Having decided, remarkably, on the bifurcation of the museum's ground plane as a first-order design move, Fehn turned to the proposed building's section for unifying the museums and connecting them to the shared spaces of the new exhibits, storage, and offices. This was primarily accomplished through a roughly cross-shaped set of elevated walkways that issue from the second story of the three bounding existing buildings and that gently slope toward the project's center.[7] Given similarities in the slope and form of the walkways, it is reasonable to wonder if Fehn had seen Yannis Xenakis' early proposal for the courtyard at La Tourette, but no direct connection has been established (Figure 4.7).[8] Sets of stairs, habitable landings, and ramps connected those upper vestibules to the double-height exhibit spaces below (triple-height at the area to the southwest labeled "multipurpose"). At this upper level, the elevated walkways transversed the exterior pedestrian street through glazed, skyway-like passages—the street passed underneath without compromising the integrity of the controlled climate of the museum. This set of upper conveyances bore similarities to the ramps at the Hedmark museum. Some of that likeness can be attributed to the sectional proportions and detailing, though it is hard to determine because the Tullinløkka design was never fully developed. It is the curious relation between the walkways and the ground-plane, though, which is most reminiscent of Hedmark. The elevated walkways were massive, their guards and railings solid, but they were also hovering. The three branches of the tree of upper walkways at Tullinløkka each sloped down slightly from the perimeter of the site toward its center. The rationale for the slope is not obvious. At the Hedmark Museum, too, one critical interior stretch of the elevated walkway subtly undulates—an effect wildly difficult to achieve in cast concrete. For what purpose, such effort? There is scant evidence of Fehn's thinking on the matter, but he did offer that the "slope of the bridges activates the pedestrian's view" – apparently the sloped walking surfaces at Tullinløkka were intended to animate the ambiance of the space in some way. There is a point to be made here about measured discord in architectural design and the urban purpose for which it might be used—I will return to that later in this chapter. The walkways appeared pendular, hanging, here as at Hedmark describing a zone of movement between the lower limit of the paved ground-plane and the luminous upper limit of the sunlight-admitting roof. The effect was to stratify lines of circulation, distinguishing them from the more contemplative spaces of the galleries without fully separating the two kinds of occupation. The activity and movement of the upper layers contributed to the life of the galleries while the order and character of the galleries was legible from the circulation above. As with the horizontal divisions between gallery and circulation along the pedestrian street, the sectional stratification was likewise productively weak at its margins, so that each of the juxtaposed conditions—active, contemplative—mutually informed the other. Whereas museums are typically designed to bracket all externalities to object and viewer, in Fehn's design the viewing of artifact is integral with urban circumstance, and the communicative nature of art viewing is rendered receptive and projective with regard to its surrounds.

Sverre Fehn, the City, and the Architecture of Participation 105

Figure 4.7 Tullinløkka, wooden model with resin roof removed, looking north. © Sverre Fehn. Courtesy of National Museum, Architecture Collections.

Figure 4.8 Tullinløkka, long section drawing, looking west. The curved shells of Fehn's proposed museum addition are visible to the right (north). © Sverre Fehn. Courtesy of National Museum, Architecture Collections.

Fehn's sloping elevated walkways connected to the two existing museums at preexisting circulation corridors (Figure 4.7). That was not the case, though, with the university building to the south. Passing over the sidewalks and vehicular traffic of Kristian den IV Gate, this southern viaduct connected from the expanded museum to the existing building directly through the back of an existing stage (Figure 4.7, bottom of image)—the institutionally revered auditorium known simply as "Aula" ("The Hall"). That inventive proposal appears somewhat less audacious when the details of the existing building are considered. Added as an appendage to the back of the building to commemorate the university's centennial in 1911, the Aula's auditorium was adorned with a series of 11 large murals in oil by Edvard Munch.[9] Fehn's proposal brought those murals within the ambit of the museum, effectively transforming the Aula into an art gallery that could still be cordoned for occasional use as an auditorium.

The appropriation of the Hall would have completed the interconnection of a long pedestrian sequence that was apparently important to Fehn. That sequence appeared in his competition entry as a section drawing that spanned the top of its board (Figure 4.8). The scope of the drawing was unusual. The section extended not just across the site's streets to include the bounding buildings, as might be expected, but cut south all the way through the university building to include its opposite facade, extended across *that* street—Karl Johans Gate which defines the city's center—and continued southward through the recognizable form of the Norwegian National Theatre and its park on the city's most important public venue, then further south across the next street, Stortingsgata, and through the facade of the commercial buildings there, from which the museums—much less Fehn's proposed addition—would not have been remotely visible. Keeping in mind Fehn's comments about the city's floor, the unusually long section shows Fehn's proposal as belonging to, responding to, and modifying a series of urban conditions that a single view could not possibly capture, but that can be understood as the character of the city revealed through the movement of its citizens. In reference to Tullinløkka, Fehn described the idea by asserting, "The city has a rhythm, each beat reflecting the temperament of its individuals. [...] The walking figure is a man activated...Only he can transfer the rhythm from one building to the next."[10] Here, the slip between city as a representation of universal order and city as street, which characterizes the chapter's opening quotes from both Vesely and Fehn, is architecturally embodied in the Tullinløkka section. The layered-ness of the city is represented in the sectional differentiation described above, defining different temporalities, movements, uses, and kinds of occupation in relation to each other; and the layered-ness of the city is at once activated for daily life, rendering parts of the city operable and available while relating those parts within the rhythm and recollection of pedestrian movement.

Building the Non-Building

The long site-section and the previously discussed deferential design decisions are emblematic of a design less concerned with giving the city a monument than with providing it an apparatus for the representation and staging of its urban life, an endeavor in which monumentality figures only partially. Fehn expressed this idea in the text of his competition boards, as if cautioning the jurors, writing that it would be "unfortunate if the new museum rejected the old, with a large entry and monumental façade."[11] Describing the ideas driving the Tullinløkka project in an interview in 2001, Fehn said:

> You open up the museum for the main street in Oslo instead of making some acrobatic building there with a new entrance and a park and a little garden and so on. Then we moved into this construction with the

roof, and it became a non-building-- a structure made to connect these three buildings to one big museum.[12]

One might protest that Fehn's Tullinløkka design had its own "little garden"—a sculpture garden on a terrace at the second floor overlooking the southern pedestrian street entrance—or that "acrobatic" might be an apt descriptor of Fehn's sloping walkways and intersecting lines of movement. But those observations only point to the complexity of Fehn's concern with the divergent conceptual aims of, in his words, "acrobatic building" and "non-building," and their respective implications for the life of the city. This directs us to an architectural province that is not easy to see or to discuss, but that is essential to understanding Fehn's urban work. Part of the difficulty stems from our culture's habit of making form and image primary in architectural analysis. Elaborating on how this problem complicates an analysis of Fehn's work, Peter Cook wrote:

> Such is our current preoccupation with slick iconography and the hard-hitting rhetoric of partisan symbols of the technologic, mainstream, or vernacular, that we are unused to a building that collages together devices, as in the tradition of the clockmaker, so that they seem naturally interdependent.[13]

As frequently the case in his projects, Fehn's decision-making at Tullinløkka has not much to do with form or image as ends in themselves, but, rather, with the anticipation of occupation and its concomitant orientation toward circumstance and other. Consequently, the architecture and the set of decisions that shape it only make sense in light of occupation, movement, continuity, cultural practice, and cultural improvisation. Such considerations are not antithetical to the more image-driven ends of monumentality, but they cannot be properly subsumed within that architectural domain.

It would be a mistake, though, to read Fehn's comments as a straightforward critique of monumentality. Fehn's work does not everywhere shy from monumental gesture, and even at Tullinløkka the design is not uniformly subordinate. While I have argued that the project defers to the primacy of the three existing buildings, it also projects its own distinct character into the ensemble, and parts of the proposed museum are designed to be not demure, but rather surprising, even spectacular.

For instance, Fehn's model-based light studies of the project's interior, as dramatic as they are in black and white imagery, are reserved relative to what the actual experience would have yielded: the glazed-tile interior surfaces of the oculi-fitted domes were meant to be sky-blue. If "non-building" was meant to indicate "pavilion," it would have been a remarkably non-neutral and non-rational one (Figure 4.9).

Instead of a general polemic against monumentality, then, Fehn's appeal to "the non-building" makes sense as a calibration of the project's role and

Figure 4.9 Tullinløkka, image of model, gallery interior. © Sverre Fehn. Courtesy of National Museum, Architecture Collections.

degree of participation in the city, suggesting, as his quote indicates, that an overemphasis of "the acrobatic" in architecture might undermine that calibration. Echoing Palladio's balancing of the project's proposed "bigness" within the city's existing one, the term "non-building" describes a project that balances assertion of identity against receptiveness to given circumstance, including cultural circumstance, to the point that, at least at Tullinløkka, its very definition as a singular building is demoted—one might say that the building's definition at its perimeter is productively blurred.

As described above, Fehn takes as a primary task the realization of a design that participates in and extends the ongoing city, a structure that, as he put it in this section's opening quote, "will reveal the thought of generations" by affirming and reinterpreting established patterns. At Tullinløkka, lines of movement and conflations of boundary are intended to sustain and enrich the ambiance of the city, and the citizen is implicated in the construction: "The new city floor is at peace with its predecessors. The functions added are gifts to the people participating in the landscape."[14] Three key points in Fehn's two short sentences warrant consideration. First, Fehn understands the success of his design to depend on reconciliation with what precedes it. Second, functions are of course added—that is, the given condition is enhanced. But the term "function" is qualified here by the predicate, "gifts," positing a definition of function not limited to utility and efficiency, but, on the contrary, suggesting excess—in this case, a productive and positive excess—like a gift. Parenthetically, if we think of love, similarly, as excessive (in a mostly positive sense), then we are not far here from Aristotle's previously cited consideration of φιλία as the essence of the city. Third, in Fehn's formulation, this structured excess is made available in support of participation in the urban setting. In that sense, the proposed museum's "added functions"—the cafés, the amphitheater, the street, the elevated walkways, the terraced sculpture garden, the gallery windows—can be understood as props or sets poised for social and communicative uses that include but exceed the more narrowly defined functions of the museum proper. Those "gifts," though, are part of an enveloping urban atmosphere that the museum inherits as much as it invents: the two museum buildings, the university, the streets, the lines of circulation, the character of the city's center, its ambulatory signature, the gallery of Munch's murals, all preexisting, are marshaled in the design of the new construction and re-availed "to the people participating in the landscape." One way to summarize this idea would be to assert that Fehn's museum is designed to actively and measuredly participate in the city so that its occupants might, through its structure, better participate in the city. The possibility of fuller participation is the gift.

For further consideration of the architectural structure of excess and participation and their relation to urban life, it is useful to proceed to Fehn's proposal for the Royal Theater in Copenhagen.

The Room the City Gives

In Denmark there is only one city and one theatre.
Søren Kierkegaard

Of all of Sverre Fehn's unbuilt projects, none were so poignantly *almost* as his proposal for the Royal Danish Theater. Having won the architectural competition in March of 1996, Fehn was set to finally realize a major urban project at the heart of a large city (Figure 4.10). The proposal again demonstrated Fehn's determination to balance daring architectural assertion with an attuned care for its fit within the site as given, and, now a seasoned designer, Fehn calibrated that balance to a degree unequaled elsewhere in his work. But by the end of December in 1997, in the wake of a series of political maneuvers that demonstrated their own kind of urban theatrics—it was clear that the project would not go forward.[15] According to Per Olaf Fjeld, it amounted to a defeat for Fehn, one from which he would not recover.[16] Fehn's health declined soon thereafter, which was perhaps coincidental, but the sense of loss surrounding the unraveling of the project was compounded. Worse still, Copenhagen had thereby forfeited an urban

110   *Sverre Fehn, the City, and the Architecture of Participation*

Figure 4.10 Royal Theater, image of model showing lobby entrance. © Sverre Fehn. Courtesy of National Museum, Architecture Collections.

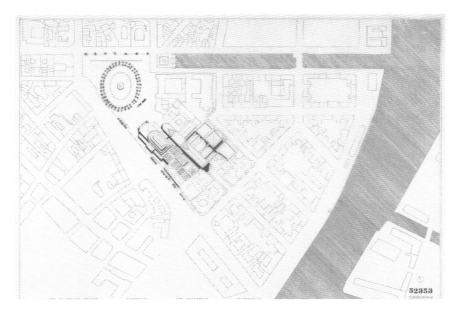

Figure 4.11 Royal Theater, site plan. © Sverre Fehn. Courtesy of National Museum, Architecture Collections.

project without equal and had lost a potential to become something the existing city was not, something better.

Given the design's orchestrated participation in its urban circumstance, its study benefits from a brief examination of those conditions and their historical formation. In 1670, as the city grew in population and prominence in the early baroque era, King Christian V developed plans to expand the city eastward from its medieval center. Loosely based on the successes of the Parisian example of the experimental Place Royale (c.1612), the plan was organized around a new baroque plaza, Kongens Nytorv (lit. "King's New Square"), and included ambitious plans for digging a new adjacent harbor (the long slot appended to the main canal, top of Figure 4.11) which would assure the square's rise as an important cultural and economic center. Opposite the square from the public gallows and flanking the end of the new harbor, the Charlottenborg Palace was among the first of the square's formative buildings. Having been converted to the Royal Danish Academy of Fine Arts in 1754, the Charlottenborg remains just to the northeast of the extant Royal Danish Theatre, which was designed by Vilhelm Dahlerup and added to the perimeter of Kongens Nytorv in 1874. That theater replaced an outmoded one (famously instrumental in Hans Christian Andersen's early career) that once existed on a contiguous parcel directly to the west, and which was demolished upon completion of its replacement. Almost immediately, the 1874 theater proved to be inadequate to the growing demands of the groups it served, and various proposals were solicited for its expansion. It was not until 1930, however, that an addition was realized to serve the needs of a contemporary theater group and also a nascent radio-based orchestra. Designed by Holger Jacobsen, the auditorium for the additional theater was built immediately to the north, nestled behind the Charlottenborg across a flanking street from the main theater. The unorthodox solution positioned the stage space for the new theater directly *over* Tordenskjoldsgade street, like a bridge, forming an elevated connection between old and new theaters (Figure 4.12). Matching the towering height of the existing theater, this bridge-like stage-box was the dominant architectural feature added to the urban ensemble, and its facade and soffit over the street were adorned with Art Deco ornamentation and detailing to characterize its public countenance.[17] At the time of its construction, the street-spanning stage with its Art Deco facade was regarded as an oddity, and because the original design reminded many of a birdhouse, it was nicknamed "Stærekassen" (lit. "starlings' nest box")—a moniker that persisted until it was made the building's official title. The history of Stærekassen is central to Fehn's efforts to expand the theater complex 65 years later (Figures 4.12 and 4.13).

The architectural competition of 1995 was, at least in part, a bid to address problems the 1931 renovations never fully solved, namely, how to adapt a 19th-century theater to the needs and potentials of a thoroughly modern and expanding theater-culture and city. In 1994, after years of failed efforts to proceed with renovations, political opportunity opened for a new theater to be appended to the existing group of theaters, and a competition was promptly launched. Five internationally recognized designers were invited to participate, including Fehn, Richard Rogers, and Enric Miralles; and five additional participants were selected by qualification. The competition jury voted unanimously in favor of Fehn's design. That plan was based on constructing a new theater in the depth of the block, and then tying it to the existing theaters through a grand unifying lobby and vestibule to be created by enclosing the corresponding section of Tordenskjoldsgade street beneath a lofting wing-like structure of glass and concrete. Fehn intended that lobby to maintain select characteristics of the street it would displace, but the street would effectively be transformed into a giant public lobby. The existing Art Deco stage box was to be incorporated as one of the key elements of the scheme by using it as spring-point for the wing-like roof-structure that would extend east and west from atop each of its existing facades, incorporating the earlier Art Deco addition into the interior of the towering new lobby.

Figure 4.12 Royal Theater, view of Stærekassen, straddling street, looking east from square. © Susanne Nilsson.

Figure 4.13 Royal Theater, view of Stærekassen from below. © Peter Mulligan.

Sverre Fehn, the City, and the Architecture of Participation 113

Collectively, the effect generated one of the most sculptural architectures of Fehn's opus.

Fehn's proposal sought to cohere a daunting set of site factors. First, there were the manifold pragmatic issues associated with inserting a large theater into the existing fabric of a dense city-center. Then there was the problem of combining new and existing theaters into a cohesive, functioning group. Relative to that concern, the existing street dividing the sites of the old and new theaters was relatively dark and had doubled as a service corridor with loading docks and back entrances which would need to be modified. Also, Kongens Nytorv is one the most important squares in Copenhagen, and its relationship to the new theater needed to be addressed. Lastly, the design's relation to the important tourist and commercial waterfronts of Nyhavn ("New Harbor") to the east and the main harbor to the south, each about a block and a half from the site, required consideration.

Fehn's design was lauded by the competition jury for finding a solution to that set of problems, a set that some had considered unsolvable.[18] But it was the proposal's perceived relationship to the existing historic fabric of the neighborhood that opened a path to its demise. Preservationists feared that

Figure 4.14 Royal Theater, full-scale mock-up of entry from Kongens Nytorv. © Ukjent. Courtesy of National Museum, Architecture Collections.

114 *Sverre Fehn, the City, and the Architecture of Participation*

Fehn's bold and contemporary insertion would detract from the revered historic buildings on the square and in the depth of the surrounding blocks, and they mounted that argument with increasing vehemence and political machination. It was this confrontation that finally led to the ordering of a full-scale mock-up of the entrance to the proposed street lobby facing the square. A daunting enterprise in its own right, the mock-up was fabricated in Poland, shipped to the city by boat in November 1996, and maneuvered into position using a flat-bed trailer and crane (Figure 4.14). The effort became a public spectacle, and Fehn was understandably concerned that the necessarily reductive mock-up would misrepresent the carefully balanced design. But if critics of the winning entry had hoped the mock-up would trigger a public outcry against the project, they appear to have miscalculated—the installation was generally deemed a success. As one account put it, "The sculptural high-heeled wing was just beautiful."[19] The preservationist camp, forced to change tactics, launched a campaign against the process by which the competition had been conducted, and began promoting the idea that a location detached from the city's historic fabric would be preferable. Local media began running stories amplifying claims that the process had neglected to seek adequate input from the citizenry. Key politicians stepped in to champion the community against, ostensibly, the pronouncements of the architectural and artistic aesthetes that had chosen Fehn's design. Nationalist sentiment exacerbated that critique. Consequently, momentum shifted, and, ultimately, the project was lost to another site and to another designer (Figure 4.15).[20]

Ironically, Fehn understood one of the most important features of his design to be the recognition and strengthening of the beauty of the existing

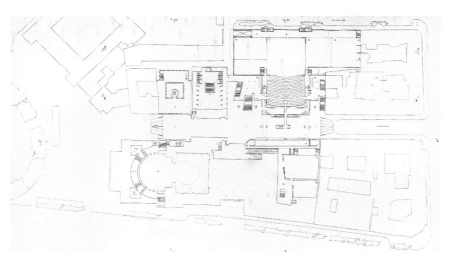

Figure 4.15 Royal Theater, ground floor plan. © Sverre Fehn. Courtesy of National Museum, Architecture Collections.

Sverre Fehn, the City, and the Architecture of Participation 115

city and its buildings, so that old and new would be mutually invigorated. Fehn explicitly expressed this concern in his competition text, writing, "The important point about this project is that the entire new project must be able to communicate with the great square [...] Inside the foyer, Stærekassen will lie like an illuminated jewel." Furthermore, in an interview at the time, Fehn described how the proposed roof configuration would frame the older Art Deco structure, help preserve it, and bathe it in a showcasing light, adding, "Finally Stærekassen will be protected—for the first time properly."[21] Apparently lost on the critics was the further irony that the building with which the preservationists were chiefly concerned, Stærekassen, was at the time of its construction a risk-taking assertion of modern design into the historic context of the square. At any rate, we are left to study not a building, but a proposal for one. As Kenneth Frampton put it,

> How could the Danes not build the superb galleria that he designed for the Royal Theatre in Copenhagen in 1996? All of these losses are irredeemable even if we may comfort ourselves with the superb pavilion he added to the Museum of Architecture in Oslo shortly before his death.[22]

Still, by the advent of the project's demise, Fehn's design was enough advanced so that careful attention to his drawings may yet yield an instructive understanding of Fehn's urban priorities, and of the project's correspondence with its urban milieu.

Scales of Participation

At the largest scale of architectural thinking, Fehn was concerned with his design's connection via Kongens Nytorv to the city and, via the harbor, to the world (Figure 4.16). In an interview with Fehn in the aftermath of the mock-up installation, a reference was made connecting the Copenhagen project to Venice's San Marco.[23] With its maritime context and balanced collection of buildings from different eras vying for presence and fit, the Italian configuration makes an apt comparison, and, given Fehn's studies of Venice, it is reasonable to wonder if it was specifically on his mind as he developed his solution for Copenhagen. In that spatial syllogism, Fehn's winged roof works similarly to San Marco's bell tower, projecting the plaza from distant vantage while, in its more local setting, receding sufficiently to strike a balance with the other buildings participating in the immediate urban ensemble. As Fehn described the lobby design, "On one side is the outward journey, represented by the great ships in the dock, and on the other side the inward journey, to the pulsating life of the city."[24]

Regarding its fit within the site's middle-ground, the proposed new theater along the project's eastern portion strengthened the relation of the clustered theaters to the harbor, while the enfolding and transforming of the street

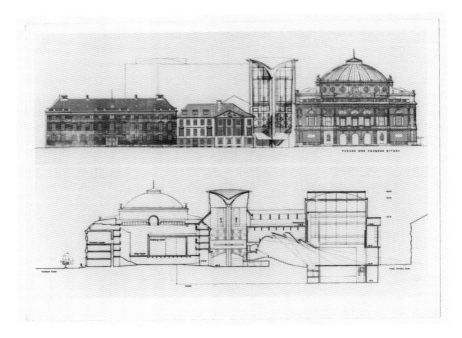

Figure 4.16 Royal Theater, west elevation, and cross-section looking west. © Sverre Fehn. Courtesy of National Museum, Architecture Collections.

into a lobby provided a new interior public space that enhanced pedestrian circulation and provided a potentially vibrant and weather-protected public event space (in a climate that can be extreme), an enclosed extension of the public square. If the winged roof served as an architectural beacon from distant points in the city, its role within its more immediate vicinity was more complex. In plan view (Figure 4.11), Fehn's lobby entrance and roof are set back into the block 30m behind the plaza-fronting facades of the existing theater (now commonly called "the Old Stage") and adjacent buildings, creating a buffering entry court between Kongens Nytorv and the complex of theatres. Viewed from the square, though (Figure 4.10), the towering wing-like roof interjected itself into the experience of the plaza, amplifying the role of the recessed theaters and announcing their point of entry. Restated, if the plan withdrew somewhat from participation in the life of the square, the roof interjected.

While the proposed street enclosure established a grand lobby serving the collected theaters, it also served as a vestibule connecting the harbor area to the south with Kongens Nytorv to the north. In that capacity, as one approached the square from the lobby, having passed beneath Stærekassen's mosaicked soffit, the winged exit and flanking buildings framed the equestrian statue of Christian V that anchors the center of the plaza—fortuitously, the opposing street facades along Tordenskjoldsgade almost perfectly center it. As one moved in the opposite direction, away from the plaza, the framed streetscape terminated in the harbor two blocks to the south. The new lobby doubled as urban vestibule and urban frame.

The next scale to be considered in the project involves more discreet experiences orchestrated at or within its perimeter. I will describe a handful of those, making a case for their relevance to the project's urban engagement, and then try to summarize what they collectively demonstrate.

Starting near the top, directly above the new theater and intersecting the upper space of the large hall, Fehn proposed a large restaurant. Nested between the highest extents of the existing buildings and the new flyspace, the dining area offered interior views down into the lobby, while its expanses of glass and convex roof-form presented a vista toward the harbor with, as Fehn put it, "views across the familiar domes and towers of Copenhagen's beautiful skyline," providing "a perspective very different from the floor of the foyer and the urban situation beyond."[25] The public room at this upper limit also presented the closest encounter of the lofty, enveloping ceiling of the wing-like roof structure. Fehn understood the roof as bringing coherence to the assortment of surrounding facades, which he described as "unbelievably airy under its white shell structure, in contrast with the more enclosed facades that surround it, it will float like a kind of bird's wing over some of the old buildings." That wing-like form is rehearsed in the smaller, lower roof-structures associated with the new theater on the east side of the plan. The scalar contrast between this hybrid grand space and the entrance to the auditorium of the new theater was to be mediated by a pair of flanking concrete shell structures that define and frame the formal staircase climbing diagonally between them (a third structure of the same kind was situated at the south side of the new theater to negotiate the fit with the existing buildings there). Whereas the top of the wing-roof reached to 35m from grade, this smaller pair rose to almost exactly half that height, each with its own wing-like inverted vaults springing from a sculptural column and extruding eastward to roof the lower levels of the new building. While Fehn did not describe them, these intermediating pieces served a role similar to the baldachins and choir-screens that were sometimes deployed to reconcile the immense scale of cathedrals to the more localized activities that were staged within them. One of Fehn's interior perspectives demonstrated that relationship, but his model image of that condition was strongest (Figure 4.17). Describing the character of the space in which the family of unusual roofs were the primary contributor, Fehn wrote, "when you emerge from the theatre you will step into an atmosphere which hopefully provides a lively contrast to the world of illusion you have just left".[26]

One of Fehn's building sections that cuts directly through that "world of illusion" of the new theater includes, not surprisingly, regulating sight-lines and light-lines relative to various depths of the stage and the furthest limits of the theater. Atypical, though, is how one of those sight-lines was taken not from within the theater, but from the sidewalk across from the street that the stage backs onto—Peder Skrams Gades (Figure 4.16). That sight-line extends from the sidewalk, across the street, across the stage, over the seating, to the furthest side of the theatre. While this feature was not highlighted in the competition entry, the back of the stage area would also have been, on the outside, a secondary facade. The unorthodox sight-line and section suggests that Fehn intended that wall to feature a large two-story window that would frame the theater from the street and the street from the theater. That portion of the plan shows a circulation area between the exterior and the stage—a hallway presenting views into the theater on one side and, on the other, views onto the street. This connection was further enforced by the decision to vertically position the stage to be coplanar with the sidewalk. It is of course possible that those decisions were largely pragmatic—perhaps facilitating deliveries to the stage, for example. However, as part of a 1994 proposal for the Hydroelectricity Museum in Sudal, Fehn designed a theater with an operable rear stage-wall that, when opened, provided framed views of the landscape, and the Copenhagen design suggests a similar exploration at a larger scale.

Figure 4.17 Royal Theater, model, south portion of enclosed street-lobby. Theater entrance at stairway. Restaurant was under winged-roof at upper right of image, with the new fly-space beyond. © Ukjent. Courtesy of National Museum, Architecture Collections.

That idea—the relation of theater to street—manifests itself more prominently at the other side of the theater with the appropriation of the actual street. Fehn's enclosure there is judicious in the detailing of its perimeter, eliminating much of the alley-like character of the street as given while also bringing select portions of those preexisting conditions into the ambiance of the new configuration. For instance, Fehn's design called for the reconfiguration of the ground floor of the building opposite the new theater in order to accommodate a street-level café (he referred to it as "book-café" in the competition text) that would open onto the grand foyer. Above the café, though, Fehn maintained the existing character of the facade at the upper floors, bringing it into the interior of the new enclosure, rather like a proscenium.

Also belonging to this intermediate stratum, Fehn designed a pair of elevated walkways that spanned the cross-section of the large hall at about 8m above its floor, connecting the new theater to the preexisting dressing rooms and support spaces across the street that already served the older theaters (Figure 4.18). For Fehn, this move was not simply pragmatic, but also a means of inscribing another layer of activity onto the urban scene of the lobby: he envisioned the movement of actors across these bridges as enlivening the larger space and establishing conditions where, he wrote, "the actors will therefore also have the possibility of participating in the busy life of the foyer."

These architectural edits and additions contribute to the creation of a type-defying space with characteristics of street, foyer, lobby, arcade, theater, and nave, but not accurately reducible to any one of those. As cited above, Fehn understood the roof as providing coherence. A different priority guided this set of decisions beneath the roof, where Fehn seemed to be cultivating a productive incoherence, a measured amalgamation of diverse contributors to the scene. For what purpose?

Figure 4.18 Royal Theater, perspective drawing of lobby, looking north, showing one of two elevated connecting walkways bisecting the main structural pier as it spans the space. © Ukjent. Courtesy of National Museum, Architecture Collections.

Theatricality, Architectural Discord, and Participation in the City

If the balance between architectural acrobatics and the anonymity of the street tilted toward "non-building" at Tullinløkka, acrobatics seems more prominent at Kongens Nytorv, though, as discussed above, less so than it first appears. It is perhaps more accurate to argue that in the Copenhagen proposal, attention to both of these architectural considerations was magnified: Fehn's design of the relationship between building and street was at its most complex in Copenhagen, and, at the same time, perhaps no other of Fehn's designs presented a more strikingly monumental image. An apt description for that experience is *dramatic*. Characterizing the sequence of movement from the theater into the grand foyer, Fehn wrote that "in this space you become part of the real theatre of life."[27] The phrase transforms an examination of architecture, *theatre*, and city into speculation regarding architecture, *theatricality*, and city.

Architectural analysis commonly makes use of tropes borrowed from theatre. Architectural settings are often said to *stage* certain activities, or may be described as *dramatic* or *scripted*—even the phrase *architectural setting* itself carries allusions to theater. Especially in consideration of urban architecture, the phrase *mise-en-scène*—referring to the selection and arrangement of the contents of a stage to structure a particular dramatic ambiance—has been used to describe how architecture anticipates and structures various urban encounters. Similarly, architectural configurations have been described as *rehearsing* cultural practices. This relation of theater to architecture can be simply understood as analogically convenient—a set of terms borrowed from a sister-art and applied descriptively to architecture. But a closer examination of that relationship can help us better understand the architectural territory in which Fehn was consciously operating and how that approach can be understood as particularly urban. To begin, consider the premise that life among others has a naturally theatrical quality to it. To say that we *act* socially, *perform* publicly, or that our lives delineate narratives or evoke archetypes is less about an analogical appeal to the art of theater than it is to recognize something essentially theatrical to experience, which is always necessarily experience in place. Theatricality, in this way of thinking, is not merely an artistic quality that can be applied analogically to daily life; rather, theater derives its art by distilling a primitive theatricality already latent in quotidian conditions. Kierkegaard echoed this idea in his description of theater as "kunstige Virkelighen"—literally, artificed actuality. This is how I understand Fehn's appeal to "the real theatre of life," and it offers a further way to understand the urban intent of his architectural decisions, and not only in regard of his Royal Theater design.

Deeper considerations of the relation of theatricality and daily life in several disciplines have sometimes appealed to the term *methexis*, from the Greek, μέθεξις, originally referring to a form of theater in which the audience was implicated in the performance they had gathered to see. This meaning is closely related to the cognate verb form, *metechein*, which meant something like *partaking*. Platonic philosophy has perpetuated the use of the term in a narrower sense, detached from theatricality and used to elucidate concepts relating forms to particulars. Its origins in theater, though, are traced in its less common use (also in diverse disciplines) in consideration of ethos, which is the sense wherein its architectural significance lies. While theatricality in architecture has been more often approached by way of mimesis—like, for example, by employing theatricality to explicate 18th-century *architecture parlante*—methexis shifts focus from issues of representation to ones of participation. This contrasting of mimesis and methexis has a long history, generally hinging on the difference between *orientation toward*, which implies distance from, and *participation within*, which implies a giving over of self, to the degree that *participation* presupposes *participation amongst others*—hence the ethical cast of methexis, in this sense of the term. Hans-Georg Gadamer helpfully summarized the distinction this way:

Sverre Fehn, the City, and the Architecture of Participation 121

When the stars bring the numbers to representation through their paths, we call this representation "mimesis" and take it to be an approximation of the actual being. In contrast to this, "methexis" is a wholly formal relationship of participation, based on mutuality. "Mimesis" always points in the direction of that which one approaches, or towards which one is oriented, when one represents something. "Methexis," however, as the Greek, *meta*, already signifies, implies that one thing is there together with something else. Participation, *metalambanein*, completes itself only in genuine being-together and belonging-together, *metechein*.[28]

In an architectural context, Colin St. John Wilson, for one, subscribed to a stark version of this opposition, reducing mimesis, in his definition, to a mere static copying, and then using methexis and its ethical implications as the basis for a kind of credo against what he understood to be an overly reductive tendency in modern architecture.[29] Hans-Ulrich Obrist, too, seemed predisposed to parse the two concepts, commenting specifically on Fehn's Fjærland project: "What I thought was so interesting about the Glacier Museum is that it is a performative space. It is not a representational space."[30]

Fehn, to my knowledge, never used the term *methexis*. But his theater project suggests that, at least in the context of urban architecture, pitting mimesis opposite methexis misses a critical point regarding their relation. Gadamer wrote that mimesis points "towards which one is oriented," but that may be putting cart before horse: mimesis itself contributes to orientation, where pointing-toward evokes a drawing-in, a reapportioning of attention. As shown above, Fehn's design is everywhere concerned with the staging of and staging for urban encounter, and yet, as noted, the design is undeniably assertive in its presentation, as if the building were at once stage and actor. In his writings, lectures, and interviews, Fehn consistently appealed to ideas of narrative and story-telling as essential to successful architecture. As in methexical theater, where the memory and imagination of the participant is activated and caught up in the unfolding drama, Fehn's designs set up stages for anticipated action at various scales that also work, simultaneously, as *signs* of participation—an invitation, or presentation of an opening, to participate. In Fehn's work, the architectural image can be understood as an invitation, a prompt, to participate in the unfolding spatial narrative, to "get caught-up in it." That familiar colloquialism carries surprising meaning for architectural experience. It suggests, I believe, an architectural parallel to what Maurice Merleau-Ponty had in mind in the context of an essay on dialog when he appealed to terms like *catch* to emphasize how we are drawn to participation.[31] Beyond Merleau-Ponty's intents, the word is useful here in its dual meanings—to receive, but also "a catch," like a hitch, something that invites and involves a would-be participant into the structure of the unfolding situation. The catch may be

122   *Sverre Fehn, the City, and the Architecture of Participation*

discovered by the participant. It may also be an artifice, designed, suggesting a relationship wherein mimesis, as *catch* structures, points the way toward, or incites participation.

In a particularly vexing four pages of *The Thought of Construction*, in a section titled, "Disappearance," Fehn interfuses consideration of expression, acting, teaching, design, spirit, and, repeatedly, "room."[32] For Fehn, almost always, that last term was in quotes or italics, indicating its complicated role in his architectural thinking. In Fehn's vocabulary, room may mean *a room*,[33] like in daily usage; it may mean a local ambiance, or, as he sometimes wrote, "shadow," given by an object or entity, or that exists between object and entity; and it may indicate something more ontological, a place imbued with human spirit, perduring, but also receptive and mutable. Fehn's "Disappearance" is not easily reducible, but two passages are pertinent. First, Fehn writes:

> To imitate the completeness of facts is a violation of humanity. The actor takes away some of his nature by placing a mask over his face. He learns about the movement of arms by imagining their use.

And then, in the section's concluding paragraph:

> The clearer an architect is able to express a room's personality the more it belongs to everyone. Within these limitations there is a generosity that no one owns, but which remains an inspiration to every person. The physical manifestation of spirit belongs to the highest order of architecture. The room effects behavior, that is to say it influences the inhabitant's spirit. To these places people return. They are an offering to mankind, an impulse to let the spirit emerge. [...] Man as an object releases himself only in a place where that spirit is present.

The passages describe mimesis effecting methexis. The second one emphasizes the concept of a designed catch or invitation: the room, effecting behavior, is an offering. Returning to the curious image from Fehn's Tullinløkka drawing (Figure 4.5), surely this is the set of ideas Fehn had in mind. Not only does the sketch read as a theatrical mask, but also specifically a comic one, a totem of the fusion of theater and the theatricality of day-to-day existence, of the life of the city and its art. This figure's presence at the entry to the pedestrian street amounts to a prompt, a marquee. With the Royal Theater, too, Fehn made overt references to the project's theatrical potency, beyond the purview of its type, saying of the entryway to the project (Figure 4.19):

> I have a feeling that if you stand far from Stærekassen, you will see the square reflected in its glass. And this can be both beautiful and symbolic, when urban life is reflected in the theater. This is the function

of modern drama. And behind it all is Harlequin, holding up the entire structure – like an umbrella above the people who want to enter.[34]

Fehn's Harlequin comment was a reference to one of the three towering piers that figure strongly in the ambiance of the foyer (Figure 98)—here again, a reference to comedic theater and its intersection with day-to-day life, and a restatement of the component's duality as both actor and stage. The allusion to "Harlequin" also invokes caprice, an observation I will return to. The plan of the base of each of the three sculptural piers reveals a two-sided configuration: the columns have a front and a back, and, owing to their convexity, also an inside and an outside. This interior-exterior orientation, together with their centrality, symmetry, and glass veil, lends the structure a subtle physiognomy. The facade is a mask. As

Figure 4.19 Royal Theater, image of model showing lobby entry from the square, simulating nighttime. © Ukjent. Courtesy of National Museum, Architecture Collections.

at Tullinløkka, here at the project's entrance is a symbol drawing together theatricality, architecture, and participation.

Fehn's approach to urban architecture is predicated on the observation that, yes, we are immersed not only in "'room'" spatially, but also as one immersed in conversation, oriented toward it, committed to it, lured forward through it, or not. This suggests that urban architecture—rather like Simmel's door being at once the symbol and the means of elsewhere—might reach out to us, invite us to find what's there, and what may yet be there, while also providing architectural conditions for immersive participation requisite to those possibilities. Restated, Fehn's work shows how in architectural settings (at least), mimesis structures and prompts methexis; or, shedding the Greek terms and their Platonic complications, how architectural representation at once structures, and gestures toward, participation. The architectural structure of participation emphasizes the immersive quality of being in place, and casts architectural design as an instance of *emplotment*,[35] or stage-setting, for the rehearsals and improvisations of daily life. The quality, multiplicity, and expansiveness of those structures prefigure the character, creativity, and reach of that rehearsed and improvised living.

While less intensive but similar structures can be found outside of cities, and while cities do not guarantee them, nowhere is the potential intensity and aggregation of those structures more multivalent and available than in the city. The Oslo and Copenhagen projects resonate with the potential fulfillment of that condition. It is a condition replete with the uncertainty endemic to immersive improvised action. An invitation to participate might be answered with withdrawal—anonymity being as central to urban life as community. The improvised actions of individuals and groups can only be weakly anticipated; the specific effects of their irruptions cannot be foreknown. Public venues can be invaluable for purposes both at ease and contested, even violent. Such tensions, contrasts, and uncertainty might be regarded as undesirable, and surely coherence and concinnity are highly valued in design in general, no less in the design of urban settings. Fehn, too, saw value in those principles, for example, in his design and description of the Royal Theater's roof. But the theatricality of the urban setting that Fehn recognized and endeavored to provide was, for Fehn, as dependent on discord as on unity. It is a point worth elaborating.

Because the Royal Theater design never advanced toward a construction phase, details about surfaces and materials were never developed, and only hints of those decisions were presented in the competition images. During the project's period of public debate, Fehn was asked in an interview about his intentions regarding materiality:

> We will use oak, concrete, marble and glass. It is too early to say exactly where and how. But the wood will be close to the people, near your hands and legs, while the strong concrete will be further away. And the marble, which is delightful and cool to the touch – almost like a woman—must also be part of the balance of different materials, which makes a place pleasing.[36]

Twenty-five years later, Fehn's gendered characterization of material qualities—the masculine concrete, the feminine marble—can sound a bit dated—perhaps worse. But what is striking here is that, presented with difference, Fehn anticipates that decisions regarding materiality will not be aimed at projecting unity, but at emphasizing division: high and low, tactile and visual, warm and cool, massive and light, and, yes, in his terms, masculine and feminine.

One of the most common oppositions that Fehn amplifies in his Royal Theater design is that of day and night. We saw in Chapter 3 Fehn's interest and facility with the effect of luminous conditions. Those concerns are especially evident in two aspects of the Royal Theater design. First, as previously alluded, Fehn uses daylight to enhance the participation of the Stærekassen facades in the architectural ensemble—remember, he referred to it as an "illuminated jewel." In order to achieve this, Fehn modified the concrete-shell wing of the roof at its juncture with the older building, substituting glass for concrete at these locations so that the facade would receive more daylight relative to the rest of the interior, effectively washing the Art Deco facades with north and south light, respectively. Fehn described the effect:

Sverre Fehn, the City, and the Architecture of Participation 125

> For Stærekassen we will cut out some of the future concrete roof, and put glass up there on the roof so that light can shine in from above. It will bathe the façade in light, so you do not end up with a black wall. It is an important architectural point, and an exception, as the only other light that will slip in from the heavens along this long and covered theater street will be from the side. The light must not fall upon the heads of the guests from above. It must shine in gently from the sides, upon the old building facades that will be left from the original street.[37]

The glazed portion of the roof and the resultant day-lighting effect relative to the Stærekassen facade was anticipated in photographs of one the project models. The second case stems from a more general observation about Fehn's design and its representation: the image just alluded to is anomalous—most of the model photos in the project archives are staged as if at night, lit from the interior. Thinking about the urban night, Fehn once wrote that "at night when the lights are dispersed, the city is released to its maximum spirit. Humanness overflows, expressing everything but nature. The city becomes a sphere that conquers the night."[38] Specifically in regard to the Copenhagen proposal, Fehn said,

> The theater belongs to the night, especially in the north, where it is cold and dark. The theater should be a luminous lantern at Kongens Nytorv. It must project life toward the square, not least at night and winter, where the artificial light from the lobby will announce that here is the National Theater.[39]

Fehn's description of how the lobby would function like a lantern is clear. His statement about "expressing everything but nature," though, merits further thought, if only briefly.

That quote might lead one to believe that Fehn subscribed to a common and rather simplistic understanding of the relation of humanity to nature. He did not. His words and his architecture consistently resisted that too-easy dichotomy, and, studying his work, one comes to understand that Fehn was especially wary of romanticized regard of nature, and, generally, of architecture's frequent indulgence in it. Perhaps to counter that current of thought, he frequently emphasized the violence of nature, and also the inevitable violence of architecture with regard to nature. When Fehn wrote of the city at night "expressing everything but nature," I am inclined, then, to read the quote not as a fallacy, nor as a declaration of the city's victory over darkness, but, in the context of the oppositions discussed above, as further recognition of the multiplication of possibility that inheres in the address of difference, its harnessing rather than its elision: the lantern-like lobby recognizes and amplifies the heightened accent on artifice that the urban night, like theater itself, already held.

Fehn's propensity for typological ambiguity and juxtaposition of difference at the Royal Theater is a restatement of operative principles at Tullinløkka. As argued in the previous section, Fehn's Tullinløkka design does not so much blur the line between the high culture of the museum and the daily life of the city as it renders that line productively porous—a reciprocal porosity that deforms inherited types in order to renew their shared purpose: bringing art to life. That renewal depends on simultaneous reference to familiar types and also the purposeful distortion of their definition. The result—a familiar ground from which to act, coupled with the provocation to exceed familiarity—yields an especially potent urban situation. Measured discord is preliminary to participation. As Fehn said, "It may sound absurd, but it has to do with human creativity." Further understanding of Fehn's thinking here can be found in consideration of less comic forms of discord. The extended passage to which that quote belongs will help.

Violence for the City (*et in urbanus ego*)

"It is better to hate nature."

–Sverre Fehn

Already evident in the examples cited above, for Fehn, discord was not always a design problem to be reconciled, but an essential feature of a robust urban architecture. His embrace of opposition was emphatic and should not be discounted. Peter Cook made a useful bridge to that topic. After commenting on the collage-like effect of Fehn's Hamar project, Cook wrote, "Yet the building is heroic. Fehn [...] never surrenders his mandate as choreographer, and the whole has a fascinating violence in its configuration."[40] Moving through thoughts on monumentality, passivity, and staging in Fehn's design, Cook arrived at violence. Though I have not explicitly addressed the idea until now, I have alluded to three kinds of violence that subtend Fehn's work. As previously depicted, violence with regard to wilderness is apparent in several of his projects—his Weldens Ende proposal comes to mind, and Mari Hvattum has keenly taken up the topic with regard to Villa Schreiner.[41] But Fehn would likely have argued that a violent relationship to nature obtains in all of his projects, that it must, because such violence is endemic to architecture. Of the many versions of Fehn's expression of that idea, the one I find most helpful appeared in his assessment of Mies van der Rohe's National Gallery:

> It is a masterpiece in the handling of light. And he brought nature into the museum – trees and objects that fight together, creating a sort of duel between nature and culture, in a way. The object itself fights to live together with nature and also culture. Nature was having a dialogue or a duel.[42]

Sverre Fehn, the City, and the Architecture of Participation 127

Fehn recognizes a mutual violence, a duel, that might also be a dialog. "The object" seems positioned at that threshold, an idea equally potent if the object is a museum piece or the building itself: artifact, at the boundary of violent juxtaposition, arranged to structure and sustain dialog. Difference is elided at the expense of dialog.

Also evident in many of his projects, but, as Cook observed, especially at Hamar, is a mutual violence between past and present. Fehn was similarly cognizant and forthright about the role of this kind of violence in his work. Asked in an interview about the ramp cutting through the Hamar courtyard, Fehn mused that one "could say that it is brutal, or aggressive," before elaborating more generally about architecture and the impotence of harmony:

> I see museums as an aggression into the present, or posing the past against the present. There is no harmony. This is a violent thing. But the greater your aggression towards it, the more you are in harmony with the past. It may sound absurd, but it has to do with human creativity. The worst thing is indifference, harmony the second worst. You can never really reach a harmony. You could say museums should show a *greater* aggression. An aggressive attack on laws and everything. That would set off a dialogue. [...]The worst thing is indifference. Aestheticization, you might say. That is a dangerous word, but things can get too pretty.[43]

In addition to the architectural violence against wilderness and the past, a third violence is demonstrated in the Tullinløkka and Royal Danish Theater proposals—violence with regard to the city. In both projects, harmony is countered with dissonance, but it is especially clear at the theater: for all its cohesion and attentiveness to what is already underway at Kongens Nytorv, the project is equally disruptive of that setting and its patterns. All construction is violent—that is a truism. The kind of violence that Fehn refers to, though, includes a violence of narrative, the imposition of a new coherence on top of an already operative one, without erasure. Here again is the idea of renewal and its dependence on an active dialog, facilitated by calibrated discord and productive uncertainty. As Fehn's quote indicates, the purpose is invigorated dialog.

There is a final piece to be considered in Fehn's thinking on the ratio of serenity and discord and its relation to the potency of urban situations, one that completes a conceptual trajectory from comedy to tragedy. Allusions to death pervaded Fehn's architectural explications. The occurrences were too frequent to enumerate, but Fehn's use of the concept in his architectural thinking was well summarized when he wrote, "The manifestation of death embodies the largest construction. The mystery of the irrational clarifies man's situation, and accords honesty to his expressions." The archival record includes several versions of that expression, from diverse points

128   *Sverre Fehn, the City, and the Architecture of Participation*

in Fehn's career. Importantly for the subject of this text, Fehn goes on to connect the idea to his understanding of urbanity:

> The places created under the sign of death are those in which people gather. [...] The unity of urbanism can be accepted. Death has a myth that is constant and possesses everyone. It is the 'room' around the mystery that creates peace and togetherness. The concept of death is clear to all.[44]

It is hard to know exactly what Fehn meant by "sign of death." But it is clear that he had in mind something legible (mimetic) and shared (methexic). The quote indicates that "togetherness" is served through the recognition of death as urbanity's most basic layer—a baseline commonality discovered in a mutual confrontation of death. In that sense, death operates similarly to Edmund Husserl's "ark:" no less than our shared world, our shared fate provides a deep basis for communion.[45] As for locating that idea in Fehn's proposal for Kongens Nytorv—if it can, in fact, be found there—there *is* something undeniably ecclesiastic about the scale, proportions, symmetries, lighting, and loft of the great lobby hall: the space feels like a nave. Fehn has made a cathedral of the street. Fehn alluded to this idea in the competition text, and, later, in several interviews. In the following extended quote, Fehn describes the foyer as reminiscent of both church and stage:

> The design of the foyer that provides a link between all the theatres emerged from listening to the old buildings… I believe Pierre Boulez will recognize motifs from St. Mark's Church in Venice, where Palestrina created his orchestral works by placing his musicians on the bridges between the domes so that the sound would fill the room from many directions. I believe Danish composer Per Nörgård will find a home for his compositions here, or Norwegian Arne Nordheim… and the spacious wooden floor could provide a setting for Grotovsky's productions of medieval drama—in fact for the entire modern movement, which really came to a halt because of a lack of spatial challenge.[46]

In his design for the Royal Theater, Fehn's understanding of a successful urban setting relies on both caprice and continuity, quotidian conditions and transcendent ones—that is to say, comic and tragic modes—to establish stages for various forms of dialog. It is a vision that recognizes an inherent theatricality in urbanity, and architecture's mimetic and methexic roles therein.

What Fehn's designs emphasize in these two city proposals are how an urban architecture can structure forms of complementarity, participation, and openness through an engagement of difference in the city. Fehn's talent, his underpinning design approach, call it his style, is no doubt evident in the proposals—the projects depend upon it—but expression of the

Sverre Fehn, the City, and the Architecture of Participation 129

architect's imaginative conceits is not the projects' highest goal. An architect studying these projects, in order to make sense of the way decisions are being made, has to first understand a good bit about the city as given and about the city as it might yet be, including a host of givens and natures that are not easily grasped with many (perhaps any) of the methods we commonly associate with the work of urbanism, including concepts of excess, theatricality, participation, and violence. It is clear in these projects that when Fehn means to open the project to the many levels of the city, he is not advocating passivity nor, less, a tabula rasa approach to receptivity. It is an urban approach that is not just similar but, I think, identical to the one we find at Hamar, where the project is the frame that gathers setting, artifact, self, and other, orienting them to the unfolding, uncertain present. In doing so, these projects materially facilitate the fulfillment of the promise of the city. In closing this chapter, I offer the following thoughts from Fehn. In light of the above analyses of Fehn's two urban works, I trust that a clearer intent is discernible without my further explication:

> In general, cities mean a lot to me. Cities have a strangeness, a fear, the grand urban architecture, density, symbols, the difference between architecture and culture. And most of all the city possesses a calmness. Out in the country it is never calm. [...] but the city possesses a great calm and a sense of waiting. [...]The city is a waiting room: the soldier that waits for his girlfriend, the sailor that awaits for the arrival of his ship, the actor that waits for the curtain to go up, the priest that waits for the church bells to ring and to start his sermon. Paris, for example, is one great bench on which all sit and wait, with their books and newspapers, with café au lait. Compared to this, nature is one great prison... I love the theater of the great city. Therefore I am very involved in designing the Royal Theater on Kongens Nytorv in Copenhagen.[47]

Notes

1 Dalibor Vesely, "The latent ground of the natural world: introduction to the communicative role of architecture," paper presented at the Communicative Role of Architecture conference, June 2010, Leicester School of Architecture, De Montfort University, Leicester, UK. The excerpt is taken from Vesely's unpublished typewritten lecture notes, p. 7. The lecture was written during a period when Vesely and I were exchanging thoughts on street, building, and city, and so he provided me a copy of his essay.
2 *Løkka* is an old Norwegian word for a gathering place, which comes from an older word that referred to a place where a stream broadened and deepened and slowed. Etymologists have noted that it could, then, be related to *lacuna*, as with *lagoon*, but is more likely related to the English *lock* or *loch*, from Old Norse *loka*, which meanings included "concealed place," "closed-in place." For a history of the site, see, Leif Thingsrud, "Tollinløkka: problematisk løkka

I byens centrum." *Tobias* no. 1 (1997): https://www.oslo.kommune.no/ OBA/tobias/tobiasartikler/t1972.htm.
3. Recently, the site has undergone substantial change as the museum buildings were adapted for new uses. Changes included construction of a new university building on the north edge of the square, preserving some of the paving and recasting the rest of the square as a green campus quadrangle.
4. In that sense, Labrouste's grid of domes at the Bibliothèque Nationale make a more apt comparison, especially considering that Fehn specified glazed tile for the domes' interior surfaces; though Fehn's domes were flatter and less grand, more like the soffit of Soane's breakfast room.
5. Sverre Fehn, Tollinløkka competition boards, 1972, object number NMK.2008.0734.060.001, Fehn Archives, Architecture Collections, Nasjonalmuseet, Oslo.
6. Sverre Fehn, Tullinløkka competition boards, 1972.
7. The museums were also connected through proposed subterranean parking and storage. Ref. building sections.
8. Kenneth Frampton recounts that Fehn recognized the influence of both Amancio William's Corrientes Province Hospital project, 1953; and Paul Nelson's *Maison Suspendu*, 1936. Frampton also recognizes Prouvé's influence. See Kenneth Frampton, in Fjeld, *Thought of Construction*, 16.
9. For history of the three Aula competitions and subsequent installation of Munch's paintings in 1916, see the University of Oslo's collection catalog. Ulla Uberg, et al, *i Aula* (Oslo: 7-Gruppen, date unknown), 7.
10. Per Olaf Fjeld, *The Pattern of Thoughts* (New York: Monacelli Press, 2009), 124.
11. Sverre Fehn, Tullinløkka competition boards, 1972.
12. Sverre Fehn, 2001 interview with Hans Ulrich Obrist, *Abitare* (March 2009).
13. Peter Cook, "Trees and Horizons." *Architectural Review* (1981): 106.
14. Fjeld, *Pattern of Thoughts*, 124.
15. For the fullest history of the theater, including Fehn's proposal's demise, see Hanne Christensen and Erik Wassard, eds., *Stærekassen—et omstridt bygningsværk: En antologi* (Copenhagen: Foreningen til Gamle Bygningers Bevaring, 1997). In Danish.
16. Per Olaf Fjeld, *Patterns of Thought*, 164.
17. Likewise, the 1931 interior included many Art Deco works, notably a marble relief by Jean Gauguin of a figure buoyed by radio-waves and flanked by theatrical masks.
18. Hanne Christensen and Erik Wassard, eds., *Stærekassen – et omstridt bygningsværk: En antologi*, (Copenhagen: Foreningen til Gamle Bygningers Bevaring, 1997), 115–118. In Danish.
19. Christensen, *Stærekassen*, 124.
20. The Royal Danish Playhouse, designed by the city-based firm Lundgaard & Tranberg, was constructed on the waterfront just north of Nyhavn in 2008. The Copenhagen Opera House, designed by Henning Larsen, was constructed across the channel to the east of the Nytorv site in 2004.
21. Sverre Fehn, interviewed by Peter Mose, "The Building Will Reflect the Drama of the City," *Politiken*, April 22, 1996, section 2, page 1. In Danish. Full translation at appendix.
22. Kenneth Frampton, "The Tectonic Form of Sverre Fehn." *Area*, no. 116 (2014): https://www.area-arch.it/en/the-tectonic-form-of-sverre-fehn.
23. Sverre Fehn, interviewed by Peter Mose, 1.
24. Sverre Fehn, "The Royal Theater, Copenhagen." *Byggekunst* no. 2 (1997): 66.
25. Sverre Fehn, "The Royal Theater," 66.

26 Sverre Fehn, "The Royal Theater," 66.
27 Sverre Fehn, "The Royal Theater," 66.
28 Hans-Georg Gadamer, "Plato as Portraitist," trans. J. Findling and S. Gabova, *Continental Philosophy Review* no. 33 (2000): 262. The essay was originally delivered as a lecture in Munich, Feb. 1988.
29 Colin St. John Wilson, *The Other Tradition of Modern Architecture* (London: Academy Editions, 1995), 41.
30 Hans-Ulrich Olbrist, "Interview with Sverre Fehn," *Abitare* (August, 2001). Also, in a short documentary on the Glacier Museum, Fehn said, "The walls of the valley are like the walls of a great cathedral. The building is like the altar. It is like a great natural room." *Sverre Fehn: Four Buildings*. Directed by Guy Fehn. Oslo: Spinnin' Globe Studio, 1997.
31 Maurice Merleau-Ponty, *Prose of the World* (Chicago: Northwestern University Press, 1973). There is reason to believe that M.M.-P., too, had in mind a broader application for the concept. In a report to Martial Gueroult in which he described the idea of his book, he wrote of his aspirations to "elaborate the category of prose beyond the confines of literature, to give it a sociological meaning."
32 Fehn, in Fjeld, *The Thought of Construction*, 147–151.
33 Note that in Norwegian there are no definite articles, so Fehn did not typically write *a room*, only *room*.
34 Sverre Fehn. Interviewed by Peter Mose. Full translation at appendix.
35 I have borrowed this term and concept from Paul Ricoeur. See, Paul Ricoeur, *Time and Narrative* (Chicago: University of Chicago Press), 31–51.
36 Sverre Fehn. Interviewed by Peter Mose. Full translation at appendix.
37 Sverre Fehn. Interviewed by Peter Mose. Full translation at appendix.
38 Sverre Fehn, in Fjeld, *The Thought of Construction*, 144.
39 Sverre Fehn. Interviewed by Peter Mose. Full translation at appendix.
40 Peter Cook, "Trees and Horizons." *Architectural Review* (1981): 106.
41 Mari Hvattum, *Villa Schreiner*, eds. Nina Berre and Mari Lending (Oslo: Pax Forlag, 2014), 36.
42 Sverre Fehn, 2001 interview with Hans Ulrich Obrist, *Abitare* (March 2009).
43 Sverre Fehn, interviewed by Ragnar Pedersen, "The Worst Thing is Indifference," *Arkitektur N* (June, 2014). Interview conducted in 1989.
44 Sverre Fehn, in Fjeld, *Thought of Construction*, 150.
45 Edmund Husserl, "The Earth, the Original Ark, Does Not Move," in *Husserl: Shorter Works*, eds. Peter McCormick and Frederick Elliston (South Bend, IA: University of Notre Dame Press, 1981), 222.
46 Sverre Fehn, "The Royal Theater, Copenhagen." *Byggekunst* no. 2 (1997): 66.
47 Sverre Fehn, interviewed by Henrik Steen Møller, in *Living Architecture* no. 15 (1997): 211–213.

5 More Oslo

As introduced in Chapter 1, the National Museum of Architecture stands in the southern part of Oslo's city-center, where the dense street-grid begins to give way to a set of parks, public institutions, and a portion of waterfront that is gaining refinement in its ongoing transformation from its industrial and military origins. Fehn's involvement with the project began in 1997. The goal was to create a new archive and exhibit space for Norway's Museum of Architecture, which was incorporated as a subsidiary of the National Museum in 2003, and which now bears the title, Nasjonalmuseet-Arkitektur.

The term *new* here, is qualified. The proposed site was a disused building dating to 1830, originally the Norges Bank, though the building had been appropriated for more pedestrian usage in recent decades and was in disrepair. Designed by prominent 19th-century architect Christian Grosch (who also designed the University of Oslo buildings associated with Fehn's Tullinløkka proposal) with neoclassical detail, the bank building had undergone many earlier modifications, most notably a wing that was added to the back of the building in 1910 that made an L-shape of the old and new parts and formed an open courtyard. The entrance to that ensemble was on Kongens Gate, facing southeast. Starting with that inherited condition, I want to return to Fehn's interventions there, now carrying urban concepts explored in Fehn's works from the preceding chapters.

The Building as Constructed and as Designed

In this text, I have alternately turned to proposed projects and to constructed projects. In this case, it is useful to do both at once. There were roughly three design phases associated with the project, spanning ten years, with significant changes at each step. The first set of drawings are dated October 1997,[1] and are titled "Conceptual Project." They are hand-drafted on mylar, with spare annotation, at 1:200. That set includes plans, sections, and elevations. The second set, dated October 2001, comprises a similar array of drawings, but in more detail, and includes a model. The 2001 version was commissioned to help secure funding and governmental

More Oslo 133

approvals necessary for advancing the project. The third set, from 2007 and 2008, brought the project to reality. Complicating that sequence, by the time of the third phase—in which the address of late demands, unforeseen problems, and creative opportunities associated with actual siting and construction were critical to the success of the project—Fehn's health was failing, and it is reasonable to wonder about the impact on the project's development and construction.[2]

At the time that Fehn first became involved in the project in 1997, the existing building was historically protected but unoccupied and in poor repair. Additionally, some of the modifications to the building's interior over the decades had been poorly conceived.[3] Fehn's basic plan was to refit the existing buildings for new uses as archive and museum, restore much of Grosch's original details in the building's most public spaces, and add a new pavilion for temporary exhibitions in the courtyard of the existing L-form plan. Fehn proposed a square plan for the pavilion, and to bring the old building and new addition into relation by preserving the original entry sequence and reinforcing its axis. Reminiscent of Fehn's entry sequences at the *Vasa* and Tullinløkka projects, the body of the old building was to serve as vestibule to the new addition. Old and new entries in this early proposal were axially aligned, but the square plan of Fehn's pavilion was not centered on that axis—the line of entry, while bilaterally symmetric to the old building, was tangential to the new (Figure 5.1). This shift was accompanied by the establishment of a peripheral exterior space, defined by an inner glass wall and a concrete outer one that were to wrap in tandem around the pavilion at a uniform interval. The result was a roughly 2m zone (3m in the constructed version) between exhibit area and site that might also be described as threshold, except that it was not meant to be crossed; or that might be described as garden, except that it was decidedly bereft of flora, stone, or water. I will return to those observations below.

The proposed relationship of the pavilion to the existing building in the early scheme is best seen in the section drawing and elevations. The springpoint of the pavilion roof was set to match the given older one, and the perimeter concrete wall mentioned above was relatively imposing (largely opaque and over 4m tall), but still shorter than the glass wall immediately behind it that defines the heated building-envelope. That glass counterpart, in this version, was to rise fully to the roof line of the existing Grosch building, making a sharp contrast between the pavilion's base and top when viewed from the street (Figure 5.2). The scale and form of the proposed building might have overpowered the existing one, but that possibility was checked by the lightness of the glass volume, and by decisions evident in the design of its roof. Though the spring-point of the addition's roof was to match the existing one, the new roof itself was to be significantly lower in profile, though not exactly flat. The drawings suggest an unusual structural design that combines a two-way lenticular roof-truss with a low-slope shed-roof at the perimeter (Figure 5.3). Such a design accomplished several goals related

134 *More Oslo*

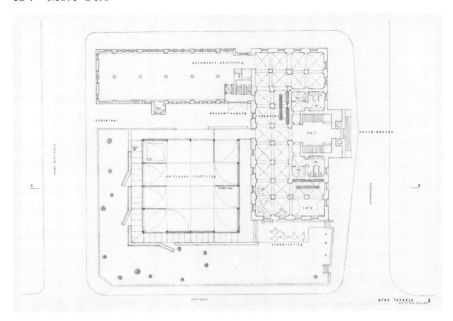

Figure 5.1 Architecture Museum, 1997 scheme, ground floor plan. Entrance at right. © Sverre Fehn. Courtesy of National Museum, Architecture Collections.

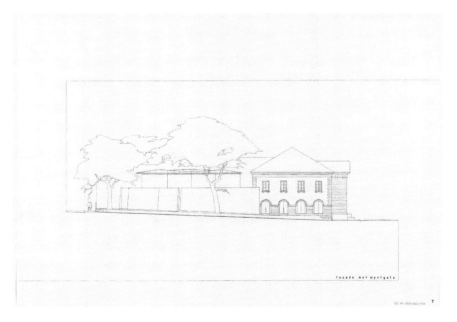

Figure 5.2 Architecture Museum, 1997 scheme, south elevation. © Sverre Fehn. Courtesy of National Museum, Architecture Collections.

More Oslo 135

to lighting, discussed below. Relevant to the building's massing, though, is how the double curvature of the lenticular truss provides an unusually low-profile roof-structure. Combined with the setback from the sidewalk, the effect is to maintain the continuity of the bank building's roofline as an upper limit and unifying datum, nesting the new building within the old while maintaining a striking contemporary identity. This set of decisions is thoroughly consonant with previous points regarding Fehn's calibration of novel assertions measured against given conditions, reaffirming an architectural propensity for dialog rather than either dominance or subordination.

That set of relationships was reworked in later versions. In 2001, the conceptual project of 1997 found new life as interest in the proposed museum gained momentum, and Fehn was asked to prepare a more detailed set of drawings in order to assist with the securing of funds and governmental permissions. The 2001 version of the design is more detailed—for example, the newer drawings reflect some consideration of the building's environmental systems—but makes few departures from the basic approach in the 1997 design. An important exception is the building's profile. The 2001 drawings dropped the height of the pavilion below the existing spring-point and, consequently, also lowered the height of the perimeter concrete wall, changes that would carry through to the constructed version in 2008. The overall effect of this modification is debatable. The pavilion's reduced stature arguably not only further balances the relative weights of old and new,

Figure 5.3 Architecture Museum, 1997 scheme, building section. © Sverre Fehn. Courtesy of National Museum, Architecture Collections.

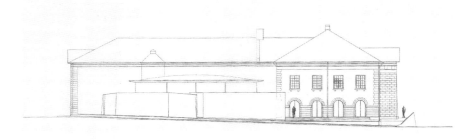

Figure 5.4 Architecture Museum, 2001 scheme, south elevation. © Sverre Fehn. Courtesy of National Museum, Architecture Collections.

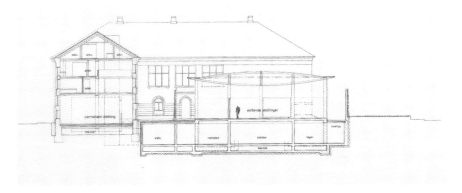

Figure 5.5 Architecture Museum, 2001 scheme, building section. © Sverre Fehn. Courtesy of National Museum, Architecture Collections.

but also dispenses with an opportunity to establish commonality in a shared roof-line (Figure 5.4). The section drawings for the 2001 scheme also depict a slightly more complicated roof, one that would now require an internal rainwater collection system. The advantages of the new roof proposal, perhaps, are an even more diminished roof profile, and the elimination of the need for perimeter guttering, while the general proportions and dimension of the roof and its relationship to the glass walls remained consistent with the 1997 roof design (Figure 5.5). In general, the 2001 design reduced the volume of the proposed pavilion, in both senses of the word *volume*: the building would be more compact and would have a more reserved voice in the urban ensemble.

Before considering the new pavilion's interior and the progression of its design, a minor observation regarding adaptive reuse is worth noting. Fehn's interventions within the existing Grosch building are both restorative and assertive. The design called for many of the surfaces and details of the old building to be rebuilt in accordance with its original configuration. Where new walls, floors, and caseworks were needed, Fehn's designs do not replicate the existing details, but neither are they incongruous with those details. Consider, for example, the design for a new partition within the existing structural vaults (Figure 5.6) where the early 20th-century wing adjoins the original 19th-century building. Rather than center the door within the vault, where there would have been ample room for a standard panel, Fehn shifts the door in correspondence with the line of movement given in the plan, even though that necessitates a custom-fabricated door with an off-center arced header. It is a simple design decision of tertiary importance in the scope of the project. But instead of defaulting to an easier solution, the doorway *is designed*, serving to help reconcile the given misalignment of the two arch systems from 1830 and 1910, using, in 2008, the configuration of an otherwise innocuous doorway to contribute to the larger pursuit of bringing old, older, and new into coherence. While minor, the detail embodies an understanding of old and new that informed several decisions in the project's reconfiguration of the existing interior.

Returning attention to the interior of the proposed new pavilion, the supporting roof structure in the 1997 and 2001 schemes consisted of 16 slender columns distributed evenly around the perimeter of a 16-square grid of 4.5m × 4.5m modules (Figure 5.1). The floor plans in both schemes show large operable panels hinged to these columns, so that an array of partition configurations could be arranged according to the needs of each exhibition. The section drawings show the panels extending upward to about 3m in height and, below, terminating on rollers a few centimeters above the finished floor. Similar to display options shown in drawings for the Venice pavilion, and echoing the spatial adjustment allowed by the sliding panels at Villa Norköpping, Fehn's proposed pivoting panels at the Oslo pavilion allowed for variation in both the configuration of exhibits and in the degree of enclosure at the pavilion's perimeter.

The deployable partitions here, had they been built, would have been more overt than the retractable ones at Norrköping, but their function as a means of modulating and subdividing the major spaces to suit the particulars of a situation makes them similar to their domestic siblings. This feature brings the moniker *pavilion* into question. The

Figure 5.6 Architecture Museum, detail of exhibition area in existing building. Photo by author.

138 *More Oslo*

term is apt here, in the sense that it describes a space that is relatively open, empty, and ready for manifold uses only vaguely anticipated. In such spaces, the building typically serves as armature, its compartition left for others to design, install, and then eventually remove. But Fehn's early designs for the Oslo building show an unwillingness to let the divide between permanent armature and transient installation be so clearly defined. As mentioned above, at a domestic scale, David Leatherbarrow has described this domain of architecture—somewhere between building and furniture, between fixed and fleeting—as "dwelling equipment." Such installations are given to the modulation of the protean ambient condition, where that condition is understood to include social practices. Pursuing those observations, Fehn's proposed hinged partitions might be thought of as "urban equipment." I do not believe that the principal concern here can rightly be understood as having to do with anything that might be described as efficiency, pragmatism, or flexibility: the proposed panels could arguably have actually hampered those ends. What they would have achieved, though, had they been implemented, is a more active participation of the building in shaping the events that would unfold there, and a greater continuity in the character of each successive event. That is, the design would simultaneously facilitate

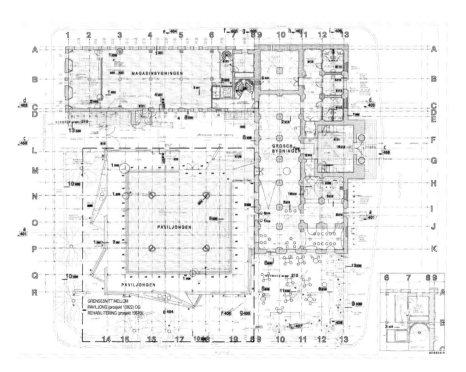

Figure 5.7 Architecture Museum, 2008 scheme, main floor plan. © Sverre Fehn. Courtesy of National Museum, Architecture Collections.

the adaption of the setting to the peculiarity of present needs, while also connecting each event more directly to its setting and to each successive event as an unfolding historical set. Had that part of the design been realized, its effect on the character of the space would have been decisively less formal than the constructed version, suggesting a more general idea about "dwelling equipment" and its public iterations: such furnishings have the tendency to render the rooms to which they belong less monumental and more available to present dictates. As argued in Chapter 4, this "availability" of the architecture can be understood as facilitating urbanity.

The pivoting panels do not appear in the 2008 plans, nor does the field of columns to which they were attached. Instead, the 16 thin columns of the earlier proposals were replaced with four massive piers, not at the perimeter, but positioned 4.5m in from each of the four corners. The switch to the pier system effectively withdrew the line of structure further from the perimeter, creating another concentric zone of space, this time along the interior of the glass walls (Figure 5.7). The piers also provided easily utilized chases to run service lines—it is unclear how that was to be addressed in the earlier schemes, though the wall at the entryway would have been a likely candidate for that purpose, and earlier section drawings show extensive use of the basement level for environmental systems. The form of the 2008 version's four piers is important in the experience of the pavilion's interior. Their roughly c-shaped plans are rotated 45 degrees relative to the pavilion's governing geometries, with a convex side made of rough-shuttered, vertically striated concrete oriented to the exterior corners, and a flat side of infilled gray brick oriented to the pavilion's center (Figure 5.8). The piers seem somewhat anomalous to the design as a whole, though Fehn's early design for the King Hågens Church (1956, unbuilt) adopted a similar approach. It is unclear if the elimination of the lenticular truss in the constructed version of the museum pavilion coincided with decisions about the supports, but the piers were not a natural fit with the earlier proposal for a trussed roof system, and the constructed building substituted a thin concrete shell structure for the roof. Importantly, as the earlier drawings suggest, and as the 2001 model makes clear, Fehn had envisioned a large oculus comprising most of the pavilion's roof area, to be fitted with translucent sheathing that would have increased daylighting and decreased shadow and glare, whereas the constructed shell structure is opaque. The combined opacity and concavity of the roof condition as constructed in the 2008 scheme is unusual for Fehn. Almost always in his projects, Fehn designed a way to release the ceiling plane to the sky, using devices like clerestories, skylights, and convex soffits. That proclivity is only evident here at the perimeter of the pavilion, where the roof tips up slightly like the brim of a hat.

The pavilion's roof details open a broader consideration of the project's relation to the sun, and it is here where the greatest design changes occurred between the three schemes. In the 1997 design, the amount of glazing at the project's upper limits—much of it south-facing—was certain to create

Figure 5.8 Architecture Museum, pavilion interior. © Ivan Brodey.

problems for the goals of evenly distributed lighting and comfortable interior climate. It seems likely that Fehn would have had solutions to that problem in mind, but, if so, those are not apparent in the drawings, except for the consistent appearance of large trees along the sidewalk to the south. In the 2001 version, the problems of solar gain and glare were substantially mitigated by the lowering of the roof and the concomitant reduction of glazing—it is plausible that the looming problem of solar gain helped inform that adjustment. As mentioned, the perimeter concrete wall was also lowered in this second version, but comparatively less than the glazed perimeter wall. Combined with the overhang of the lenticular truss and its creation of an eave condition at the top of the glass wall as it appeared in the two early schemes, the amount of space available for direct sunlight to pass between the top of the concrete wall and the bottom of the eave was reduced to about 2m in the 2001 version (compare Figures 5.3 and 5.5). Taken together, the eave, the perimeter walls, and the translucent roof section would have provided generous and even daylighting. The changes made to the constructed version of 2008 are especially important here. First, the gap between concrete and glass walls was enlarged to about 3m, increasing the glass wall's exposure to direct sunlight. Of greater consequence were changes made to the eave condition, where not only were the overhang

More Oslo   141

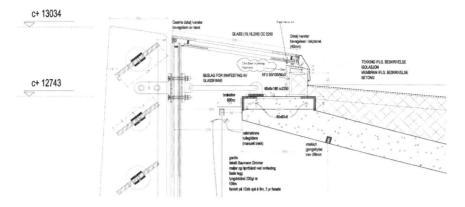

Figure 5.9 Architecture Museum, pavilion roof detail showing structural glass fins, glass louvers, mullion-less glass wall, skylight at inverted eave, concrete shell roof, and curtains. From construction drawings. © Sverre Fehn. Courtesy of National Museum, Architecture Collections.

and oculus both eliminated, but the outermost section of roofing was now glazed, fashioning a perimeter skylight around the top of the exterior wall (Figure 5.9), effectively doubling the size of the gap between the opaque components—the top of the concrete wall and the edge of the concrete roof. Among the consequences of that set of decisions was a pronounced increase in the amount of solar exposure and heat-gain. That may have contributed to the decision to develop the constructed building's defining glass-louvered brise-soleil—a feature that does not appear in the earlier work—and to include a line of fabric curtains at the perimeter of the exhibition space.

These decisions about glazing and lighting can be understood, in one sense, as merely pragmatic responses to the programmatic needs of an exhibit area and its thermal regulation. They also, though, belong to a consideration of the building's fit within its existing milieu. The pragmatic understanding can be connected to a consideration of urbanity in much the same way that the practical considerations of the Norrköpping house were in Chapter 2. That is, architectural provision for the functions and expectations of daily life and instilled practice serve to establish continuity and normalcy, a condition conducive to, and necessary for, participation. It is the second understanding, though—the one that pertains to an urban ambiance—that I want to further consider in relation to Fehn's project.

On Perimeter Definition, Ambiance, and Participation

To begin a shift from an account of the Oslo pavilion's configuration and the trajectory of its development, and toward a consideration of the building's further relevance to points made in the previous chapters regarding urban

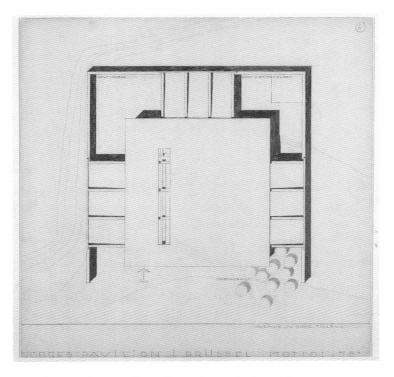

Figure 5.10 Norwegian Pavilion, Brussels, roof plan. Nine opaque extensions at perimeter depict roof-tarps. ©Sverre Fehn. Courtesy of National Museum, Architecture Collections.

architecture, it is helpful to turn to an earlier pavilion project. The design of the Norwegian Pavilion for the 1958 World's Fair in Brussels was the project that launched Fehn's career onto the international scene. The two buildings are similar enough, in scale, purpose, and form, to be thought of as bookends to Fehn's career. And while the earlier work was more experimental in nature, it offers insights into several of Fehn's decisions 50 years later, especially on matters of perimeter definition. That architectural idea—perimeter definition—is useful for making a general account of the complexity of any building's limits with regard to its urban situation. Whereas concepts like "building envelope" and "skin," for example, tend to obscure that complexity, a building's perimeter definition, as a concept, more clearly maintains a concern for the building's multivalent fit within its immediate urban context (which may involve decisions about scale, form, appearance, and lines of movement, for example), its selective orientation to what is far and near (which may involve framing, aperture, facing, or foreclosing), and its creation and regulation of an ambiance appropriate to the kinds of sociation the building is intended to sustain. It is in those senses that I want to try to better understand the perimeter definition of Fehn's Oslo pavilion.

As with the building in Oslo, the Brussels pavilion was square in plan, with a perimeter exterior zone between a glazed interior wall and an opaque outer one.[4] The floor-to-ceiling fenestration of both projects forgo mullions, substituting vertical structural transparent fins—tempered glass in Oslo, Plexiglas in Brussels. In the Brussels pavilion, that outdoor zone was wider than at Oslo and meant to be furnished and occupied. At Brussels, in lieu of Oslo's brise-soleil and curtains, Fehn used sets of translucent tarps (which the text on his competition drawings described as sails) made from an experimental nylon composite that could be deployed to span between the eave and the perimeter pre-cast composite concrete walls (Figure 5.10). The ceiling of the main roof, too, was fitted with translucent sheets (though of a different proprietary material), and incorporated concealed fluorescent light fixtures: "the ceiling," Fehn said, "functions in the evening like one great lamp."[5] Advancing designs that would eventually inform various parts of the Venice pavilion, the camera shop, and the Hedmark Museum, the Brussels project especially corresponds with the Oslo pavilion, sharing concentric zones with a controlled garden-like perimeter, a luminous

Figure 5.11 Norwegian Pavilion, Brussels, northwest corner, looking through Plexiglas wall to exterior perimeter zone. © Sverre Fehn. Courtesy of National Museum, Architecture Collections.

mantle meant to stage the encounter of displayed objects, and a relatively darker core. Illustrating this point, Fehn included an unusual drawing in his winning competition proposal for the Brussels pavilion—a plan-diagram that showed how he was anticipating the creation of three different qualities of light, how those zones would overlap, and how each different lighting condition might relate to different kinds of display and occupation (Figure 5.11).

The resultant project could be summarized, then, as a garden-perimeter between a selectively bracketed site and a luminous interior pavilion, where the ambiance of the interior is largely given by the garden which its glass walls at once exclude and admit.

Fehn's design for the pavilion in Oslo achieves similar ends. Might its own perimeter zone, too, be best understood as garden (Figure 5.12)? That will be a stretch for anyone inclined to identify gardens with flora, rocks, water elements, or some combination of those. The emptiness of that perimeter space is important to the experience of the pavilion's interior, and we can assume that its character was important to Fehn. He could easily have designed that area to be a garden in the traditional sense, but nowhere is that possibility evident in his designs. Of course, that empty space is not truly empty. The temperature and shadow of the concrete surfaces vary with the temperature and intensity of the sunlight. For viewers inside the pavilion, as at the *Vasa* design (though the effect was decidedly more dramatic in the Swedish proposal), the wall's bracketing of the middle-ground has the effect of presenting the sky and the cast walls as protean backdrop. Can a garden consist *only* of air, sky, and light? If so, mirroring the exploration of similar themes at Villa Norrköping, we may credit Fehn with inviting wilderness—that is, all the things the building ostensibly forecloses (rain, light, uncertainty, decay, boundlessness)—into the experience of a highly sophisticated room near the heart of a city. To a degree, that could be said of any building: all architecture necessarily admits, in some ratio, by design or happenstance, what it endeavors to forestall. What Fehn's architecture asks us to consider, I think, is how the artful expression and calibration of that ratio might contribute to an urban ambiance.

To further develop that point, a related example can be found in the design of the museum addition's perimeter wall itself. Like the remnants of

Figure 5.12 Architecture Museum, view of perimeter zone between glass and concrete walls. Photo by author.

its 17th-century predecessor across the street, the wall appears fortress-like: its mass is exaggerated by the cant of its outer faces, and the 3m high wall presents mostly as impenetrable. Having established opacity and a degree of perimeter control suitable for an exhibition space, Fehn compromised that separation with flap-like openings in the walls, a feature that figures prominently in all three versions of the plans. These are unusual. Though the openings are of a scale and proportion that suggest entry, and while the 2001 designs show hinged shutters at those locations (Figure 5.13), in none of the design schemes were they ever intended to conduct passage, and the constructed version is emphatic in that regard: tempered glass sheets fixed within the openings were substituted for the gate-like closures from 2001 (Figure 5.14). Published photos of the project frequently go to some length to depict these openings as framing devices, but to do so the camera must be placed in positions not comfortably occupied by an actual inhabitant. As the chosen angles and positioning of the openings' walls afford little by way of view from even the most advantageous standpoints along the sidewalk (looking inward) or from within the pavilion's interior (looking outward), one is left to conclude that these openings are less about view than about the suggestion of interpenetration, an intentional interjection of discontinuity in the boundary between within and without. One cannot physically pass through the openings in the wall, but the idea, the presentation of where you aren't, appears from the exterior as a kind of invitation or allure, and from the interior as a compromise of the perimeter enclosure, a circumstantial leak. Georg Simmel described that phenomenon as the possibility of elsewhere, writing, "Exactly because the door can be opened, its being shut gives a feeling of being shut-out that is stronger than a feeling emanating from just a solid wall. The wall is silent but the door speaks."[6]

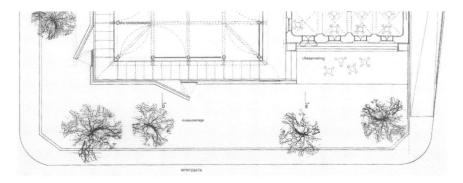

Figure 5.13 Architecture Museum, 2001 scheme, plan detail showing proposed recessed hinged shutters at openings. Note also divisions in the floor surface of the perimeter zone, which represented the proposed glass-block system (not built) to provide light to basement. Pivoting display panels shown at interior. © Sverre Fehn. Courtesy of National Museum, Architecture Collections.

146   *More Oslo*

   Similar to what was found at Villa Norrköping, and paralleling the preceding observations about garden, Fehn's pavilion in Oslo is designed to oscillate between what is closed and certain on the one hand, and what is open and changeable on the other. As previously suggested, this is a ratio. Compared to Fehn's less mature work at Brussels, the calibration of that ratio at the Oslo pavilion exhibits high degrees of finesse and mastery.

   The glass walls play another role in characterizing the pavilion's interior ambiance. As given to Fehn, the Grosch building, though vacant, was not a ruin, at least not in the typical sense. But, like the district as a whole, the building was a relic of Oslo's past, antiquated and removed from its original purpose. Returning to ideas developed in discussion of the Hedmark Museum and Trondheim Library, Fehn endeavors to neither erase the building as an anachronism, nor embalm it as a historical fragment, nor bracket it out of the experience of the new project, but rather to activate it for participation in its reinvigorated contemporary context. At the north and east sides of the pavilion, the existing building provides the solar protection and sense of enclosure that the glass walls forgo. Accordingly, the exterior facades of the original bank are appropriated, effectively, as walls of the new pavilion's interior, marshaled as important contributors to its ambiance.

   The glass walls' role in the exterior appearance of the building and its engagement of its surrounds is no less significant. One of the most readily apparent features of the glass facade is its contrast with the concrete wall that partially eclipses it. The smooth surfaces and crisp lines of the glazing system and its glass louvers emphasize the coarser tolerances and textures of the concrete. If we can understand the forgoing of mullions as making the glass glass-ier, then the concrete, too, has been worked in a way that accentuates

Figure 5.14 Architecture Museum, view of exterior wall. Photo by author.

More Oslo 147

its relative coarseness (Figure 5.14). This presents a related but less obvious point of contrast between the two kinds of structure, a point that has to do with the building's engagement of chronology. As seen in many of the previous examples, Fehn's architecture is often concerned with the inclusion and overlay of varying scales of time, and some of the previously discussed architectural strategies for accomplishing that feat are again on display in the Oslo pavilion. Barely fifteen years since its construction, while the glass has predictably registered no readily legible signs of aging, the concrete's weathering is already noticeable: two scales of time are on display in each of the two primary materials of the building's facade. Because the concrete walls are not responsible for containing heat or resisting water, the need for careful maintenance is diminished and the contrast between the condition of the surfaces can be left to become increasingly pronounced. In the materiality and detailing of its facade, the new structure's different components engage different scales of time and anticipate their divergent effects.

What such engagement of chronological variegation embodied in a building's appearance might contribute to an urban setting is difficult to assess. Does greater chronological variegation in a building correspond with heightened urbanity? Fehn seems to believe so. Perhaps here is another instance of multivalence as a property contributing to urbanity. Different scales of time sustain different kinds of activities, different kinds of thinking and creativity. An architecture that endeavored to embody that multiplicity may indeed contribute to an urban setting's potency by availing a more extensive menu, so to speak, of possible relationships and ingredients to be brought in dialog to the unfolding present.

Lastly, the glass wall also structures a more basic connection to its urban surrounds: it reflects it. That property is hardly unique to Fehn's

Figure 5.15 Architecture Museum, view of rear corner. Photo by author.

building—reflectivity is endemic to the material. But designers can exercise some control over that property by specifying additives or films in the production of the glass to minimize its reflective property, or, in some cases, to increase it. The glass specified for the pavilion in Oslo exhibits a slightly greenish hue (typically achieved by adjusting the glass's iron-oxide content) and high specular reflectivity. The color, evident in most daylight conditions, heightens the material contrasts considered above. The effect of the reflectivity is best seen on the north-facing facade where the concrete wall steps down and the fretted-glass louvers are not required (Figure 5.15). It is another minor point, but the effect does further extend the building's receptiveness to circumstance. While the glass's role in the appearance of the building within surrounds is receptive during the day, it is projective at night. Again, the general effect—a glass volume illuminated from the interior at night—is not novel. But because the pavilion's glazed interior is partially wrapped in concrete, the effect is amplified: reminiscent of Fehn's description of the Brussels pavilion, the glass volume of the Architecture Museum awakens at night. Further anticipating the shifting experience of the pavilion in the evening from the perspective of the interior, in a detail carefully described in the wall-section, the perimeter space between the glass and the concrete is lit at night with outside lighting installed under the lip of the floor, projecting light on the inside face of the concrete, thereby preempting the blackness that would otherwise result from expanses of glass in a lit interior at night.

On Fehn's Cafés

The Brussels and Oslo projects both feature cafés. In fact, several of the projects discussed or mentioned in this text included in their designs a place for pausing and socializing over coffee: the Brussels pavilion, the Royal Theater, the Hydro-electric museum, the Glacier Museum, and Trondheim all incorporated cafés into their designs; the Tullinløkka proposal had two. At the architecture museum, the café is located on the ground floor at the southeast corner of the existing building, with an associated patio immediately adjacent (Figure 1.1).

As constructed, the patio's relationship to the project as a whole appears somewhat casual—it could be mistaken as an afterthought. But the café and its patio appear in the earliest drawings, and there is evidence that Fehn afforded its role in the project a surprising degree of attention. Consider the structural gymnastics required to place a patio in that location. In all the schemes, including the constructed version, adjustments were made to the museum's first floor level, thereby allowing an existing window to be converted to a patio doorway without substantially modifying the historically protected facade. In the earliest scheme, that accommodation involved raising *the entire first floor*, as attested by the riser count at the stairway at the museum's main entry, which shows three fewer risers than the original stair. The 2001 version maintained the original floor level at the museum entrance and, instead, proposed interior ramps at the approach to the café—requiring a ramp-run that would have been difficult to accommodate. In the constructed version, the difference was split: one riser was eliminated at the museum entrance, the entire first floor was raised accordingly, and a short interior ramp was installed to access the café's floor level, which is two additional risers higher. Notably, Fehn left visual evidence of that set of decisions by designing a window of sorts into the floor of the main entry foyer that reveals a portion of the original floor, with its original tile, at its original vertical position (Figure 5.16). Moving from the main entrance toward the new pavilion, one cannot avoid walking over that structural glass case. It is a detail that belongs with the "floor-window" onto the ruins beneath the old town hall at Trondheim; it is also, I think, reminiscent of the placement of the *Vasa*, albeit a dramatically different scale. Given the effort invested in its realization, it is reasonable to take more seriously the patio's potential importance.

In both the 1997 and 2001 drawing sets, the patio's boundaries are inscribed within the datum of the new concrete pavilion wall parallel to Myntgata and the existing building. A subtle sense of enclosure and separation from both museum and street was achieved by setting the patio slightly below grade—enough for the required retaining walls to double as benches.[7] In these early schemes, no wall separated the new pavilion's

Figure 5.16 Architecture Museum, Architecture Museum, entry foyer. Glazed flooring area at bottom left reveals original flooring detail below. © Ivan Brodey.

150 *More Oslo*

perimeter "garden" from the slightly sunken al fresco seating area. That boundary, instead, was marked by a set of wide steps that might have doubled as seating, or that might have allowed access to the pavilion's perimeter zone—there is no indication in the drawings of any barrier. Consequently, occupants of the patio were presented not just the current view onto the two bounding city streets, but also a view behind the concrete wall and an oblique, somewhat furtive view of the pavilion's interior (Figure 5.17). In that sense, the patio area functioned in part as a terminus for the pavilion's perimeter zone. It was a condition that balanced the patio within a set of thresholds: old wall and new wall, museum and street, public view and privileged view, interior and exterior, active and calm, above grade and below grade. This reflects a design intent recurrent in each of the projects previously considered: establishment of a degree of openness to and engagement of circumstance, balanced against internal definition and interiority, familiarity balanced against uncertainty, and the development of spaces that straddle those reciprocal conditions. Paraphrasing Voltaire, to occupy a position of uncertainty is difficult, but to occupy a certain one is absurd. Fehn's designs suggest an architectural counterpart to that assertion, in which inhabitable liminal spaces are valued as especially conducive to sociation owing to the indeterminate ambiance, socio-spatial porosity,

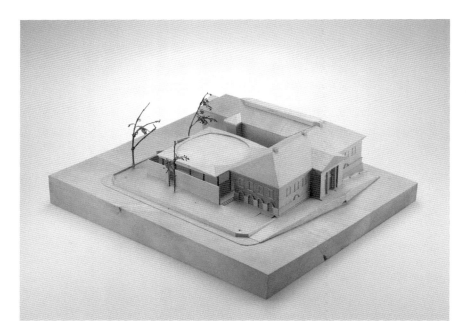

Figure 5.17 Architecture Museum, 2001 scheme, wooden model showing detail of cafe patio. © Sverre Fehn. Courtesy of National Museum, Architecture Collections.

and productive discord that mark such spaces, as discussed in Chapter 4.[8] The café patio at the Oslo pavilion embodies that idea.

The Nature of the Building's Urbanity

Returning to the question posed at the beginning, what can now be said, in summary, about "the nature of the Architecture Museum's urbanity?" The project is a contemporary insertion into the historic fabric of the city. But it is designed so that its identity is checked and informed by the larger setting as given. This can be seen in its conformance to the setback lines of the buildings immediately to the east, and in the way the concrete walls mimic the texture and canted form of the walls of the 13th-century fortress to the south. Within its more immediate site, the pavilion addition is scaled so that it neither dominates nor is dwarfed by the historic bank building to which it belongs. The new building's detailing, form, and materiality also serve to establish an even footing conducive to its participation in its milieu: not an aberration foreign to its setting, and not a replication of what is already there, but an instance of what I have described above as the concinnation of parts calibrated for participation in the setting. If what at first appeared as a fortress-like form appropriated from its designer's earlier, more rural projects are now understandable as communicative with respect to its unique urban setting, has the form of the building nevertheless taken too many of the characteristics of its fortress neighbor? Has Fehn, in his effort to enter into architectural dialog with other constructed figures in the vicinity, unwittingly replicated the problems he had previously associated with the citadel-like modern museum? No. The imposition of the walls is relieved with oblique openings, and their coarseness and opacity are balanced against the lantern-like character of the glass volume nested behind them. The building reaches. Its allure or presence—what I have described as the volume of the building's voice—has been designed to vary with the lighting of the hour, the weather, and the season. Pursuant to that idea, the building, as described, is also designed to gather still larger scales of time: years, eras, eons. As I have argued, this expanded chronological engagement renders available more of what is latent in the urban condition. And here, as with the previous analysis of Fehn's design for the Royal Theater, we are already passing across the hazy line between building as a participant in its setting and building as a setting for participation, where its personification as urban actor, as citizen, translates into its contribution to the lives of actual urbanites. The building interweaves the strata of the city—excavating its historical traces, edifying its daily patterns, staging its various modes of theatricality, modulating its atmosphere—and thereby invigorates the lives unfolding within the settings it shapes. Central to this expanded horizon of possibility is orientation toward the other, in which architectural configurations relate us to those with whom we are immediately among, and also to those who are spatially and chronologically distant, all of whom with which we share a world, and the immediate world of the city.[9] Fehn's architecture, I hope I have shown, is attuned to each of these, showing how a building may be designed to sustain an urban entelechy in which the city becomes more of itself.

An orientation toward the fullness of the city is ultimately an orientation toward others. The quality, character, and reach of those relationships is prefigured by the settings that stage them. Sverre Fehn understood that architecture, at great loss, might neglect that phenomenon. His architecture sought to engage it.

Notes

1. The National Museum's website for Fehn's archives gives 2001 for the project's origins. In the exhibition catalog, *Intuition, Reflection, Construction*, Fehn's project supervisor for the museum design, Martin Dietrichson, also puts the initial date as 2001. The drawings from the archive's earliest set are clearly labeled "Oktober, 1997."
2. Fjeld recalls drawings and site photographs being brought to Fehn's bedside. See Per Olaf Fjeld, *The Pattern of Thoughts* (New York: Monacelli Press, 2009), 276.
3. Martin Dietrichson, "The National Museum—Architecture," in *Intuition, Reflection, Construction*, eds. Marianne Yvennes and Eva Madhus (Oslo: National Museum, 2009), 139.
4. In this text, I have found it helpful to consider select details of the Brussels pavilion in order to better illuminate architectural decisions in the Oslo pavilion. For my fuller account of the Brussels pavilion itself and its relevance to urban architectural thinking, see Anderson, Stephen. "Of Artifact, Urbanity, and the City: Sverre Fehn's Norwegian Pavilion and the Structure of Urbanity," in *Projecting Urbanity: Architecture For and Against the City*, ed. David Leatherbarrow, chapter 6 (London: Artifice Press, 2023).
5. Sverre Fehn, "Pavilion in Brussels," *Byggekunst* no. 4 (1958): 85–94.
6. Georg Simmel, "Brücke und Tür," *Der Tag*, September 15, 1909.
7. As constructed, the outdoor grade-level of the patio was raised to that of the interior—probably, again, a response to codes for accessibility.
8. The social potency of liminal conditions has been taken up in the disciplines of sociology and anthropology, and helpfully so, but typically recognizing a physio-spatial component while stopping short of explicitly exploring it. On *communitas* and liminality, see Victor Turner, *The Ritual Process* (Chicago, IL: Aldine, 1969). On the productive uncertainty to be found in the thresholds of social boundaries, see Georg Simmel, "Soziologie der Geselligkeit," *Frankfurter Zeitung* no. 292 (1910), 22.
9. These different relationships to others were categorized by Alfred Schutz as *Umwelt, Mitwelt, Vorwelt*, and *Folgewelt* (roughly, knowable world, immediately shared world, past world, and future world), each implying respective forms of participation. Each of these, it can be argued, carries distinct architectural implications, and, perhaps, obligations—certainly, at least, distinct creative opportunities. See Alfred Schutz and Thomas Luckmann, *Structures of the Life-world* (Evanston, IL: Northwestern University Press, 1973), and, Alfred Schutz, *On Phenomenology and Social Relations: Selected Writings*, ed. Helmut Wagner (Chicago: University of Chicago Press, 1970).

Afterword

Perhaps it is delusion, or hubris, but I feel that there are architects for whom I might adequately summarize the gist of their architectural efforts in a few paragraphs. Not so for the works of Sverre Fehn. Even with respect to this book's focus on a particular theme within his opus, even after several years of research and many pages of analysis, I remain unprepared, I admit, to reduce to a few sentences the understanding of urbanity that Fehn's work presents. Furthermore, here at the end, I have no concluding definition of urbanity to profess. Knowing that the reader may regard that as failure or evasion, I offer, tentatively, at least the following summary notes.

Starting simply, Fehn understood architecture to stand against nature, in the sense of resisting wilderness and natural forces. For Fehn, that fundamental architectural task was already a base stratum in what can be thought of as a vertical, multilayered spectrum of urbanity. Also for Fehn, and not at all surprising, urbanity involved not just presence alongside, but orientation toward, the other. More than recognition, juxtaposition, or awareness of others, Fehn emphasized what emerges between two (or more) people but which could not belong entirely to either alone, an idea that Fehn, like many other students of urbanity, located in active and balanced dialog in which commonality and difference were both essential. For Fehn that dialog involved others present, others distant, and others past, for which architecture served as medium. Fehn also recognized fecundity as essential to urbanity, a sense of openness and possibility and uncertainty, of a churning and nascent present, dependent on creativity, conflict, and participation in a cultural-spatial milieu, at once prefigured and improvised, with attendant lineaments of theatricality. As evident in Fehn's projects, degrees of that milieu could be found outside of cities, but the potential for fullest expression was to be found within them. He further believed that architecture had the capacity, even obligation, to engage, sustain, and amplify those phenomena; that, as he asserted, architecture's role therein was critical and indispensable (remember, he went as far as stating that architecture was the only means of achieving those ends), and his designs reveal an endeavor to architecturally recognize and embody those premises. As I have tried to show, central to that architectural role in the structure of urbanity in Fehn's work was the expansion of dialog and awareness through engagement of and attunement to circumstance—circumstance in three interwoven senses: historic, ambient, and cultural. That expansion involved architectural strategies for drawing attention to those circumstances in ways that amplified their presence, or, as I've argued, facilitated their participation in urban settings by bringing them to consciousness, including the counter-intuitive readmission of what the architectural project initially and ostensibly foreclosed. As alluded to above, one of the results of that heightened inclusivity in urban settings is the conveyance of a self-aware, performative cast that Fehn understood as an essentially theatrical component of urbanity. As we have seen, Fehn's urban architecture advanced this notion of urban theatricality in diverse ways. And lastly, it is important to remember two related points that were critical for Fehn's thinking on urbanity. First, that the maintenance of a robust urbanity was not guaranteed—he repeatedly emphasized challenges to urbanity, to ways that some architecture and features of contemporary cities had neglected urban promise or had diminished the fullness and vibrancy of urbanity. For Fehn, the key threats were instrumentality, an exclusive rationalism, indifference, and, most surprisingly, the pursuit of harmony over difference and confrontation. And second, that the sphere of urbanity, though dependent on rational structures, was essentially extra-rational, involving aspects of spirituality, humanness, humility, and, especially important for Fehn's approach to the city, regard of death.

No part of that preceding summary, nor all of it taken together, amounts to a definition of urbanity. And neither did Fehn ever attempt a concise definition. Perhaps the necessarily reductive nature of any such definition would, in any event, render it counterproductive—there are benefits to allowing the term to remain complex, contested, elusive. Attempting to describe the dream-like ambience of a living room central to a formative childhood memory, Anne Carson wrote that it was like "something incognito at the heart of our sleeping house." She then explicated her own phrase: "Both words are important. Incognito means unrecognized, hidden, unknown. And something means not nothing." I hope it can now be recognized that there is something hidden in Fehn's work pertinent to consideration of the architectural structure of urbanity; that, for Fehn, that concern was central to his architecture and to architecture in general; and that attention to how Fehn sought to materially engage those concerns in his projects should prove instructive to any designer who might share Fehn's urban concerns. We should expect to find the rudiments of urbanity in any city and in many places beyond. There is no contradiction in observing that urbanity can be diminished, and that, in the contemporary city, it is demonstrably under threat. If our cities are to fulfill their promise—which may rightly be understood as the promise of humanity, and upon which the principles of equity and the health of our world depend—we will need more than rudiments and vestiges. Architecture's role is essential.

Appendix 1
The Building Will Reflect the Drama of the City

The following interview of Sverre Fehn was conducted by Peter Mose one month after Fehn was awarded the Royal Danish Theater commission. The interview was published in *Politiken*, April 22, 1996. This form of the interview was provided by the interviewer, and is longer than the published version. Translated into English from the original Danish by Alan Frost.

The Building Will Reflect the Drama of the City

By Peter Mose

Kongens Nytorv is in need of a cathedral, in the opinion of the architect behind The Royal Danish Theatre's reconstruction. Finally, a foreign architect is allowed to build something in Copenhagen, and to top it off, it is a compelling, unpredictable, and masterful work, which will turn The Royal Danish Theatre into one of Europe's largest theaters.

This was the enthusiastic response one month ago, when a panel of judges led by the Minister for Culture, Jette Hilden (S), awarded this difficult task with a price tag of DKK 720 million to the renowned Norwegian architect Sverre Fehn. The judges were all in agreement that his stroke of genius stood head and shoulders above the other 10 heavyweights who had been allowed to participate in this prestigious architectural competition.

But now, there are whispers of discontent about the 71-year-old Norwegian—a band of skeptics has started to hurl verbal criticism towards the 34-meter-tall glass construction in which Sverre Fehn would like to enclose Stærekassen. The protected Art Deco theater stage from the 1930s would only become an indoor fixture, encased in a big glass incubator. And Sverre Fehn is not just elbowing his way into Kongens Nytorv, but also encroaching upon sacred architectural treasures such as Charlottenborg and Harsdorff House, the mother of classical Copenhagen. This is why the large construction should be moved further away from Kongens Nytorv. The ambitious cladding, which would house a gigantic theatre vestibule the size of a Gothic cathedral, should be placed all the way behind Stærekassen's facade—hidden away from the side facing Kongens Nytorv. This is the opinion of the critics, which include architects and supporters of preservation.

156   Appendix 1

Sverre Fehn himself says that his suspended construction, which will have a concrete roof of bird wings, would enrich both Stærekassen and Kongens Nytorv—and that there is room for his large construction, which, by all accounts, will open on New Year's Eve in 2001.

"Among city planners, there is the basic objection that this is the wrong place to build. How would you respond to this criticism?"

Lots of Room

> Well, if you have to build in an urban landscape, you have to accept the space you get. And if you have a somewhat mystical outlook on the city, then Kongens Nytorv is the place where citizens have experienced the world's drama for generations.

says the Oslo architect, who can look back on a glorious career that has thus far spanned 47 years. "Copenhagen would lose something if one suddenly packed up and left this place. Then the blind would not be able to find their theater again."

"Could the new construction, for example, be place in an attractive location by the waterfront?"

> I do not know much about that discussion. I just have the feeling that Kongens Nytorv is yearning for more. A new city motif. There is lots of room here – now that you mentioned a lack of space. And all great squares around the world have tall buildings. For example, cathedrals that shoot up. Here…you get Magasin, Hotel d'Angleterre and The Royal Danish Theatre together with a number of more modest buildings.

says Sverre Fehn, who is the childhood friend of our own Jørn Utzon and known as one of the most soulful world-class architects in the Nordic region.

"In your own sketches, it could seem as though you are encroaching on Kongens Nytorv?"

> I am sorry, but it is not like that. I should have made some perspective renderings to better show the situation. The thing is that the 34-meter tall vestibule is far from Kongens Nytorv. We are not placing the building right up against the square, and we are generous, both in relation to the theater's old stage and the Brønnum building.

says Sverre Fehn. The slim, gray-haired Norwegian stands tall—and he has that special Norwegian blue gaze.

> The height and width of the future construction is not random. "The height and width come from Stærekassen itself. That was the point of

departure. And for me, it is about that the theater should be a shining beacon towards Kongens Nytorv. It should breathe life towards the square, particularly at night and in the winter, when the artificial light from the vestibule will announce that this is the national theater.

After all, the theater belongs to the night, particularly in the North where it is cold and dark. Stærekassen must be warm and well lit. Now, it is just a dark cave, a tunnel with a draft where it can be icy cold. This way, Stærekassen – which scholars have loved and hated for 60 years, but which is finally protected – will be properly highlighted for the first time.

The tall building mass, which is like a bridge over Tordenskjoldsgade, is the key element in Sverre Fehn's project.

Terribly Calming

"Inner Copenhagen is otherwise renowned for its low buildings on a human scale…"

"Yes, all that homogeneity is terribly calming. But, on the other hand, Copenhagen also loves its towers. Suddenly, the monotony of the street is broken, for example with golden onion domes or with a winding spire."

I remember as a young architect that I saw a wonderful panoramic drawing of the old Copenhagen behind the moats. The low houses did not stick out, but the towers and the masts of the ships in the harbor did.

"And now Kongens Nytorv is getting a tower?"

Yes, the place will get a symbol of a spiritual and creative theater world, which may even make Kongens Nytorv bigger. After all, the dimensions of the squares are defined by the buildings that surround them. And when you walk into the vestibule, you will also get a view of the beautiful trees in the square – behind the large glass wall, while you are waiting in the ticket line. Guests of the theater do not experience this today. Now Kongens Nytorv will also play a role as an interior motif. I would call it a green vestibule, where you – at the other end – can also look out over part of the harbor.

"How would you respond to the avid criticism that Stærekassen will be packed into a large glass case?"

Well, it will be highlighted thanks to the project. A stage built over a street is a fantastic urban event. Imagine doing that. Those kinds of buildings are some of the largest there are in urban environments. They are like cathedrals. It has inspired us tremendously. When you walk under Stærekassen, you have the feeling that just above your head great drama is being played out. It is amazing. You can almost feel the lines drop down to the street. Now, it will be even greater when we build Stærekassen with the vestibule. This is no weak glass case, but great architecture. The building will stand as a new architectural drama, staged differently than before. We did not shy away from the dimensions. We could have just slinked away with our heads down, leaving Stærekassen dark and sad.

"Glass can otherwise be a dangerous material to work with. It is far from always transparent and translucent, and it can seem dark and unapproachable."

Correct. But for Stærekassen we will cut out some of the future concrete roof – and put glass up there on the roof. So that light can shine in from above. It will bathe the façade in light, so you do not end up with a black wall.

says Sverre Fehn.

It is an important architectural point and exception, as the only other light that will slip in from the heavens along this long and covered theater street will be from the side. The light must not fall upon the heads of the guests from above. It must shine in gently from the sides, upon the old building facades that will be left from the original street. I have a feeling that if you stand far from Stærekassen, you will see the square reflected in its glass. And this can be both beautiful and symbolic, when urban life is reflected in the theater. This is the function of modern drama. And behind it all is Harlekin, holding up the entire structure – like an umbrella above the people who want to enter.

By Harlekin, Sverre Fehn is referring to the three concrete pillars that will hold up the structure like an umbrella—without static stress on existing structures. Everything will hover in this giant cathedral, which may be somewhat reminiscent of the famous city arcades in Italy, for example in Milan. Sverre Ferhn will not exclude the possibility that the vestibule will be used for total theater during special occasions if the management of the royal theater so wishes. Just as St Mark's Basilica in Venice can be filled with music, and the sound of voices and instruments come from different places in the church. The architectural layout will certainly allow for it, promises Sverre Fehn, who is expecting a lot from the pair of bridges that will cross high up above the theater guests and connect the changing room of the old stages with the new stage. Here, the actors in costume will walk above the people—and allow themselves to be admired if they so wish. The Norwegian architect, whose best works have been repeatedly described and admired in the leading architectural magazines worldwide, is also known for bringing different materials together. Soulfully and delicately. Wood against steel. Concrete against marble. Some have even compared him to the Italian Carlo Scarpa, a world-renowned virtuoso in this field.

> I am probably more primitive, but I have learned a great deal from him. In The Royal Danish Theatre we will use oak, concrete, marble and glass. It is too early to say exactly where and how. But the wood will be close to the people, near your hands and legs, while the strong concrete will be further away. And the marble, which is nice and cool to the touch – almost like a woman – must also be part of the balance of different materials, which makes a building seem pleasant.

Appendix 2
Lecture Transcript

The following is a transcript of a lecture given by Sverre Fehn at Cooper Union, March 19, 1980. Fehn was introduced by John Hejduk. It is likely that Fehn was drawing at times as he was speaking. Lacking the images, it is difficult in some places to know what he is referring to. Also, the transcript was interrupted at a point where the audio tape was changed.

Several projects are discussed. It is unclear exactly which residences Fehn is describing at the beginning of his lecture, at least until he identifies Villa Norrköping. One of the residential projects he describes but does not name is likely Villa Schreiner (c.1963). He proceeds to a lengthy description of the Skådalen School for Deaf Children (1975), then turns to the Nordic Pavilion in Venice, including a brief description of his Brussels pavilion. Next is a consideration of the Hedmark Museum, which is the longest section of the lecture. Thinking, he says, of the city, he then turns to the Tullinløkka and Trondheim Library projects. Getting more rushed toward the end, Fehn quickly presents his Osaka Pavilion proposal (1970), his recently completed Medieval Gallery in Oslo (1979), and his proposal for a church in Honningsvåg, North Cape (1965).

Fehn closes with one of many versions of his imagined dialog with Palladio.

JOHN HEJDUK: I am pleased to introduce Sverre Fehn, who is the Carnegie Mellon professor for the spring semester. I think that we are very fortunate to have him here for a funny reason, which is that generally over the last ten years the shift has been to the west, I mean East of New York, and that we've never had anyone come to us from the North, in my recollection, over 15 years. I bet we did, and that someone is going to point that out to me later, but Sverre Fehn is a Norwegian, and I think that he is a Norwegian architect in a certain quality, and I think that he made my introduction, or he made his introduction to me, in a telephone call about three years ago. He wanted to come down to see the Cooper Union school of architecture, and he told the secretary that he was also interested in Le Corbusier. And I said, Look I'm so tired of hearing that people are interested in Le Corbusier, tell him to forget it.

And she did so. She said, Look, we're not interested in seeing anyone who is interested in Le Corbusier. Then about five minutes later he called up again and said that he wanted to speak to me, and I knew that I was going to have to talk to him for the next ten or 15 minutes, so I said I'll talk to him and tell the guy off. I'll get him on the phone myself. He got on the phone and said he was interested in Le Corbusier and that he wanted to come down and see Cooper Union. And I said, OK, when can you come down? He said he could come down tomorrow. So I said, well I'm not going to be here tomorrow, so I guess you can't come down. So I said, what are you doing Thursday? and he said, I'm busy Thursday, so I said, "well, you can come down Thursday." Then he hung up. Then about five minutes later he called and he said, "look, I can come down tomorrow."

And he came down the next day, and that began what I consider a marvelous friendship with this gentleman, and I had seen some of his work in some magazines, which he showed me. I didn't know of his work, which was another advantage, probably, that he had, my not knowing of his work. And then I had the incredible experience of having the opportunity of going to Norway about two years ago, and I went up north with Fehn to see a museum in Hamar which he had been working on for ten years, on the site of a twelfth- or 13th-century cathedral, where he was commissioned to do a museum. It was an archaeological dig. On the one hand it was the unearthing of Norwegian history through a number of centuries, and for me it was devastating. You see that someone was working somewhere that I had no knowledge of, who had simply created what I considered to be a masterwork and a masterpiece. And I went away extremely jealous that somebody could build the way he could build, and that someone who incorporated all the history and all the formal propositions, and all the exquisite detailing. And I had never seen the kind of architectural detailing that went into Hamar since I had paid a visit to the works of Albini when I was a student and the work of Gardella in the early fifties. And also to see the works of Jean Prouvé, the marvelous engineer, whom… [missing] …of working with. And I think that it is extremely appropriate at this particular time in architecture, that we see a man's work who is really in the grandest sense of the word an architect, who incorporates all the art that he can muster up into our particular art of approximation, because that is what architecture is, the art of approximation, and it is just what architect is more approximate than what other architect. And I think we have today one of the first rate architects of this generation. I give you Sverre Fehn.

[applause]

SVERRE FEHN: Thank you very much for this introduction, and I'm very glad to be here and teaching at Cooper, I must say so, because you gave me a phone call one year after. I was in class teaching and was told that I had a call from New York, and it was my first call from New York. I picked it up and heard "Can you come to Cooper?" "Yes." I said, and I think that was the whole conversation. It was very rapid. And I am very pleased to be here in New York talking about my work. So thank you for that.

I think in a way that every person is an architect, because when he moves through nature, through the landscape, you don't go from one point to another point directly, but he moves like that, and here is the light, and it slopes down a little, and here is a hill, and you walk up the hill and look around and go to that point. And in that movement he makes footsteps on the earth, and that is his letter to the next, and in that moment he has broken a branch or destroyed some grass. He has made a sign to another person. And in that sign he has made poetry, written on the earth. And I think that in that way all of us are creative, and in that way we are all architects.

The next slide, I had to show one of my own first buildings, and it's really a little building at the end of that kind of walk. It was a little wooden house for one of my friends. And you know wood is a very dangerous material to work with, because it's always in movement. So the detailing for that little house was like that with the wood connections like that, and in between we could use, just as they constructed the great airplane runways, concrete with tubes, and without the air in the tubes we put the wood together that way and it works perfectly. So the roof and the floor are kind of resting on air. So here you see there is no touch point here, it is just air on the top and on the floor. So that was the idea, and I had a beautiful contractor who used to build boats, so he made all this detailing very carefully, and all those windows and doors could be opened and closed. You see this corner can go that way and the other half can go like that, so it can be opened in the summer time and closed in the winter. Because the summer is so short, the house must be able to greet the summer very quickly. The plan was like that. Very simple. In the middle I have all the utilities, the kitchen, two bathrooms, and the sleeping lofts. And on the main roof, here we have these mechanisms, so the house could change with the seasons. And here you see more of the detailing. It's quite extraordinary. I've never reached that quality in my life in wood. I was only able to do it because of this contractor. As a matter of fact, it was an idea of Jean Prouvé, that he worked with in the early fifties, and this is one of his ideas—to put the wet section in the middle, and the cooking facilities were on the bay in the middle of the house. That was also the idea for the plan of my house. But then I realized that that was a very bad idea in a way. Because this is a difficult way to manage a house like that.

So I proposed another problem in an even smaller house. You made this kind of house that was prefabricated so you could put it in, and it seemed that when you moved back a little, it was like the way you lived before, when the candle and the light was following you. I mean, you had the candle in your hand and were going from one room to another. You were the owner of the darkness. And also the water, because water was cooked in each room and not bound to one special room. This was the kind of association I was thinking of when the water was put outside the structure. And that way the house could grow, when the children grew older you can add to the house. So that was the idea of having the unit outside. And this is the section of the house, and this box is on the outside. Because, you see, I come from a country where the green grass is covered with snow in September. It's a terrible climate from that point of view. And in my mind, in those days I was thinking of…[missing]… but it doesn't work in that country. It doesn't work at all. So I had to get rid of that. And I was thinking of the bear. He has an eternal summertime, because in the winter he goes in his winter lair and doesn't see any snow at all. For him it is summer all the time. And that was the way of thinking when I was thinking about these houses. To be able to create a space that you could hide in. You can hide from the winter. And look at that. That little lamp is always on. It's always night where that lamp is, even in the middle of the day. A 40-watt light in the daylight. Well, I was thinking of that bear, that could creep in and nearly go into a house and sleep without thinking about the climate. But I ended up in a construction like that. You have these walls that protect you against the site, and in the middle, again, I constructed the bathroom and the kitchen. But here I came to the very point in that house that is important. Because of the plan, you can make that house into one big room, and you could change into nine separate rooms. And by using these sliding doors, you can change the room qualities and also play with the light, always. And look at the corner. Here is the sliding door. It closes like that, to the column, and that room is facing completely out, J mean, out from the house. And look at that. I was young at that time. And that door leaves that point so that there is nothing there, if everything works. And so the mechanism of the house was really that corner. And then you were able to create and gain back again what is gone by all this modern architecture. What is gone is to be able to change the light, I mean that the artificial light creates walls, the walls came up where there were artificial lights in the house.

So here is the house, It is built in Sweden, and this part is higher and gives light from all directions. Here is the corner, with one of the doors open. It is closed from inside when you want to be completely isolated. And there you see the detailing for the ventilation. And the light comes through. I remember thinking that I was like the bear, not looking out on reality, just yourself in the house. And here is the kitchen. And we broke through the brick walls with all the activities, that correspond with the other rooms. And this is the sleeping room, with the bed, and here are some secret rooms for books. Directly into the bathroom. And again, this is what the whole story was about. And that is the house again, and here my friend's son is now 20 years old, so you know how old this house is. But this house was for four children, actually, as well as the grownups, so the corner could fit the table looking out.

And I went from that picture to the children. I constructed a complex of buildings near Oslo for deaf children. Half of the architectural experience is gone when you can't listen to sounds. Because in this room you hear a certain sound, the street is a certain sound, New York is a collection of sounds. If you close your eyes you can really listen to New York, or to Paris, or whatever it is. It is fantastic how hearing is how you live in a room. And I observed that that is one thing, and another thing is that when you deal with a little child, from two years old up to 18, and in these little houses you deal with the formation, you put it into the hill, and this is a school, and this is a dormitory where they sleep, and this is for the grownups. But I said, "Don't touch the nature, don't touch the trees." So we put them in with the cranes and the digging machines so that they would not touch a thing. So you nearly can't see the buildings. And this is a plan of the little house where the small children live, and they have to learn a little here, and here is a room for the person that teaches here. But the tower is there, and you know when you are a little man, and when you can go to that room, to the bathroom, alone, you have reached a certain point, I mean the most important point, I think, and so you put a little window in there so they can look out and not be so alone. You can look out into the sitting room and out into nature. So that was the idea of that tower, in the building. And you see, the building itself, was built up to the slope, so when you are so little, you walk up here, and at that point is the end of the world. You have really made a journey. And so you go back, and the building takes you into its heart again. And half of the time something happens so that the small people inside can do the same movements with their sickness as the healthy ones outside. And another thing, we made very small windows, very near the floor, for as an architect, you always calculate it from the age from 20 to 45, that is, all buildings we figure for that age and the rest is something that you have to grow up and reach that very point at 20. But no one has calculated that if you are two years old, you are a person, a little man, and you have a right to look out. But for grownup people all the windows are the same height. And all the grownup people are saying "oh, it's snowing outside, and do you see that?" What! And the child grows angry and destroys the furniture. So I put the windows down there, and I was visiting the school afterwards, and what was in the window? Yes, telephones. Because they feel that they've grown up, and that each window is a little telephone. So they are grownup people already. But we made a mistake, because each of these roofs was to be roofed by grass, but

Appendix 2 165

the government cut it out and said it was too expensive. So It's just papered, which is too bad, because in this silent world, with people that can't talk, and there you have the water and the silence. It's beautiful. I think we made this place more beautiful in winter time. And we put color there. And you see, you are as small as that. And that is for the small ones. So the teachers couldn't see out. They had to bend down on their knees. It's raining outside! And that is the story of that little room with the low windows. And the teachers were angry. Oh my God, I was nearly killed. But I must say, that the children like the school very much. And the dormitory goes directly like that. You are nearly in the trees. And from the ages of six to 12 you have a room that you can participate in, It's a room for everybody. You just walk from your own room to the common room, and the building is following the slope like that. And for the very grownup ones, they are in another position, because the room itself became the main space, and there you can stay, and the common room is split by a garden. Because now you like to be alone. But something happens here. It's glass all over, and the handicap for people who can't talk is reversed, For me, it's a handicap that I can't talk with the person up there, because he can't hear me. But for the people without sound, they talk with each other through the windows. So that's the architect's answer to that question that the handicap of the deaf becomes a pleasure. Here is the kitchen and the room. And this floor is heated, so when the snow came the stones melted the snow. And this is the school. It is an open school, and this remains, you see, when you are a little person and tell stories, everyone sits around you in a half-circle, so when you tell a story the children sit around you like that. But you have to educate these small fellows to reach the world of the grownups, the rectangular world. But it's left still in small rooms where you can tell two or three persons about how to learn or whatever. This is the section of the school. And the light is very important, because you are dealing with sight always. It's like designing rooms for artists. And every piece of furniture was designed in my office to be used in these rooms and in the whole building. This is a very long building, because it's kind of a fence between the ordinary housing and the school. And here is the kitchen and the restaurant. I love to play in wintertime because the snow is a beautiful thing. When there is a lot of snow, it creates islands. When you have a very bad car, that makes a lot of noise, and winter comes, it's like driving a Mercedes Benz without a sound. Because of the snow. And when people move around in the snow, I find it's beautiful.

Well, the next building is just a story about the trees. And the sun. Because the sun has a certain angle to the earth, and the structure of that building is to make a roof that can catch the sunbeams before reaching the ground. That is the story of the Venice pavilion I made between the United States and Denmark. For Sweden, Denmark, and

Norway. And to obtain this and protect the trees, because Venice is without trees nearly, and when they have a garden, they are so proud of it, that it is nearly forbidden to cut trees. It was a competition, and I really did the competition because of the idea of the trees. And here is the structure. You see, you have beams in that direction, and in the other direction and you cut the sunbeams and for the orchids that are so sensitive to light, they won't be disturbed by the terrible sun. And this is the construction of those roofs, with the transparent plastic, so the light could get through. It's a very simple building. Here you have the Danish, and here the light comes through the construction. And here is the corner, with the very thin concrete construction, and again back to the workers, that are excellent. And here is the space before the sliding doors arrived. But what to do about the most important tree, at the end of the big structure? And I had to deport the big beam, and say, please stay where you are, I won't touch you. And the tree is still up and in good shape. And here you have the pavilion on the opening day. There was a lawyer in the city that said to me these steps are too steep, you must change this staircase. And so on the opening day, the president of Italy, who was a little man, just jumped up this little staircase with double steps just like that. And so the lawyer, who was an old Venetian man, said "Congratulations, Mr. Fehn."

And just a little interruption. With all these levels I built the Brussels pavilion in 1958. It was a more complicated plan, but really very simple, as a matter of fact, you go in here, and around, and out again. But we made this roof, and here we get three kinds of spaces, one with ordinary light, one with light from here, and the other with light from the pitched roofs. So we had three qualities of light. And the walls, you see, were prefabricated and went in like that. And in between we put the elements that lift the beams and tied the thing together, and it was 48 bolts that kept the whole thing together.

And this is constructed like a spider with these strings, and so you had a cannon shooting off these mysterious things. And it begins to be a roof, It was fantastic. But all of this kind of building is built on the ground itself. And in this thing we made a platform and on that platform, in that space, you made your structure.

But suddenly a thing happened to me and an old student of mine who was director of a museum asked me what to do with his house. To create a museum. So I had to deal with one thing that is important. Here is the ground, and I had to think of a person between earth and heaven because this is sacred, you can't touch that. And that little man must have his story told and I was thinking of New York, a place where people are between earth and heaven like that. It's like a musician that writes alone. And so you make small platforms, and here you have, nearly, the story of New York. But my story is what to do with that little man in the air, because the task was, here is a bit of land on the greatest lake in Norway, which had been in the Middle Ages a little city, or a great city, and here you see the plan of the town, and here is the church, and here is the castle for the bishop, and the school and the cloister. All the kinds of buildings that are...[missing]...and on the left of the map is the great hall, and so it ends up in the present. The museum. And so the story of that old building was due to that. This is the church. Because an old building like that is like...[missing]...and when buildings are on the way of dying, new ideas are born, and that was to create that as a museum building. And so I was thinking of how to see a ruin. You had to go up and look down to have the pleasure of the drawing. You see how beautiful this is. And even here, a little building down below these old walls too, and so you have a new part, or at least a part from the last century, here. And here is a plan of the first floor, and you see this building is only touched by a few columns, and that is the whole story. Even here. And you enter here, and so on. And next we begin to start with the bridges., that go through the building and this part. It is not so valuable, but that part is very valuable. And also this part. And you end up in that land, this is the middle age, and from the middle ages, you expose the things in three very small museums, and this is the other part, and this is the folk museum. So the section is like that, and you must be aware, in every step you take, that you mustn't touch the old things. You mustn't touch these old walls, and each construction must be separate from each other. And here you have the whole plan. And you enter from here, and this is where you look down and see what is going on in this part, because they are still digging, and out, and go up and up and come to where you have the exhibitions, go down, and look into the small museum. This is from the church, this is from the war, and that is for the very small objects, and turn this way, and if it's good weather you go out, and again to the ruin, and down and follow that route, and up and back to the beginning. This is the rhythm of the visitors.

And the director said to me "don't touch everything that is history, even the day you make history, don't touch what is happening with the wall. That should stay where it is." And so the story of the details began. Here is the entrance door. And you keep every detail and every story told, it is written in these stones. And the steps are the steps of the middle ages. And you have the stories told in the ground there. And it's a fantastic thing to work with old ruins, because you will be thinking of the fact that stones belong to history. But the wood construction belongs to the eternal. And here you are in the great story of history.

And you come to that very point where the two buildings meet and it's built of glass. I had one man I trust, and he has made all my glass work from the time I was a very young architect, and he listens to glass, I mean, glass is something to him, he can build with it, three stories high. And the big glass window was constructed like that because this supports the roof, but for the glass windows we had this thin construction. And I was worried about protecting it from the wind, but it works. When we drew this staircase, we weren't thinking so much of what happens below, but that was a job for the carpenter, and he did an excellent job. And all this construction is out of hard wood. And the size of the wood construction was a little complicated because the building turns like that, and that corner is warped. So we made those huge thick beams. And the ordinary construction leaves off and this heavyweight takes the load from that corner. And you had to have these details because the wall wasn't quite straight. And there was a certain point here where you had to decide what to do.

And here is the folk museum and before that there was a house here. With the wood construction, and you see this beam. And as I said before, you had to put the wood construction separate, and so the concrete construction came. It's like the construction itself mirrors the problems of the site. To put one thing next to the other. But this dialogue between the concrete and the stone happens to be very beautiful, because it's two centuries, I mean. I'm so tired of merely following history, without making a manifestation of the present. How can you have a dialogue that way? It's impossible. You must have a manifestation of the present. Then the past will talk to you. You see, you just screw this glass on the wall, which makes the window there. That is the old site. And he even followed the stone with his glass. It's incredible. He followed each movement of the stone. In between the big glass here and the lattice. The inspiration for this wall was that the whole thing was fallen down. So I said, "Let it be. Don't touch it. We can't reconstruct that." This was the inspiration for the big window into the lecture hall. And you see, when John [Hejduk] went up there, he was very impressed, because I said to him, you know, this little stream ends in a pier. And at that pier is a little boat, and the fisher was rowing that boat, and he was rowing to Rome. It's a fantastic thing. And he went back again with his instructions and he continued his life by this little church here. And you know, during the war between the Norwegians and the Swedes, they had surrounded the castle, but the priest or the bishop went down on the grounds and talked to everyone, to the Swedes, and continued his walk.

And so I got to complete this building because it had been standing empty for years because of money. And so we got some money so we could have some objects in the room. And the story of the object is fantastic. Because when you are going to expose things, in this light, and when you put the thing in a room, it depends where you put it, either here or there. And you must be the object yourself. You must feel it. Because the only story you can add to the object, as an architect, is how you place it. You must be the object yourself. That should be a good story. The Japanese have a word for that. Because the rooms in Japanese architecture are nearly empty. In a European house, you have

Appendix 2   169

every sort of sign, the big chair, the small chair, the table. Everything tells you where to go. But in a Japanese house, nothing tells a story. So you have to go like that, and then there you are, and you sit down. It's the same thing with the object. I have to feel good. And as object.

In this building I have four paintings. Two paintings and two drawings. How to expose them on that terrible concrete wall? Well, we had a little interaction. We made a little iron piece that could be something between the concrete and that man. And I began to think about the story of the portrait and of the painter. There are three actors in that story. The portrait itself, the painter, and the man. And the story of these three persons is fantastic, as a matter of fact, because the portrait is not like a photograph, and if you see yourself in the mirror you are like an artist, you are suddenly an actor, you never tell yourself the truth in the mirror. Perhaps when you are at the barbershop and very tired and suddenly you look at yourself. "Oh God!" But the painter is a real eye, and he can look at you and paint a frozen moment in your life. There you are, suddenly. And so he has done his job, but he is gone. And the drama is now between the portrait, which is a frozen moment in his life, and the other man, who says it's terrible, it's a mess. But that is telling him who he was. And that is a strong story, and it is in every painting in the room where he lives. The painter walks into the room itself and paints the portrait. It belongs to that room. But now something happens, that he isn't here, he is gone. What now? For the very great museum, for the great conservation, at that moment the painting belongs to him and goes down in the grave. And there is where the conservation is a kind of passion. Look at the Viking graves, look at the Egyptian, everything is perfect and preserved for years. And in this darkness is a real museum, where nobody visits these beautiful things. It's not visited by picture-people, by aesthetic people. "Oh what a man! oh what a masterpiece!" And when the people are coming back again, that is a painter, he being a god more or less. Because he has created a painting and nobody knows that that has been a famous painting by a painter called Stoltenburg. And that is the story of the museum. There you have it.

And this is a story about the earth. Look at that. You must have force to go into the ground. A little seed goes down. And this is the only place in Norway where they have enough grain. You have concrete, you have wood, and the things that are left are iron. And I'm always thinking about children, because children's stories are about thieves going in and out. And when I see these little sculptures, I think about all these thieves. And the grain gives them liquor, so they export liquor. They are still exporting liquor to the whole world. And these are small bottles for the liquor. It is put in a container like that. And you see where do you wear your watch? That is near your hand and on your warm skin. And this is the liquor, the fabrication of it. And the container was so, and we had to draw these small details. And they are famous for one thing, that is how to cut sculptures and make them out of wood. And that is a masterpiece, but it was so restored that the restoration man, after he had worked on it, looked like the sculpture himself. And also the lions that he put on, he loved it, and I said "don't touch it It's so beautiful. Let it be like that." He was eager, and what happened was that there was no lion anymore. Look at that. The lion is not like that. You can think of thieves, but that is another story.

Here you see, the museum begins to fill up with objects, and here is a bridge, and it is a very famous stone. In that particular way, you feel the material, you feel the ground. Then you begin to observe that the story itself is told by the hard thing. I mean, when you leave the earth, The first thing that leaves you is your spirit. And then your flesh and bone. And the story that is put together by the hard pieces that remain of you. The same story is true of the wooden houses. It is the iron pieces that are left in the ground that you put together and try to make the story of the house, and of yourself. And it's fantastic, for the story is not left in books, because from that time there are only 12 pages left. From the whole century of that town and that church. So the story must be told by the hard pieces.

But in between these hard pieces we found a little finger of silver. And I was shocked, because when the director came and we opened the coffin, I said, "here is something. Would you like to expose it?" And he said "Oh my God, that finger is real. It is the exact finger of an old person." And you see what is happening with this finger. This part of the finger is small, because the hands have been touching some loving thing, for a whole generation, and so that part is really worn out. So I said to myself, I have to expose that. We would like to see that object in a certain way.

And what to do with the war? How to expose the war? And I happened in that period to go to the cinema and see a film by Stanley Kubrick, "Barry Lyndon." Fantastic film. And in that film is a duel, and you know, I suddenly realized what was the war. Because at that moment when the assistants for the duel came, and opened the box and the man looked down and saw the bullets arranged in it, and the revolver with it, then he is broken, I mean, suddenly, in that moment, the whole duel is lived through. And after that it's over, it's gone, he can't shoot. The duel is going on, but the terrible thing with war is the silence and the order before. So we exposed the bullets of stone, put like in a bullet box, each bullet with its own room, and that is also the story for the thieves, because with the glass here, you can't steal it. It's impossible. There is this mechanism here, and if you wanted to steal it, it would be so much trouble that it wouldn't be worth it. This is much better than the keyhole. It's terrible in museums to have keyholes. You can't trust them anyway. And look at this war, with these

Appendix 2 171

stones shooting out in this war. And this is a cannon. It's very valuable. I think it's one of the few pieces left in Europe. A little cannon like that. You put the bullet in, and the powder and everything, and you burn it down, and suddenly it shoots off. It's nothing. Just Boom. A lot of noise. And here is that tragic thing. These little pieces of iron.

And then you come to the last room. That was the church. And we have very few pieces, because if you have a beautiful piece, it ends up in Oslo. It's nearly impossible to keep. But we have a few pieces left, which are exposed like that. And the Madonna here. And happily, she has no face—because of that, she still remains in Hamar. Not in Oslo or in New York. And that is the tragic story of the object, because I can't think about the museums and the objects. They belong to the land where they have been created. And if you remove them from the life that has created the objects, you make a very great, terrible mistake.

And this museum job made me think a little about what happens in the towns, and what is our past or our future, as architects. Because you see in Oslo, we have three main buildings. Beautiful. That is the old university building, that is the museum for the Vikings, and that is the museum for painting, called the National Gallery. And these three buildings make a square. And on this square now is a parking place. So there was a competition to make a museum that connects these two buildings and also connected that one. So that was the proposal. What to do? And you had to leave this building, and be very careful, because it tells the story, and even tells you what to do. Here is the plan. And each of the old buildings has a beautiful thing, because the entrance door is something valuable. I mean, it's not only the little entrance door. Down in the street level, it continues up and up and ends on the roof with the lions up there. It's the story of the whole building. Each of these has the same story. Look at that. It's the story of the opening of the entrance. And all the other competition entries have neglected that. And what a terrible thing to come here and find the door is closed, turn around and go to the new entrance. And I said, no. Keep it. I would even work more with that. Keep this as entrance to that organization. And another thing is important, that every city have a floor of the city. It's the floor that everybody knows. They have known it from childhood. And every citizen knows the floor of the city. So we didn't touch that so much. We made a little passage on the floor itself, and this is the entrance, the other one, and the last one.

And I said, "cut it over here." So we made an entrance here too. So you see, we have this pedestrian going like this, and he reaches it like that, and to this we add small museum buildings. You see, here is a museum, here is another little museum, and so on.

So this was connected with the city floor, and this was for the promenade. And we had a structure like that, which goes through the building, and we curved it a little, so it wasn't alone on the bridge. This is the structure. And everything could be done connecting to it. And you see, the section through the town was beautiful. Here is the great cafe on the corner, where everybody eats. And this is the National Theatre. And here this architect had made a wonderful building like a tunnel, through the square, and this tunnel is leading to the university, so the old professor who came here would go down three or four steps, you know, they are very old, and the heart has nearly stopped, you go down here, and you have help to get out, and you are in the auditorium. This is the structure. That is the bridge, and here is our Gallery for Modern Art.

And another thing that happened, when we did another competition after Hamar, is that in old days, a town's story was written in heaven. You could see that this is a castle, this is a windmill, that makes the energy, that is a boat, there is its mast, and this is the church. I mean, every single building made its story against the blue sky. But now, we are more or less looking down, even in New York, where the most beautiful things happen out, you are always like that looking down, because of the street and the cars and everything. And so we were to build a library, and it so happens that it was to be built on a ground that was full of ruins from the Middle Ages. And what to do? Again the city floor. And here we took a corner of the city floor and just dropped it a few meters down. And then you open it up like that. And there it was. You can say the library was already built, because in the old ruin, you had these thick walls. And so you could put children in part of the library, because the thick walls held the silence. And this is the silence of the old churches, and so the library is a place of silence, and so are the ruins, a place without noise. And so we put these two things together to make a story out of the letters, and there you are. This is an important thing, because you really in Europe can open the ground, and there it is.

And in Osaka there was a competition that you should make an exhibition hall, about bad air. I mean, of polluted air. What to do as an architect to express polluted air?...[missing].... So you came in the space that is flexible. It's breathing like a lion. And it's filled with that kind of ozone, and everybody will be happy down there, and there will be pictures on the wall that are out of focus, and that was the story of the Osaka project. And I hoped it would make noise of breathing. And you enter here, stay on that platform looking at something and go out.

Back to the middle ages. I can't get rid of it. And this is a bark made in the Middle Ages. It's fantastic. More fantastic as an art object than as a ship. And this is from my last work, which was an exhibition of medieval objects in Oslo. And this is a little piece of wing, made of gold. But I had been thinking about wood as a material, when it talks with the water. I mean on land, it's not the same story. But when wood is connected and talking with the waves... It's made of extraordinary construction, the Viking ship. Look at the mast. And the exploration at the sea was so very big. I mean, the structure that was in Paris and in the Atlantic ocean and everywhere. But suddenly the church of Rome arrived, and all the spirit went ashore. And the carpenters built this church. And look at that. It was built like a boat, it doesn't go into the ground itself, it's like a keel. And wood construction has never been as good as that, after the carpenter went ashore from the boat. Here you can see how it ends in the ground. It's boat builder's work.

And this is my last expression. This is the door, the gateway into the church, and they are not Christians. The doors are telling the same story as on the boat. But past this door, you came to Jesus Christ. And look at him, he is an old man now. The king, and tired of life. And this is the beginning of the Middle Ages. And further on he became more human, and is crucified with his clothes on. Fantastic. And on his stomach he has a jewel. It's a great difference from this one to that. And so I made an exhibition, and that last one is slipping down a long perforated iron base, and he is nearly human. I mean, he is blood and flesh all over. And the only thing that he has left as an illusion is his hair, which is silver and colored like gold. And now the time was ready for Martin Luther.

And my last commission was to build a building up on the very North of Norway. And look at this. This is from the Middle Ages, created up there. It's quite a story. It looks beautiful and it's not the masts of the fisher boats. It's a church. And it's people that are well educated that can manage a structure like that. And so they are living on fish, and the climate is so strong that after the war, the Germans destroyed the whole country, so it was rebuilt by architects from the south. And when they built the doors for the houses, they were going out like that, and that was a terrible mistake, because the people were so tired that when they entered the house, that when the doors went out the people coming in the door would fall down. And in ten minutes, it was so cold that they would freeze to death, immediately. So I have this story to tell you about how strong that climate is. So I had to make this construction by making these huge walls here. Of concrete, that could protect that little wood construction inside. And when the fisherman came from the sea, and came into the church, it's really very difficult to be talked to about heaven and hell and all this intellectual talk. And it would be very beautiful if you could look in the roof, and see something similar to your boat. Because your boat is your home, more or less. So we created this little construction on the roof. We decomposed the ordinary elementary wooden beams, and we put the pieces in this curve like that, which could challenge the rain and water, and that part of the beam goes down and supports the roof. And also these secondary beams were split in two and this corresponds to the language of the engineering of these thick beams. So this whole thing was to create the beautiful wood construction in the shell of the concrete. So when you sit in the church and the story is too complicated, you can look at the mast beside your seat. Because for the fisherman, if the mast breaks, you are out. And the plan of the church is to have these small houses in the big room itself, and here you have the entrance, which should have two separate rooms, so when one part is open, the other part is closed. And here is a detail of the church roof, with the beam and the wall that cuts this beam in two, to make two rooms.

And it is written that I should talk today on from the fifties to the eighties. And this is many years for an architect. And I will end my talk here with a little project in 1951. It's a cemetery, and the cemetery is like a building, like a man that has lost something valuable. He has lost a friend, he has lost his nearest. And so the composition was like that, that you had a wall here and you came from this part to that part just through the walls. And you miss something. And the openings in the walls are just openings, so like a blind man, you can nearly feel your path through the whole thing. And your only friend, of course, is your own shadow on the wall. Because when you are up in the North, the sun is in the horizon itself, and it creates that shadow which follows you into the room where the dead body is. That's all. And in that shadow, I met Palladio. And I said, Palladio, it's beautiful the things you have written about the sun slipping through your house. Because the sun in your house tells you whether you have built a good building or not. I think that is beautiful. But Palladio was very tired, and he said to me, Well, you have put all the utilities in the middle of the room. In my house it was completely open. Even the dome was not covered with glass. The room was still open with air and with rain and fog. Oh, he said, but you have opened the four corners. Oh, yes, we were on the point of losing the horizon. And he became smaller, and said, Oh, but you opened the corners, you are losing the glow. And then he became very weak and I said, "Please tell me more." And he just whispered, and his voice was very weak, "All constructive forms are related to death." And then he was gone.

Index

Note: Page numbers followed by "n" denote endnotes.

Aasen Center 3
Architecture Museum 1, 132; design phases 133–141; perimeter definition 141–148
Aristotle 6, 7, 12, 17, 51, 109
Asplund, Gunnar 8, 10

Banham, Reyner 4, 9
Bookchin, Murray 7
Bourdieu, Pierre 54
Brussels *see* Norwegian Pavilion

camera shop in Oslo 61–67, 80, 143
Casey, Edward 54–55
Cook, Peter 107, 126–127
Copenhagen *see* Royal Danish Theater
Corbusier 9, 16n17, 56, 70, 160–161

Dahlerup, Vilhelm 111
De Carlo, Giancarlo 9, 26
diegesis 52, 57

Eliot, T.S. 54–55

Fjærland *see* Glacier Museum
Fjeld, Per Olaf 4, 25, 56, 70, 109
Foto Huset *see* camera shop
Frampton, Kenneth 32, 76, 87, 115

Gadamer, Hans-Georg 120–121
Galärvarvskyrkogården 22
Glacier Museum 3, 121, 148
Grosch, Christian 132–133, 136, 146
Grung, Gier 9, 26

Hamar 18, 26–29, 42–43, 48–49, 61, 97, 126; *see also* Hedmark Museum

Hedmark Museum 18, 26–35, 48, 57, 61, 104, 160; exhibit and installations 35–42
Heidegger, Martin 54
Hillman, James 12, 57
Homansbyen station 15n1, 31
Hvattum, Mari 72, 126

Jacobsen, Holger 111

Kahn, Louis I. 10, 16n18
Kierkegaard, Søren 109, 120
Kongens Nytorv *see* Royal Danish Theater
Korsmo, Arne 8
Kropotkin, Peter 7

Leatherbarrow, David 76, 138
Loos, Adolf 17, 25, 49, 57

Malraux, André 27, 40
Merleau-Ponty, Maurice 35, 53, 59n37, 121
methexis 14, 120–123
Mies van der Rohe, Ludwig 85–86, 126
Miralles, Enric 112
Mumford, Lewis 7
Munch, Edvard 1, 9, 105
Murcutt, Glenn 29, 41
Museum of Hydraulic Energy 31, 118

Nasjonalmuseet-Arkitektur *see* Architecture Museum
Nesjar, Carl 63, 93n1
Nordic Pavilion 81–87; urban engagement 87–93
Norrköping *see* Villa Norrköping

176 *Index*

Norwegian Pavilion 9, 36, 63, 93n5, 98, 142–143, 146, 148

Obrist, Hans-Ulrich 121
Oslo 1–3, 28, 96, 106, 131, 171; *see also* Architecture Museum; camera shop; Tullinløkka

PAGON 8
Palladio, Andrea 56, 71–73, 76, 92, 160, 174
Preus Photography Museum 36
Prouvé, Jean 8, 56, 161–162

Rogers, Richard 112
Royal Danish Theater 96, 109–111, 128–129, 155; competition 111–114; scales of participation 115–119; urban theatricality 119–126

Scarpa, Carlo 9, 82, 159
Schelling, Friedrich 1, 13, 53, 59n37
Schutz, Alfred 59n37, 152n9
Selva, Giannantonio 83
Shimmerling, Andre 8
Simmel, Georg 59n37, 61, 123, 145
Spitzer, Leo 13
Smithson, Alison and Peter 9, 70

Stackhouse, Max 6–7
Stærekassen Theater 111–112, 122–125, 155
Stockholm 8, 18, 20; *see also* Vasa Museum
Storhammer *see* Hedmark Museum
Sudal *see* Museum of Hydraulic Energy

Team X 4, 9, 26
Trondheim 42–43, 46, 48; *see also* Trondheim Library
Trondheim Library 42–50, 56, 95, 146, 148, 160
Tullinløkka 96–105, 148; on "non-building" 106–119; urban theatricality 119–126

Van Eyck, Aldo 9, 26, 99
Vasa Museum 19–25, 32, 50, 133
Venice 61, 81, 85, 115, 128, 158; *see also* Nordic Pavilion
Vesely, Dalibor 95, 106, 129n1
Villa Norrköping 14, 68–76, 86, 91; casework 77–81
Voegelin, Eric 54

Wasa see Vasa Museum
Wilson, Colin St. John 121